GOING UNDER

KIDNAPPING, MURDER, AND A LIFE UNDERCOVER

JOHN MADINGER

WILD BLUE
PRESS

WildBluePress.co

D0887101

GOING UNDER published by:
WILDBLUE PRESS
P.O. Box 102440
Denver, Colorado 80250

WILDBLUE PRESS is registered at the U.S. Patent and Trademark Offices.

ISBN 978-1-957288-52-9 Hardcover
ISBN 978-1-957288-51-2 Trade Paperback
ISBN 978-1-957288-50-5 eBook

Interior Formatting by Elijah Toten
www.totencreative.com

Book Cover Design by VilaDesign

GOING UNDER

TABLE OF CONTENTS

DEDICATED

To the memories of those in law enforcement whose lives touched my story and who aren't here for the end of it. James Birdsong, Troy Leathers, and Lonnie Wright of the Oklahoma Bureau of Narcotics and Dangerous Drugs. James Pat Grimes, Billy G. Young, and Houston F. "Pappy" Summers of the Oklahoma Highway Patrol. Terry Glen Lawson of the Oklahoma City Police Department. Kenneth Elsworth Miller of the Beaver County (Oklahoma) Sheriff's Department; Clifford Payne of the Washita County (Oklahoma) Sheriff's Office. Larry Wallace, Paul Seema, George Montoya, Allen Winn, and Carol "Chip" Fields of the Drug Enforcement Administration. And Troy Barboza of the Honolulu Police Department. It's a sad list and way too long, but thank you all for your service and sacrifice. R.I.P.

CHAPTER 1

BOOKENDS

"You hanged them. The Mexicans." I felt the first stirrings of a headache coming on, maybe the stack gasses from the paper mill about a hundred yards away, but probably the eighteen-year-old psycho in the back seat with the puzzled expression on his face. "I just want to make sure I've got this right. You hanged all three of them..."

"Well, yeah. They knew about Tommy and wasn't telling us, so what else was we supposed to do?" Terrell asked reasonably, like somebody might offer some other alternative to kidnapping, torture, and maybe murder. "But we didn't really *hang* 'em, on account of nobody knew how to tie one of them knots." Terrell, who said he wanted to be called "T.W.," made it sound like the most normal thing in the world, lynching three people. Just something that could happen to anybody. As if murder didn't count unless you'd properly mastered the subtle complexities and the thirteen coils of a hangman's knot.

"And not all of 'em at once. We could only find the one rope long enough," he added for clarity, like cold-bloodedly letting one down before moving to the next made the thing somewhat less outrageous.

"But you strung them up. Hung 'em high," I said. This sounded like a real enough hanging to me, even without the advantage of an authentic and properly tied noose. "And this is after you shot at all of them a bunch of times..." I looked at Lewis, the Oklahoma Highway Patrol trooper sitting next to T.W. in the back of the OHP cruiser. Lewis just rolled his eyes and shrugged. He'd heard the story before from Psycho T.W., maybe more than once on his drive down to the paper mill. Judging from the casual retelling here in the parking lot, T.W. clearly didn't think he'd done anything problematic or even awkward, much less something illegal as all hell, like torturing and killing people for information. He definitely wasn't apologizing, but maybe sensing the palpable air of disapproval coming off the three law enforcement officers in the car, he backpedaled a little.

"Not real high," he said, my allusion to the Clint Eastwood film of a few years before wafting unnoticed over the unkempt mop of ginger hair and vanishing into the ether and the paper mill vapors. That film featured a pack of vigilantes too. Those boys had only strung up one innocent man. Terrell and his buddies had gotten the hat trick. "You don't need to get 'em much off the floor before they start chokin'. We just jerked 'em up. It's harder than you'd think. I guess 'cause they're heavier, but it takes more'n a couple o' people pulling," T.W. said, giving us some helpful hints on lynching.

"The first one, he's all wiggling and shaking and kicking and turning red and blue, so we let him down and threw some more questions at him. He still wasn't sayin' nothin' so we strung up the second one. Same deal, so we did the third one too. Didn't do a damn bit of good, all that *por favor* 'n shit. That's all we got. They all pissed their pants, so we scared 'em pretty bad, but they wouldn't tell us jack."

I didn't investigate homicides. Kidnapping or lynching either. Neither did Lewis or the other man in the car, OHP Lieutenant Pat Grimes. We were all state police officers with jurisdiction in every corner of Oklahoma, but as a Narcotic Agent (II) of the Bureau of Narcotics and Dangerous Drugs,

I tried to stay in my own lane. That path carried me all around the world, to plenty of funky parking lots and cheap motel rooms, to glittering nightclubs and lonely stretches of empty highway. I'd sit through a few thousand other huddles like this one in places strange with people stranger before I left it all behind three decades later. That morning, though, I didn't think they came much more outlandish or depraved than the apparently conscienceless criminal mastermind in the back seat. Terrell took the cake.

Occasionally the road led to something I'd never investigated before and had no experience with. I'd see kidnapping and murder again, and a hundred other crimes less serious or immediate than this one, always trying to leave them to the professionals, but if what Terrell was saying was true, I wasn't going to have much choice this time. I'd been told when I drove down to McCurtain County that one life was at stake. Now Terrell was saying there might be three more.

I took off my glasses and rubbed my eyes, pushing against the forming headache. "Okay... Okay. Tell me again how you wound up in somebody's barn down in Frogville, Oklahoma," I said, and I remember thinking later that somebody could ask me exactly the same question. Maybe Terrell had a better answer. "Let's start at the beginning."

SOUTHEAST OKLAHOMA CITY, OKLAHOMA
FIFTEEN MONTHS EARLIER

It began bad a year before, in a sweltering little box in southeast Oklahoma City in June 1976, the stifling torments of an Oklahoma summer already starting to boil the people who lived under the tarpaper and asphalt roofs in the neighborhood. The box wore an ugly coat of green siding, asbestos shingles, chipped and broken, with patches of white showing in puffy, cancerous lesions that made the whole house look like it had psoriasis. Individual shingles—and in some places, whole sections of them—had fallen off the walls, revealing the insulation underneath, a sort of white, corrugated material. Something or someone had, here and there, punched holes in that too, and replaced one window opening with a sheet of unpainted fiberboard. A corner of the board had rotted off and collapsed on the ground outside. Another window had a piece of dirty white fabric hanging over the opening, half in, half out. No breeze stirred the stifling air enough to move it.

Somebody years before had surrounded the front of the house with a chain-link fence, three feet high, maybe protection for a dog or small children. Now, though it no longer had a gate, it imprisoned a sad little yard, all gray dust, an occasional thirsty-looking weed, some rusty children's toys, and dried leaves from one lonely tree. One of the tree's branches had fallen and lay bare and leafless across the fence onto the chipped sidewalk in front. It had been there a while.

A hundred feet away in the lot next door, behind a much more substantial chain-link fence topped with barbed wire, a pump jack sighed and thumped as the big horsehead bobbed up and down, nodding knowingly as it sucked up the only thing of real value in the neighborhood: oil from some ancient sink deep beneath the house. The stench of petroleum—from the pump or the industrial area just across the next street to the north—hung over everything in the still air, reeking even before I shut the car's AC off.

Following the informant's directions, I pulled the car onto the sidewalk next to the fence, staring at the front of the house, wondering, if the outside looked this bad, could the inside be worse? The informant already knew. He'd been here before, done business with Franklin, the man we'd come to see, and understood it wasn't important, gesturing at me impatiently to get out of the car.

What was important was that Franklin had methamphetamine for sale and I had two hundred dollars; those were the only things that mattered. I switched off the motor and opened the door, stepping out into a face full of Oklahoma summer, instantly sticky, immediately sorry to be leaving the cold comfort of the car. Walking toward the house, getting close enough to get the full effects of the sights and smells of poverty, wreckage, and despair, I had the answer to my question. Yes, things could always get worse.

The informant didn't stop at the front door, just pushed on through, leading me into a place meaner by far than the outside. The dead air inside, loaded with the odors of cooking and waste, assaulted us in a steamy wave. A baby, wearing only an obviously full diaper, crawled away from us across a bare floor strewn with tissues, old fast-food wrappers, empty prescription vials, and the leavings of what looked like a medium-sized dog, the un-housebroken canine not in evidence.

Franklin, shirtless and sporting several homemade tattoos, BIC pen ink or soot souvenirs from a previous stint at Oklahoma's Granite Reformatory, glistened with sweat though he didn't seem bothered by the heat, and he moved quickly to greet us. Shooting crank will do that to you, keep you moving when everybody else is drained and sluggish. He had track marks in both elbows, angry black scar tissue running down his wiry forearms. I could hear other people in the house though none of them ever came into the front room. The informant introduced me, and asked Franklin if he was holding. I watched the baby crawl past the doggie landmine toward a hole in the floor. It looked big enough that he (or she—there was no way of telling from my vantage point, and what did it matter anyway?) could get an arm or a leg into it. I edged toward the hole and the baby reversed course away from my leg and headed for the dog pile. Jesus.

"What? Huh?" Franklin and the informant were staring at me, obviously expecting some kind of answer to a question I'd missed. "Listen to everything" would become one of my Ten Iron Rules for working undercover, but the whole hellish scene had been a big enough distraction that I'd lost the thread. I'd learn with experience that this, an undercover, if he wants to survive the day, must never, ever do.

"The money, two hundred for a quarter. That's a good deal," the informant said impatiently.

I shook myself, tearing my eyes away from the kid. "Yeah, sure. That's good. I got that much. Where's the stuff?"

Franklin held out a clear plastic packet with white powder inside. I took it and thought it felt about right for a quarter ounce and looked okay for homemade biker meth.

"You want to try it here? I got some works." Franklin gestured at a low coffee table behind him where three or four syringes, a glass of cloudy water, and the other paraphernalia sat next to a flickering candle. Some assorted rubbish and at least one other needle had fallen onto the floor next to the table, directly in the baby's path. Not my problem and never had been. The pump jack outside moaned and thumped.

"No, man. Thanks, but I'm taking this to do with the old lady. We gotta go." I dug the cash out of my pocket and passed it over. Hand to hand with the Man. Franklin was toast.

He looked mildly disappointed that I wasn't sharing, the usual junkie etiquette, but that was never going to happen and now I wanted to be out of this place and somewhere else—anywhere else—as fast as I could get there. I shot a hard look at the informant, letting him know it was time to leave.

That had been the baptism, an eye-opening plunge into a dark world, one that not too many sane, sober people would voluntarily go back into. But that's what the state was paying me to do. That's what undercover was all about. At least, I thought as I drove away, the car's AC on full blast, it couldn't get much worse than that southside Oklahoma City hellhole. Yeah, well, that's a rookie UC talking. I'd learn pretty quickly: it can always get worse and usually does.

When I went looking for Franklin with an arrest warrant, he wasn't at his decrepit pad.

"He ain't here. He's in the hospital," his girlfriend said reluctantly after getting a few pointed threats about harboring fugitives.

We found him at Presbyterian on the city's northeast side, but I couldn't serve the warrant that day. Not unless I wanted to suit up with full mask and gown and take custody of and responsibility for a sick man. Sick *and* contagious. Franklin had hepatitis, not a huge surprise diagnosis for intravenous drug users. And the hospital wasn't taking any chances with the "contagious" part of that diagnosis. They put Franklin in isolation, a room with prominent Do Not Enter signs on the closed door due to the "high risk of exposure for visitors."

Wonderful. Of course, I'd already been exposed, not aware that as a visitor to Franklin's house, I'd required a mask or a gown when went we'd gone hand to hand (without latex gloves). Now I needed poking with needles of my own blood tests while I watched for symptoms, wondering whether my first undercover deal was going to put me in the hospital with Do Not Enter signs on the door and a permanently damaged liver.

You learn that quickly about narcotics enforcement, especially working undercover. As terrible as things might look, as nightmarish as it can be inside the dark places where our adversaries abide, it can always get worse. The path in this case had certainly descended into ever grimmer and more desolate depths, but we hadn't reached the lowest point marked by the sign on Franklin's door.

No; the bottom, in this case, lay across the street at Oklahoma Children's Hospital, where behind another sign requiring a cap, gown, and mask, hooked up to a lot of wires and tubes, Franklin's baby crawled toward another hole in his little life's floor. He had hepatitis too.

It can, of course, get even worse. Though sick and jaundiced, Franklin and his baby were at least still breathing. That isn't the ending in store for countless lives touched by drugs and our war on them, and sometimes, someone notices. Officially caring might be a coincidence, which I discovered when I got a second beginning a couple of years later, changing jobs and returning home, the newest hire for Hawaii's Investigations and Narcotics Control Section. Now I was getting my first assignment and an unexpected one.

"Death certificates?"

"Yep. We get all of them that are drug-related. Overdoses, poisonings, whatever." Paul, the senior investigator who would be training me, pushed the stack of forms across my new desk. "Half of them are suicides. You don't need to pay much attention to those. Or street drugs, like heroin. Nobody cares about them anymore."

Gee, that was sad. I picked up the top form, saw it listed the cause of death as suicide by barbiturates. The same way Marilyn Monroe and Judy Garland had checked out. Still a thing in 1978 apparently. "What's the point? Why am I doing this?" I said.

"You're the new guy. It's a bullshit job. New guys get the bullshit jobs."

"Sure, yeah, I get that. But why do we have these things? What am I supposed to do with them?"

"Stats, mostly. We list them in our annual report and keep track of the drugs in each case, especially whether they're pharmaceutical or street. Most of them are pharmaceutical. They come from doctors and pharmacies, which we register if they want to handle controlled substances. So, for those, the ones that are listed as 'accidental' or 'unknown,' you run against the script files and see if the doctor was negligent or overprescribing. Maybe we'll open a case on him."

The script files. Ooh, I hadn't been at INCS all that long but already knew that wasn't good. INCS got a duplicate of every prescription written for Schedule II controlled substances—amphetamines, barbiturates, Quaaludes, morphine, codeine, Demerol, Dilaudid—all the heavy stuff. There were thousands of them, tens of thousands, the copies mailed to us by all the pharmacies in the state. This was long before the system was computerized and each faded copy was written in the notoriously terrible handwriting they apparently teach in medical school, some in Latin, many barely legible from well-worn carbon paper, but they all had to be examined page by page. We had boxes and boxes of prescriptions stacked in the office. Weeding through that lot looking for dead people's names sounded boring and pointless with a hefty serving of futile. It definitely wasn't the reason I'd taken this job or first became a narcotics agent on the mainland a couple of years before.

"Does that ever happen, catching a doctor overprescribing to somebody who overdosed?"

"Yeah, surprisingly. We've got four or five registrants—doctors, osteopaths, dentists—under investigation. Some of 'em write a lot of scripts and a couple of times, one of the people they're writing for has croaked." He named one, a doctor who'd just been convicted for writing illegal prescriptions. "So it's not a complete waste of time." He stood up. "Almost, but not completely," he said with a grin.

I squared the stack; 1977's total and quite a few from 1978, maybe two hundred in all, and started through the pile, pulling out every form that listed "suicide" as the cause of death, setting them all aside. Never checked the names, because sadly, we officially didn't care about them. With the "accidental" and "unknown" deaths left, I picked up my very first death certificate and stopped cold.

MATT MAXWELL.

The name jumped off the page at me, the face, the laughing eyes, and the mischievous smile right behind. Matt, my classmate from seventh grade through high school. Matt, the joker, the teaser, popular with girls and guys alike. Matt, the cool kid with the sardonic grin who surfed, drank a little, smoked some pot, and was in the middle of every crowd at every party, had lived big, lived like there was no tomorrow. The certificate said Matt had gotten that right: there was no tomorrow for him. Somebody who followed only a few steps behind me at our high school commencement ceremony and sat next to me in class for a quarter of our lives was gone from it at age twenty-four.

The certificate listed morphine as the cause of death, but I'd been to DEA school and already knew that the human body metabolizes diacetyl morphine (heroin) back into morphine after injection. Blood tests on a person—living or dead—will show only morphine. As Paul had also said, INCS didn't care about OD deaths by street drugs like heroin, only the pharmaceuticals, but under his rules, even though 99 percent of "morphine" deaths were really heroin ODs, I'd have to do the full search on Matt's name because morphine is a pharmaceutical drug: a Schedule II controlled substance. Sometimes, though, the first responders find a syringe with heroin residue at the scene, and they did in this case. The medical examiner noted that, concluding Matt died from an accidental heroin overdose. That made it official. Nobody at INCS, me included, was supposed to care anymore about heroin ODs. I could put the certificate in the pile with the suicides, forget about Matt Maxwell, and stop caring. Of course, that wouldn't ever be possible.

Matt and people like him *were* the reason I'd gone into the profession, been through the state police academy and DEA's, why I took tremendous risks undercover. I'd joined America's War on Drugs believing in the evil of the abuse of these substances and in the fight against them. I wanted to keep stuff like heroin away from everyone whose names had just landed on my desk or might in the future. I wanted to pursue the people who made money from those like Matt Maxwell until drugs killed them. In a world where all the colors are very often different shades of gray (something doubly true undercover), this seemed starkly black and white. These people were bad and wrong, and I and those on my side were right and good. You believe that sort of horseshit when you're twenty-four, harbor exactly those delusions. They go away later though, that's for sure.

Seeing a classmate's name on a death certificate made the whole thing more intimate and personal. Thoughtful and grieving, I went back to the job I'd chosen with a renewed awareness that drugs touch everyone in society. Heroin had shaded Matt and his family, and in killing him, reached across to me and everybody else who knew him. It was too late to do anything for my friend, but by God, I was going to do something for everyone else.

There was right and wrong. I could find clarity in the mist. And I could rescue somebody who needed saving. You believe that sort of horseshit too; you *want* to believe it, though even at twenty-four, I should have known better. I had a bitter experience with the rescue-saving thing already, saw close-up how evil sometimes trumps even the very best of intentions. And though I never returned to Frogville, I think back on it often, remembering the hailstorm of bullets and hate that darkened a beautiful May morning, shattering a score of lives forever. For me, it would always be blood and killing that ended my rescue story in the saddest and worst possible way on Black Friday.

CHAPTER 2

KEEP THE CUSTOMER SATISFIED

FROGVILLE, OKLAHOMA
SEPTEMBER 1977
MORNING OF THE FIRST DAY

I said my career path took me to some unexpected and out-of-the-way places, and there's almost no place in America more out of the way than Frogville, Oklahoma. You probably haven't been to Frogville. Almost nobody has. I'd never even heard of the place before my boss called me at home one September evening and told me to go down to Choctaw County. He'd gotten a request from the Highway Patrol to assist them with a very hot kidnapping case. "Be there by 8 a.m. tomorrow," he told me.

Even in 1977 Frogville wasn't a ville anymore, just a memory of one, with a few beat-up houses spread out along a couple miles of ragged county road, about as far south as you can get in the state. No more than eighty people lived in the area, a patchwork of farmland and forest riding the series of twists and turns in the Red River that marks the line between Oklahoma and Texas. What's left of Frogville sits in one of the bigger loops, almost surrounded by muddy red water and our Lone Star neighbor to the south. The man

I'd gone to meet, OHP Lieutenant Pat Grimes, told me how it got its name.

"Supposed to be frogs so big down here, they eat ducks," he said as we cruised down a dusty road, searching for Mexicans.

I mulled that one over for a moment, forming a clear, and disturbing, mental picture of this scenario and the animals in it. "Those are big damn frogs," I said.

"Our pilot says he can see 'em from the air," Grimes said, looking sideways at me, grinning a little. Pat Grimes was a kidder. I'd figured that out already.

I told him I thought maybe he was thinking about the frogs on the south side of the river. "I hear everything's bigger in Texas," I said.

"That is what they say. I haven't seen any Texas frogs myself. But if they're any bigger than our Oklahoma frogs, I don't want to run into 'em."

We'd been into Texas already that day, crossing the Red River twice, but saw no frogs. We'd spent hours talking to an OHP airplane pilot and to a passel of very riled-up folks I referred to as Frog-villains. That's because these people, like our informant T.W., were all also real villains, but they claimed to be on our side for this particular scrimmage. It had been a long day and wouldn't be over for a while longer, not until we turned up the three lynched Mexicans, hopefully still alive.

I'd gotten to the starting point, in Valliant, McCurtain County, Oklahoma, early that morning, meeting Pat for the first time over the highway patrol radio when I got to town. He directed me to a little Valliant diner, and I found out why I was there instead of an agent from the Oklahoma State Bureau of Investigation. OSBI would normally have legal authority to investigate kidnappings. They had the jurisdiction—and much more experience than I did—over murders too, which Pat told me this was shaping up to look like.

"This is gonna end up being all about marijuana," Pat said, explaining why I'd driven almost four hours to introduce myself. "And if we don't get on top of it pretty quick, it could turn out real bad."

I'd heard plenty about marijuana in southeastern Oklahoma, although I'd never worked a case there before. McCurtain County and Choctaw County, just a couple miles west of Valliant, were part of the old Choctaw Nation and in the Eastern Judicial District of Oklahoma. Our Tulsa office and DEA took all federal drug cases in the southeastern part of the state to the United States District Court in Muskogee, and they had a lot of business. Choctaw County had a reputation for producing plenty of homegrown marijuana and eradicating it was an OBN responsibility. The Tulsa agents, who usually worked eradication in the eastern part of the state, were busy on a major clandestine laboratory investigation, so the boss picked me to help out.

This corner of Oklahoma was wild and woolly even before the Civil War. It had once been the Indian Territory, the bailiwick of *True Grit's* "Hanging Judge" Isaac C. Parker, a rough and lawless place that held more outlaws and desperadoes "on the scout" than any other slice of America. From his courtroom in Fort Smith, Arkansas, Parker sentenced 160 people to hang, most of whom committed their crimes—rape, robbery, and murder—in the Territory. It was a deadly place for lawmen too, with over a hundred of Judge Parker's marshals dying in the line of duty over the years, and probably double that number in Indian Police, sheriff's deputies, police officers, possemen, and railroad cops. People said, "There ain't no law west of Saint Louis and no God west of Fort Smith," and a whole lot of dead law officers over the years bore that out.

The marijuana business was a natural for the outlaws of southeast Oklahoma, many of whom got their start with moonshining, even before Prohibition. The government prohibited liquor sales in Indian Territory for decades, and parts of the state, including Choctaw County, were still "dry" in the 1970s, where you couldn't buy liquor by the drink. In some counties, you couldn't buy it at all, not legally. Moonshiners had a century of practice dodging the law in the hills and forests of eastern Oklahoma, but that mostly ended when the rising price of sugar in the 1970s sucked the profit out of white lightning. Fortunately for the 'shiners, they had an equally lucrative alternative ready at hand, and ten thousand marijuana patches bloomed. By 1977, pot was probably a bigger business than timber, nominally the leading industry in the neighborhood.

This wasn't the laidback, easygoing, mellow-type, Cheech-and-Chong stoner marijuana business either. The people running it were old school. Their daddies and granddaddies had no problem whatsoever killing nosy revenue agents or Prohibition men who got too close to one of their stills in the bad old days—had done so on numerous occasions, in fact. The pot growers were descended from the same folks who gave Judge Parker 13,490 cases to try in only twenty-one years, something like five matters every single day. They guarded their marijuana crops with high-powered rifles and shotguns, and used booby traps made from rat traps and shotgun shells, and catfish hooks strung at face level on the paths leading to the patches. They shot first and shot straight, and they didn't like people raiding their crops; something that went for cops or crooks looking to score. Which, Pat Grimes said, it looked like our kidnap victim might have tried one time too many.

I was curious about why Grimes was there. OHP didn't do kidnapping cases either, normally getting involved in criminal matters when summoned to assist by the county sheriff or the chief of a local police department. Pat was a lieutenant with the Special Investigations Section working out of Oklahoma City, mostly handling internal affairs cases for the Patrol, and, from what I gathered, aside from a local OHP trooper, neither the OSBI people nor the area cops knew anything about our being in town. Nothing about the pairing made real sense, but he had the explanation and I got it over a late breakfast. Pat was having coffee; he'd been up early and on the road, already into his second day of this unfamiliar investigation.

"Yeah, it's an unusual arrangement all right. See, there are these two families down here." (We're going to call them the Hatfields and the McCoys, because… well, you'll see). Pat went on. "One of the Hatfields called us up and asked for help from the trooper, Lewis, that works this part of Choctaw County. He's known the family for a long time. Knows everybody else down here too. He heard them out and called Oklahoma City. I got down here yesterday and I'm starting to get the picture.

"The Hatfields say Tommy, one of their sons, eighteen years old, just out of high school, turned up missing a couple of days ago. Supposedly he went hunting, maybe out on some land that belonged to the McCoys, down by the river bottoms. Never came back. When he didn't get home, the Hatfields went looking for him, asking around too. They say they 'heard' he was last seen in a barn that the McCoys own, and then got taken somewhere else. Now they think he might be dead."

"What was he hunting? It's September. I thought we were out of season for everything right now."

"For animals, yeah. But I don't think a little thing like a license or taking an out-of-season deer would get in any of these folks' way. Anyhow, the picture I'm getting is that he was out for plants. McCoy marijuana plants. And the Hatfields are saying he might've found them."

"That does tend to piss people off," I said. "Where's this barn and who supposedly saw him there?"

"The barn's down in a little place called 'Frogville.' You ever hear of it?"

"Nope, but it sounds lovely. Frogville."

"It's right down on the river. I drove around there just after daylight this morning with our trooper. Pretty flat, farm fields and some timber. Not many people. A friend of Tommy's from high school told his folks the McCoys had him in the barn. That was the day before yesterday. The friend said he didn't know what happened to him after that."

"Use your imagination, huh?"

"Yeah. We need to find this kid and talk to him. I'm guessing the two of them were in it together, out scouting for pot to steal, and whoever got Tommy just missed the other guy."

"He may not want to talk to us if they were both out ripping off people," I said.

"Maybe not, but the family's gonna take care of that for us. He'll talk to us or he'll wind up missing too is the message I'm getting. Tommy's mom and dad aren't fooling around anymore."

I could see the marijuana angle and sort of got why the two of us, rather than a couple of OSBI agents, were sitting there in the diner, but this did raise a couple of other questions. Like, why didn't the Hatfields pursue this with the logical choice in local law enforcement, namely the Choctaw County sheriff? He's the one who's supposed to put out the call for state help, getting the OSBI and dogs and planes and agents who did murder cases down to pitch in when one of his citizens goes missing. Pat had the answer for that too.

"They say they can't trust him. According to them, he's in with the McCoys, protecting their marijuana grows, letting them do their thing. They're saying he wouldn't help and he might be involved himself. There have been some threats made."

I'd heard this kind of talk before, spending a lot of time out in Oklahoma's more rural areas. "There're always rumors like that. Listen to the gossip and every county sheriff in eastern Oklahoma's a crook or dope dealer. You must've gotten the same word, working Internal Affairs."

"Yeah," Pat nodded. "I'm inclined to believe these rumors though because the Hatfields are saying *they* used to be the ones paying the sheriff—or somebody who works with him—to protect *their* marijuana grows before the sheriff switched sides. These folks aren't exactly pure as the driven snow themselves, if you catch my drift."

"Hmm. Okay, well, my boss says I'm on board. What's your first move?"

"I'll get in touch with Lewis, the trooper that got the ball rolling. He showed me the sights as soon as the sun came up this morning and he's out looking for this kid, Terrell—T.W.—right now. The kid's been laying low, but when the Hatfields turn him up, they'll tell Lewis where he's at."

"Always good to start with an informant."

"Yeah. We'll have to meet him here in Valliant or up in Antlers. Word's gonna get out that we're in town, but we probably ought to fly under the radar as long as we can. And speaking of that, I got the Patrol plane flying out of Durant for us later this morning. We can have him scout the whole area, see if he can scare up some marijuana patches. We'll check those out and see what we can find."

"This Terrell kid can probably put us on to a couple of those. It would be nice if he could tell us which ones are the McCoy's patches and which ones are the Hatfields'. Narrow things down. And they're probably not the only two bunches down here growing weed. From what I hear, it's sort of a way of life."

Pat grimaced. "There is a lot of that happening. Enough so these folks get upset about each other messing with their action. And they're gonna be more unhappy about outsiders like us coming in and poking around. I'm not gonna lie; all the guns down here, this could get hairy. It already has, in fact."

"Well, yeah. Kidnapping and probably murder."

"Hotheads on all sides. Armed hotheads. They had a big confrontation yesterday. I don't know if it was high noon or what, but about twenty people from both families faced off right in the middle of Highway 70 in Fort Towson. Shotguns, deer rifles. Miracle nobody opened fire, no shooting. Yet. But tempers are running high. It didn't get past yelling and cussing yesterday, but it will."

"Jesus. Just like the Old West," I said. "Hard to believe this stuff's going on in 1977."

But really, it wasn't that big a stretch. Crooks and criminals hadn't transformed or gotten more civilized over the decades. A lot of the Oklahoma lawmen I met hadn't changed much either, and the biggest of these in every sense might have been Jimmy Birdsong.

OKLAHOMA CITY, OKLAHOMA

James Michael Birdsong was a legend. Even if only half the stuff people said about him was true, he was the most notable narc in Oklahoma. He taught me a lot, made me a better undercover, shot me once, saved my ass, and scared the living hell out of me a couple other times. You couldn't let Jimmy know that you'd been spooked or even much flustered by anything like that, though, or he'd never let you forget it and bear down twice as hard the next time.

I only worked undercover with Jimmy twice: eerily similar, hair-graying experiences, both of them. Jimmy didn't make the best undercover partner. For starters, he was noticeable. Six feet six inches tall, and three hundred plus pounds, with an outsized personality to go with the physique, he wasn't the kind of individual people meet and forget. And he met a lot of people. On the mostly black northeast side of Oklahoma City where he did a lot of his business, he knew—and was known by—practically everybody. This sort of notoriety isn't healthy for undercover agents. Since it might be the last thing you ever hear, the last thing you *want* to hear while you're in the middle of a deal is somebody saying, "I know this guy, he's a cop." A high percentage of the crooks in Oklahoma City could say exactly that about Jimmy Birdsong since he'd put handcuffs on many of them.

But I worked undercover *for* Jimmy plenty of times, buying dope from the people he and his informants, of which there seemed to be hundreds, sent me to. This included many cases on the Eastside, where almost all of the dealers and the junkies were black. I'd been a little hesitant about working the heroin cases there, not feeling that I fit in, a white boy from Hawaii, but Jimmy assured me that the dealers would be happy to sell to a skinny white kid, no matter where he was from if he set it up properly.

"What are you worried about?" he asked me early on. "Those dope pushin' maggots don't give a damn if you're white or black. They just wanna know if you've got the green."

And he was right. As usual in the drug business, the most important color on Northeast 23rd Street and Eastern Avenue (now Martin Luther King Blvd.) wasn't black or white, but the exact hue of a twenty-dollar bill.

At street level, the dealers sold Mexican brown heroin, a fine powder, in tiny packets called "pills," that went for ten or twenty dollars each. Each pill consisted of a child's rubber balloon, wrapped tightly, tied off, and completely waterproof, about the size of a peanut M&M candy. These were functional, but a pain in the neck for undercovers. Dealers and their customers normally carried the pills in their mouths, where they could be easily swallowed and not-so-easily retrieved later if a cop suddenly showed up wanting to do a search. The rubberized pills survived their trips through the digestive system quite nicely but buying them had its issues.

For one thing, I liked to know what I was getting, not wanting to have to explain to Jimmy why I'd paid one hundred dollars of state funds for some convincing-looking but empty rubber balloons. You had to cut the things open to view the contents, and junkies did not do this on the street. Dealers got very jumpy when I proposed to check a pill right there in the car or on the corner, knowing that only narcs violated standard junkie protocol to do so.

Normal etiquette consisted of a set routine whereby you placed your order and paid on delivery, a quick hand-to-hand transfer with a twist. The wrinkle was that the dealer, not wanting to get caught with his stash, kept it in his mouth until the moment of sale, spitting out your order and handing it over. Then he watched expectantly while you popped them into *your* mouth because a real junkie customer wouldn't want to be caught with them either.

I got very adept at palming the pills and getting them into a pocket unnoticed, often by "accidentally" dropping part of the buy money and making the move during the distraction. Still, it didn't solve the rip-off problem, which was very real, the Eastside dealer seeing a likely victim in the white boy from another part of town, passing off (or spitting out) pills full of chocolate powder or milk sugar or worse. I unwrapped one purchase to field test it, carefully taking out each knot in the tightly bound rubber pill, a junkie version of one of those endless Russian nesting Matryoshka dolls. Being careful not to spill anything, this process took almost five minutes, and when I got to the very last level, I found... nothing but a knot.

There aren't any complaint departments or other places to make a grievance over a "beat bag" or some other rip-off. People like me, white folks and junkies from elsewhere, would have a hard time bitching a bad deal on the Eastside, that being the dealer's home turf, for sure.

Jimmy told me to just roll with it. His already low, rumbling voice dropping dangerously, he said he'd later deal harshly with anybody who got the state's money under false pretenses, a non-idle threat that Eastside dealers took seriously, knowing who made it.

"Look at this boy," Jimmy said to one such pirate, grabbing me by the collar and holding me out like a restaurant meal he'd found with a bug in it. "Look at him close. I know you remember you sold five pills to him the other day. And come to find out there wasn't any fuckin' heh-rawn in any of 'em. What've you got to say about that, huh?"

The dealer looked appropriately sheepish. "I guess I'm real sorry, Mr. Birdsong. I didn't know it was for you or I wouldn't of did it."

"Damn straight. But we spent a hundred bucks on sugar, which is fuckin' useless, and now you gotta go get me some real stuff to make it up. You can take him with you to meet your connection. The real one." And another Birdsong informant was born.

The negotiations for the pills were always interesting. Prices went up for the white boys, though not for the girls, who could "tip" the difference in creative ways. It wasn't uncommon for me to pay twenty bucks for a ten-dollar pill, but I tried to convert the process into my "buy up" scenario that should allow me to get a look at a more sizable quantity, one sold in wrapped up paper squares or small plastic bags. The biggest heroin buy I made was a quarter ounce, although we later grabbed a pound from the guy. Those buys let me get a tiny quantity out and run it through a chemical test kit, hoping for the distinctive purple of the Marquis reagent.

Birdsong must have worked undercover at some point because he had the moves, but he'd mostly gotten over it by the time I hired on. I took him with me on two occasions though, and both times ended up scary close calls, although the first started off quite entertaining. That's because, as we'll see, Jimmy, a notorious practical joker and comic, always tried to wring as much fun as he could out of what might or might not be a very funny situation.

***

We'd been working the crook, Brad, for a couple of weeks and I'd made one buy from him already, setting it up for the bigger methamphetamine purchase to follow. That would be a buy-bust: see the drugs, take possession, arrest everybody. Although we might flash it at them, even let them hold it for a minute, no money really changed hands because we didn't have that kind of cash to give away, and with the case already made, didn't need to.

I'd agreed to do the deal at the crook's house, which normally I avoided. Keeping it on his turf gave him an edge and more control than I liked to cede, but setting it there meant it would be that much easier to get a search warrant for the place later. To even the odds a bit, we thought we'd bring another agent to the party, and Jimmy volunteered himself. Since Brad didn't have any track record for violence, we thought the meet was fairly low-risk, and because our target's place was on the southwest side of OKC, outside Jimmy's usual stomping grounds, he thought he could get in unrecognized. It turned out we were about half right on both counts.

I called Brad late in the afternoon and told him we were on the way over, but we waited until after dark to roll up, and not by accident. I preferred doing deals at night because it cut down on the chances of someone I knew seeing me and tipping the crook. It also let the backup agents outside get closer. Close is good. Close is comforting. Close, you don't feel so all alone. I didn't let Brad know exactly when to expect us so we'd have a chance to check his place out and see if there were any visible surprises planned.

We knew when we parked that he had company; the surveillance had spotted two other people going in. That made at least 3-2 odds, but we felt comfortable with those. Sure enough, all three of them were sitting in the living room when I knocked on the open screen door. Brad said to come in.

He didn't introduce the other two, both of whom had that coyote-lean, perpetually hungry, tweaker look, just asked straight up if we had the money. Neither of his buddies said anything, following the conversation like spectators at a tennis match, their stares flat and cold. Also tracking the conversation with interest was a large German shepherd mix dog, who we'll call Shep. He was a friendly sort, a big, playful puppy, wagging that long, fringed tail, wearing a goofy "pet me" grin, clearly overjoyed to have more company show up. I'd met Shep the last time I'd been there and knew he enjoyed having those pointed ears scratched, so when he laid his head up against my leg, I obliged him while I talked to his owner.

"I got the money, same as last time," I said. "It might be out in the car with our friend. Have you got the stuff?"

"I got it. I been keeping it here for hours, waiting for you, man. Where you been?"

"Sorry. Had to get all the cash together. We had to see a couple of people. They fronted us the money because I told them you were straight up."

"Let's see it," Jimmy said. "Not here. No offense, but I don't know these guys. Or you either, no matter how solid he says you are."

Brad looked mildly put out but not enough to shut the deal down, not with the money—$10,000—so close. "C'mon back here, I'll show you."

I gave Shep a parting pat and followed Brad and Jimmy into a back bedroom where he went to the closet and pulled out a shoebox with a bag of white powder inside. He handed it to me. It looked like speed and when I opened it, it smelled like it too; the slightly stale, sweaty, cat-pee scent of biker meth from a P2P (phenyl 2-propanone) cook. Awful, but definitely felonious. I gave the bag to Jimmy, who did his own inspection. Before either of us could say anything, including the bust signal for the transmitter, Brad, obviously concerned about losing the sale, started vouching for the dope, saying it had come "right from the lab," and that he'd been much too scrupulous to cut it.

"I'm being straight with you guys," he said. "I'll show you. Here's my ID. You'll know who I am. I'm real."

Jimmy and I looked at each other. This was... unusual. Nobody had ever carded me before, though I had a genuine Oklahoma driver's license in my undercover name. And I'd certainly never demanded identification from a seller, though that would have saved a lot of trouble over the years. I mean, it's not like there's some regulation that you have to have valid, government-issued identification to be a dope dealer, or have to prove you're over twenty-one to buy methamphetamine. Jimmy seemed amused by the concept, giving the bag back to me and checking the driver's license.

"That's real good, *Bradley*. We're pretty real too, and just to show you that *we're* on the up and up, I'll show you *my* ID; how's that?" he said, starting that familiar deep, echoing chuckle that always got increasingly maniacal as he warmed up to his punch line. And of course, he pulls out his OBN badge and credentials, handing the closed wallet over to Brad.

Who cracked open the case, peeking just far enough inside to see the gold badge, then snapped the leather shut, staring wildly up at Birdsong, who towered over him by almost a foot and was now laughing madly. He took back his badge. "That's right; you're busted, fool," he said. "And hey, Brad, don't you recognize me? I bagged you once before, just last year. Why in the hell did you still do this deal? You have got to be the dumbest dope dealer in Oklahoma."

Brad hung his head, shaking it and not saying anything.

Now I was laughing, not believing anybody arrested by Jimmy Birdsong could ever forget that minor little detail. I sent our own bust signal out, then told Jimmy I'd put the other two on the floor while we waited for the backup to get there.

Gun in hand, I went back to the living room, told them who we were, and yelled at them to get on the ground, making sure they couldn't get to the door or reach for any weapons. Things were going well so far, then a bone-chilling sound reminded me that things can always get worse undercover.

I'd totally forgotten about Shep. He'd been happy to see me come back into the living room, trotting over for another pat, which I didn't have time for, being busy at the moment, bending down to give the nearest of the two tweakers a fast frisk for weapons. But Shep let me know he was still around, though not in his usual, happy-go-lucky style. This time, he sounded off with a harsh, booming growl.

I looked back over my shoulder, seeing eighty pounds of barely contained, pissed-off pooch poised about a foot from my extremely exposed butt. There was no lolling tongue or sappy expression, no puppy playfulness now. Ol' Shep was all German shepherd, ears straight up, his whiskers standing out like he'd been plugged into an electric socket, lips drawn way back over his teeth. Lots of teeth: shiny, white, and from my point of view, about the size of a saber-toothed tiger's.

If the fangs didn't do it, the snarl did; a throaty warning of impending action that seemed to come from the depths of a very angry soul. He sounded like the Hound from Hell and looked like it too. Figuring I had about three seconds before I lost a bite-sized piece of my ass, I tried, "nice doggie," reminding Shep that we were old pals, but he barely paused for breath before starting another menacing growl, increasing the pitch, and showing about an inch of gum above the teeth.

"Call off your dog," I told the guy I was leaning over.

"Ain't my dog," he said, turning his head for a look, making sure he wasn't the one in the canine crosshairs.

Nope, it was all me. I'd clearly violated the space Shep had suddenly remembered was his job to protect, and now he was making sure I knew that I, his former friend and ear-scratcher, had worn out his welcome on this patch.

I had a distressingly short list of options, trying to run through them before Shep removed any, along with my butt. None of them had any appeal or were going to work. I could wait for the backup agents to arrive (and they seemed to be taking forever), but it sounded as though Shep's patience had about expired, and the sudden entry of another bunch of strangers seemed likely to make matters worse, not better. I could turn and shoot him—had my gun in my hand already and couldn't miss from this range—but I loved dogs and had never deliberately hurt one. And deep down, this was a good dog, just doing his job, his pack-protection thing. Very deep down. Hard to see the good, friendly side of Shep at the moment behind all those teeth. He opened his mouth a little wider and started another snarl. I could see the back teeth now and feel his hot breath. He couldn't miss at this range either.

"What the hell are you doing, playing with the damn dog?" Jimmy had come into the room, dragging Brad along by his shirt collar.

"I'm not playing. He's gonna eat me. Get him off my ass." They say you're not supposed to show fear to an animal. Too late for that. Shep was seeing plenty of fear and didn't seem too distracted by it.

"Oh, for Pete's sake," Jimmy said. "Come here, dog." He grabbed Shep by the collar and lifted him up and away, all four legs waving wildly and the snarl completely forgotten. He held all squirming eighty pounds at arm's length with one hand, keeping a firm grip on Brad's shirt with the other as I scrambled over the tweaker toward the front door.

"Okay, Brad. Let's stick him in the bedroom where he won't be eating anybody. Wouldn't want any dis-ass-ters in here." Jimmy, chuckling again, glad to find some more humor in what should have been a fairly serious enterprise.

While they turned toward the back of the house, the agents on surveillance outside came in, too late to see the whole K-9 near-miss. Nobody, including Shep, had gotten hurt and we had our case made, so everything turned out okay. I've had people rescue me from other potential "disasters" before and since, but I can proudly say that nobody but Jimmy Birdsong has ever literally saved my ass.

CHAPTER 3

LEAVES THAT ARE GREEN –
LOST IN THE HIGH GRASS

FROGVILLE, OKLAHOMA
SEPTEMBER 1977
MORNING OF THE FIRST DAY

Pat Grimes was thirty-five that year, with dark hair and eyes full of humor that smiled at me even as we talked about finding a kidnap victim and Wild West showdowns on quiet country streets. He and Jimmy Birdsong had a lot in common, both Oklahoma lawmen to the core. Pat was a trooper who had patrolled Oklahoma's turnpikes and back roads alone for a decade before a promotion to the Patrol's Internal Affairs section. He came from a law enforcement family; father Bill Grimes had been a trooper and so was Pat's twin brother Mike, who would eventually become deputy chief of the Patrol.

This thing with the Hatfields and McCoys wasn't in Pat's normal job description either; but like me, he was determined to do what he could to get Tommy back healthy and intact if possible. That was going to require a lot of road miles and taking help from unsavory characters like Terrell and some hotheaded folks whose loyalties might lie elsewhere. We could count on no support from local law enforcement, whose own allegiances, we'd been told, were also in some doubt. Tracking down three people who might already be dead would just get us to the starting line, one that already loomed in the distance as the clock ticked louder and louder on the life of Tommy Hatfield.

In the diner in Valliant earlier that morning, the breakfast crowd drifted out, leaving the two of us pretty much alone with the waitress, both of us thinking about the complications already apparent in this situation. Pat saw it clearly. "Somebody's liable to get killed over this deal if they haven't been already. That's why we need to get moving on this. We'll have a lot of driving to do today."

"More driving. Great." I had four hours in already that morning.

"We're gonna need to go over to Texas too, talk to the sheriff down in Paris."

"What's in Texas?"

"Maybe Tommy. Let me show you." He got out a folded topographic map of the area, the broad coils of the Red River twisting along the bottom, not many contour lines. The roads ran dead straight and made right-angle turns and there were very few built-up areas, and almost nothing south of State Highway 109.

"Here's the border." He ran his finger along the line. "You can see how it follows the river, but there's places like here," he pointed to a slice due east of Frogville, "where the river changed its bed and now Texas is on this side of the water. Maybe a few hundred yards of it, all river bottoms, scrub, and timber. Rough country. And over here, you got a big piece, maybe a square mile, pretty close to Frogville, that's Oklahoma, but on the south side of the river. The family says that's where Tommy was headed. He was probably in Oklahoma, but maybe not."

"Swell. So, this might be a Texas kidnapping, is what you're saying."

"It's possible. Or an Oklahoma kidnapping and a Texas murder. And we can drive into the Texas part on this side of the river, but we'll need a boat to get to the Oklahoma part on the other side unless we come at it north from Paris. Nearest bridge is fifteen minutes away, and that's from here in Valliant. Maybe forty from Frogville."

I studied the map. On the positive side, we weren't talking about a huge area, maybe only ten or twelve square miles. On the negative, you could hide an awful lot of bodies in this little corner of Oklahoma (and maybe Texas). Or dump one in the Red River and have him wash up in Arkansas or Louisiana in a couple of months. And there wasn't much in the way of civilization on the map. It showed some structures, little squares that were probably farmhouses or barns. Most were set back from the few roads running through the area, which meant driving down long private driveways to places where people might be real unhappy to see two state police officers.

"That's a start. We should have the pilot spot any buildings out there too. If they're holding him someplace inside, maybe they've got a trailer or a cabin. Something that's not marked on the map here. If we get lucky, maybe there's one close to a patch. It'd be nice to cut the search area down a little."

"We're gonna need a break is how I figure it," Pat said. "Let me check in with Durant, see if Lewis found the kid, and set up a meet." He went out to his cruiser, a plain blue OHP sedan with a half dozen whip antennas sprouting on the trunk and roof. You didn't need the white state map on the side and OKLAHOMA HIGHWAY PATROL to know whose car this was.

He got off the radio and was back in a minute, saying Lewis had T.W. in tow and was bringing him over from Fort Towson. "We'll meet them over by the paper mill. Stay in the car, less likely somebody'll see us together," he said.

I paid up and said I'd follow him, arranging the highway patrol frequency that we'd be using to talk back and forth when we weren't in the same car. A few minutes later, we were stopped nose to tail on a side road near the entrance to the Valliant Paper Plant, one of the biggest in the country. Had that lovely pulp mill aroma and fuggy atmosphere going on. A swell place for a meeting with an informant, who rode up a few minutes later in the passenger seat of a black-and-white OHP car with the antennas *and* all the markings. The trooper got out, saying something to T.W., who peered out at us through the windshield.

Lewis was the quintessential state trooper: tall, solid, crew-cut under the broad-brimmed Smokey Bear hat, bulked up under a bulletproof vest, all his uniform and equipment shiny, spotless and perfect. He looked tired though and told us why as we stood by the side of Pat's car, the morning temperature already climbing. It would be a hot one.

"Been runnin' this boy down since yesterday. Spent most of last night looking for him in Hugo. I hope it's worth it."

"Did he say anything to you about the missing kid?" Pat asked.

"Oh yeah. He's got all kinds of things to say about that. He says it's all second-hand, but I think he knows more than he's lettin' on. And wait till you hear about the Mexicans. That'll make your day."

"Mexicans? What Mexicans?" I said.

"I'll let him tell you. It's a good story, even if the guy telling it's a 12-gauge moron. You're gonna want to thump him a few times. I sure wanted to, but I didn't think it'd do him any good. Sure ain't gonna make him any smarter."

I looked sideways at Pat, the Internal Affairs guy, listening with me as his trooper talked casually about wanting to beat on a citizen. Pat didn't seem fazed by it though, keeping an open mind, and after a minute with T.W. in the back seat of Pat's car, I could see what Lewis meant as I resisted the urge to haul off and smack my latest informant. It wouldn't have done any good though. Lewis was right about that too.

Terrell (or T.W. as he preferred to be called) was, what we in the narcotics business said, "a couple grams short of an eightball." Since an eightball, or eighth of an ounce, starts out at a piddling three and a half grams, you can't be too many grams short or you end up with thin air. Which is right where T.W.'s head was at. He was a blocky kid, already starting to put on the weight that would turn into an impressive beer belly if he made it to age forty. A broad jaw gave him a rectangular face, flat and acne-pitted and dusted with the faint, wispy tracing of a hopeful but failed mustache.

I remember thinking that this kid, who probably played center on his high school football team, didn't look like he had the speed to outrun a bunch of pissed-off McCoys. But I guess he only had to be faster than his cousin. T.W. had gotten through high school somehow, graduating with the now missing Tommy Hatfield, the two of them "hunting up work" in the summer months after school finished. Neither of them had college plans, and in T.W.'s case, those would have been a wild overreach and total waste of everybody's time.

He started off lying, of course. People who believe they're smarter than you, but really aren't, mistakenly think is a good way to begin a relationship with folks who can put them in a pair of handcuffs. T.W. hadn't "seen nothin' personally," but had "heard what everybody's sayin' about Tommy."

Lewis shot that down straight off. "Cut the crap, Terrell. Tommy's momma told me right in front of you that you were along on his little hunting trip. She watched the two of you drive off together."

"Yeah, but we got split up when we got to the barn and they run us off. So I didn't see nothin' after that."

"Which barn is this?" I asked.

"Eugene McCoy's. All rundown and shitty. They run some cattle, and the cows use it for the rain and shit. Mostly they store their weed inside. Dryin' it out. It's way off behind all the other stuff on Gene's place."

"You know where this is?" Pat asked Lewis.

"Yeah. I can show you on a map. He's right. It's off in the weeds. I've never been back to this barn, but I know McCoy's place," Lewis said.

"So who ran you off, and what were you doing in the McCoys' barn in the first place?" I asked.

"Hunting hog. Don't need no license and there's plenty in that timber down toward the river bottom."

"Uh huh. Hogs. Did you happen to see any weed while you were inside this barn?" I asked.

"We never even got inside that time. It was there though. Got plants hanging so they dry out, some bagged up. It's a little early, but they're starting to bring it in already. They was the three Mexicans there the McCoys got working for 'em, and a couple of the McCoys too. When they seen us, they pulled guns and started chasing. I got back to the car. Tommy never showed. He had the keys, so I had to walk a couple miles to get to a phone. Got a bunch of the family together and we went back down there. Car was gone and so was Tommy."

"We got a vehicle description? That the Camaro?" Pat looked at Lewis, who pulled a notebook out of a carefully creased pocket.

"Yep. 1970 Chevrolet Camaro, red. Registered to Katherine Hatfield. Katie. Tommy's momma." He read off the tag number.

That could be a break. Finding a red car in this search area would be a lot easier than finding a body, and we had the plane going up any minute. Pat got on one of his radios to reach out to the pilot as T.W. filled in his story with descriptions of the place, the Mexicans, and the two

McCoys he'd seen. He gave us a good idea about what Tommy looked like and had been wearing, although we already had a picture of the kid that Pat had gotten from the family. That's when it turned weird. Or weirder.

T.W. said he and the posse got back to the barn about two hours later, the afternoon waning but the sun still up in the early September sky. Heavily armed and amped up for a confrontation, they drove in pickup trucks straight to the barn, where they fanned out, looking for Tommy and anybody else they could round up.

"No Tommy and the McCoys was gone too. Probably out moving the car. But those Mex boys was still there. All three of 'em."

Bad news for the Mexicans, who T.W. said had been hired on to tend the marijuana crop set out in the brush around the barn. He seemed rather offended by this, saying the McCoys were getting what amounted to slave labor to "do all the damn work" while "real" Americans (presumably the Hatfields) had to perform all that toil on their own illegal marijuana fields.

"Is that even legal, them usin' these wetbacks?"

"No. But that's the least of everybody's problems right now. Let's get back to the story," Pat said.

There were trails leading off to these little patches, and the Hatfield posse checked out all of them, "poking the Mexicans out front," which meant pushing them at gunpoint down the paths first to set off any booby traps that might have been laid out for trespassers or draw any McCoy fire. No sign of Tommy though, and everybody trooped back to the barn, where they held a short discussion on possible alternative courses of action.

"Somebody said we should find out what happened from the Mexicans. I told them they was right there when it happened. They must've seen something. Only they wouldn't talk. So we tried to make 'em. Made 'em dance first."

"Dance? Mexican dance?" I said. What the hell? Pat looked confused too. Lewis just shrugged, resigned. He'd evidently heard about dancing Mexicans previously.

T.W. had a good answer, seemed downright proud of it, in fact, which is also par for the course for stupid people. "Nah, we had their hands tied up behind their backs with some electrical cable and they was just standing there, not sayin' nothing, like they didn't know, so J—I mean, somebody just started shootin' at their feet. They was hoppin' around like the whole ground was on fire, but when he run dry, they still wouldn't say nothin' anybody could understand, so he loaded up another mag and did it all over."

"Jesus. Did he hit anybody?" I practically had to push my dropped jaw back in place to ask this, wondering if we were going to be looking for four dead people now, the roll of the missing starting to lengthen.

"Nope. Knocked off a bootheel though, put that one Mex on the ground. But none of 'em was really hurt."

"What did you do next?"

"They still wasn't saying nothin' more than '*por favor*,' which we worked out was 'please.' But they wasn't sayin' please *what*, so J— somebody says, 'Take 'em in the barn and get a rope out of the truck.'"

Pat and I looked at each other, wordlessly agreeing that this bizarre story could, indeed, get worse. Lewis shrugged again. He already knew it got worse. I could clearly picture the scene, three terrified young men, trapped at the center of a circle of hate, shot at, bound, and undoubtedly beaten, and now marched into a dark barn where their captors threw a rope over the first rafter.

"What the hell? Did any of those dumb sons of bitches check to see if these guys could even speak English?" I asked.

"Nah, they couldn't. They're wetbacks. Only thing they know is Mexican and how to work in a pot field. We figured that out later."

"Yeah, after you'd shot at them and hung 'em from a barn rafter, you figured out they couldn't understand what you were asking them or tell you if they did."

"They knew what happened to Tommy." T.W. shook his head stubbornly. "They was right there when it happened. I seen 'em myself."

"None of you boys spoke any Spanish, huh?" Pat said.

"Hell no. Maybe they need that Mex shit down in Texas, but up here, everybody gets by in English."

"Might've come in handy this time though," Pat said, and T.W. didn't argue it.

"So what happened next? What did you do with the Mexicans?"

"We give up on 'em. Left 'em right there where they was at, went lookin' for McCoys. At least those assholes speak English. They was scarce though. Didn't find any till yesterday morning, up in Fort Towson. I guess y'all heard about that."

"Oh yeah. We heard about that all right," Pat said. "Doesn't sound like that was real helpful for anybody either. Where can we find these Mexicans?"

"Gene's place. They're livin' in an ol' trailer out back of the house. Just down a ways from the barn, so they can walk to work."

"And you're sure we're gonna find them there? Alive and kicking..." I said.

"Unless they run off someplace. They was sure kicking last time I saw 'em." He laughed.

Nobody laughed with him. "You'd better hope so. Because killing Mexicans is just as illegal in Oklahoma as killing Tommy Hatfield," Pat said.

"Hey, they're alive. We wasn't trying to kill 'em, just scare what happened to Tommy out of 'em."

"Well, clearly that great plan didn't pan out," I said. "Show us on the map here where we can find this place."

"Those Mexicans aren't out of the woods yet," Pat said, as we headed down US 70 toward Frogville. "I don't think the McCoys are going to be real happy hearing their hired hands spent an hour or so alone with a bunch of Hatfields, telling them who knows what."

"No," I said. "Dead men tell no tales, and if what Terrell says is true, they're witnesses to the kidnapping and maybe everything that happened later. Plus, they're probably illegal and definitely up to their necks in the dope thing, so they've got legal problems of their own. I wouldn't want to leave that kind of loose end laying around."

Heatwaves rose from the blacktop in front of us as we entered Fort Towson, an even smaller and more forlorn version of Valliant, five or six faded storefronts on the highway and a few tired-looking houses. Nobody outside as the sun climbed higher and the thermometer headed toward the century mark. All quiet on the main street as we rolled through, past the site of yesterday's Wild West confrontation. I felt better about this thing. I might be uncomfortable with a kidnapping and murder investigation, but finding three people in the dope growing and selling business and squeezing them for information? That there was right smack in my wheelhouse.

OKLAHOMA CITY, OKLAHOMA

I didn't usually work in places as small as Valliant or Fort Towson, much less no-places like Frogville. Most of my undercover work went down in Oklahoma City, and much of that on the northeast side where the drugs were and where everybody else did business—out on the street. A lot of white junkies dropped in on the black neighborhoods to score, and this meant picking up from one of the many corner dealers and runners that kept the heroin flowing.

Jimmy's informants set up the buys from these people; I had little or no control over the targeting process. The informant would tell Jimmy about a connection, and he'd tell me where to go and who to look for. Most of the time, the informant would go along and make the introduction. We generally tended not to take this buy to court because it meant exposing the informant as a potential witness. Once the introduction had been made, I could go back by myself and make one or two smaller purchases before ordering up the big one for the buy/bust.

These smaller, follow-up transactions were called "confidence buys" because they were intended to build up the crook's trust and get him comfortable with the UC. This was the standard routine, and if the undercover isn't careful, it can get to be routine, which is a bad state of mind to be in.

It was this routine that took me several times to the corner shared by two notorious Eastside characters. They weren't infamous because of their stature as drug dealers; they were small-timers like everyone else who worked out on the street. No, these two were notable for their street names, Sleepy and Dopey. It's hard to write that almost four decades later without laughing, but there it is. And those weren't our nicknames for them; when you asked for Sleepy or Dopey on the corner, that's who answered. They were usually together, a matched pair. I don't know where or even who the other five dope-selling dwarves might have been, or what these two did to earn their street names, but neither of them seemed too bothered by their association with fat little cartoon characters.

I'd made the case on Dopey easily enough—the informant making the intro, and Dopey, who looked sharp enough at the time, spitting out the rubber heroin pills without missing a beat. He did the confidence buys the same way, one for heroin and one for cocaine, the two of us getting used to seeing each other in the same place and under the same circumstances. Dopey knew my car and started waving me down when he saw it, even when I was driving through the neighborhood on some other business.

This would be a problem because once we had the first three buys down, Jimmy wanted me to turn to Sleepy.

"We don't know who these two idiots are picking up from," he told me. "Could be it's the same guy supplying both of 'em. Probably is. But on the chance they've got different connections, we'll get buys into Sleepy too."

"I dunno, Jimmy. Dopey's seen me three or four times and I've been buying his pills. He's gonna want to do the next one too."

"We'll figure it out. Maybe we can put you out there when Dopey goes to re-up."

That was a thought. These guys could only hold so many pills in their mouths at one time. They had to be able to talk and, more importantly, swallow all the pills quickly if an emergency (like Jimmy Birdsong turning up unexpectedly) occurred. This meant that when they'd sold a mouthful, they had to go get some more from their stash, leaving the corner to the competition for a few minutes. If we timed it right, I could come and go before Dopey returned, and his absence would be my excuse later for giving my business to a competitor: "Sorry, man, but you weren't around when I came by..."

That's how we worked it, but as I was learning fast, undercover deals never went on time or according to plan.

We had an agent with binoculars in a parking lot a block away, keeping track of everybody on the corner or near it. Jimmy and I were parked out of sight, two or three streets further off. Business on the corner was booming, cars stopping and the slingers doing their thing at the open windows. Sometimes the surveillance could even see the money changing hands. All this was taking place about three blocks from the residence of Oklahoma's governor, almost in the shadow of the state capitol building.

I got the call to roll up after only a half hour or so of waiting, so it looked like this deal would happen more or less on time. As I got to the corner, I found out it wasn't going according to plan. The spotter had described Sleepy, supposedly identified from a mugshot taken at the time of another recent encounter with the police, and said he was wearing a gray hoodie sweatshirt to ward off a little of the late autumn chill. Problem was, Sleepy wasn't the only hoodie-wearer on the block that morning.

I told the hidden transmitter about the problem. "Dammit, there's at least three guys out here with gray sweatshirts and hoods. I can't see any faces. I'm going to the closest one and asking for Sleepy."

But the nearest hoodie turned out to be an old acquaintance, who recognized me and my car immediately.

"What it is, little brother?" The individual improbably known as Dopey leaned into the open passenger window. "What can I do you for? Coke like last time? I got the best deal."

I didn't mention that Dopey was quite the salesman, one of the more aggressive hawkers on the street. He was always on the hustle, always pushing for the upsell, and had a dozen good reasons why his pills were far and away superior to anyone else's on that corner or any other.

But Dopey wasn't supposed to be here and now I was wasting time and energy and possibly buy money on somebody who already bought and paid for but just didn't know it yet. Hoping I'd caught him empty on the heroin side, but not very optimistic, I said, "Nah, man. I'm lookin' for some smack for a friend of mine."

"Her-o-wine," Dopey said. "I can do that. Got some right here, finest in OKC." He worked his tongue around inside his mouth and made the selection from the shelf, spitting two brightly colored balloons into his hand, holding them out, the rubber shining wetly. "Check it out, this stuff come straight from the her-o-wine mine. Pure as it get." Getting into his sales rap, and...

Wait. What?

You obviously can't see my face on the audiotape, but there is a fairly lengthy pause in the conversation while I ponder this information, outrageously erroneous, and contrary to everything I'd learned at the DEA's school and in about fifty books on the opium and heroin trade. As almost everybody (probably including Dopey, but not, apparently, his less witty customers) knows, heroin comes from the same poppy plant that produces opium and morphine. It's a vegetable product. "Mines" and mining don't enter into it.

I was really, really trying to find a way to put this guy off, and finally decided to challenge him on this latest and most ridiculous sales line. "Heroin mine? What the hell are you talking about? That stuff doesn't come from a mine. They make it from a plant. Some kind of flower."

Dopey laughs. "Flower? Flower? How they gonna get her-o-wine outta a flower? Nah, I been selling this shit for years." (He was going to regret this recorded admission.) "I know all about the mine. Even seen it myself, down Mexico, one time."

"But... but..." Now I was seriously torn. Part of me wanted to buy the pills just so we'd have a chance to use this tape in court. Another part reminded me that Jimmy gave me pretty strict instructions not to mess with Dopey today or waste any more money on him. Plus, a third part really wanted to continue this entertaining conversation and the idiot's education, thinking about how the tape would play back to an appreciative audience as tales of Lost Heroin Mines, hidden narcotic Golcondas would amuse jurors. But I finally remembered why I was there and it wasn't to go chasing after nonexistent heroin mines, so I resisted the temptation, although it was a struggle.

"Whatever," I said finally. "I ain't buying any heroin comes from a mine. What about Sleepy? My friend got some from him before. He said it was good stuff."

"Sleepy? No, you for sure don't want none of that boy's shit, nuh uh." Here, he leaned in even closer, dropping his voice, obviously not wanting to be overheard speaking ill of a competitor. "He used to have the good stuff, same as me. Well, almost. He hit his a little too hard, put some bad cut on it. Word get out, people stop buying his shit. De-value the merchandise, so now he on the outs with the man. Now, I hear he mostly use Nestlé's Quik and floor sweepin'. You wanna make some dirty hot chocolate, you go see Sleepy for sure."

"Wait a minute. You're telling me the stuff you've got comes straight from the her-o-wine, I mean, the *heroin* mine, but he gets his shit off the floor?"

Dopey nodded vigorously. "He my friend and all, and a man got to make his ends meet, but rippin' off folks, mmm, mmmm. Cain't be havin' that."

"That him down there?"

Dopey looked reluctantly through the windshield to where I was pointing at another hooded figure, just going to the side of a pickup truck. "Yeah, he the one stand next to the white truck, got the gray shirt. I'm tellin' you though—"

"Thanks. I'm gonna check him out." I torqued the stick shift, letting the car roll a few inches, hoping Dopey, still half in and half out, would get the message and leave off the sales pitch.

He wasn't quitting that easily and he wasn't backing out of the window, which made it hard to just drive on. He turned to another product line. "What about some coke, then? I got pure, uncut."

I almost laughed out loud. It was grossly unrealistic that cocaine could filter down through a half-dozen layers to an Oklahoma City street corner "uncut." More likely, somebody at each level had been one nipping off a little here and there, every hand that touched it (or every nose) making up for the shrinkage by tapping a health store for Inositol or a medicine chest for some benzocaine or lidocaine. Benzo would—lido, too—provide coke's numbing features but they delivered none of cocaine's buzz. Other additives, like baking powder, looked good but provided even less in terms of active ingredients. By the time it got to the street, that coke had been hit more times than a speed bag at a Muhammed Ali training session.

Same thing for the heroin, really. Uncut dope of any kind was the Himalayan yeti of OKC. Big, bad, hairy, cold, and white (though the heroin was usually brown). And like the yeti, almost certainly a legend. When it finally landed on Dopey's corner at Kelley, it had been cut more than a steak at a Japanese hibachi restaurant and stripped down from a regular ounce (28.35 grams) to something about 25 grams. A little of Dopey's second confidence buy, supposedly an eightball (3.5 grams) of "pure" coke had turned out to be stepped on so heavy, the chemist had to run a second test just to confirm there was any coke there at all.

I shined him on, nixing another confidence buy on the wrong guy. "Can't do it. I only got so much cash today."

He still wasn't giving up. "How about high grass? I get you some a that. No problem."

"High grass? What the hell is that?" I pressed harder on the brake, curiosity getting the better of me.

"Weed. Smoke. Herb. Where you been? Only this is from the field with the biggest plants. The high grass. It get you plenty high too."

"Like sugar cane fields, then," I said, trying to sound skeptical, not sarcastic.

"More like corn. You seen those? Go five feet inside, you disappear outta sight."

"Uh huh. Lost in the high grass, huh?"

"Exackly, my man. You be lost in this shit, that's for sure. Won't come out till to-morrow. And even then, you won't know where you at or where you been. Lost in the high grass."

I contemplated the salesman's image of fields of waving Mary Jane. "Well, it's tempting, I'll admit. But like I said, I only brought enough money for a couple pills of some smack. So..." I inched the car another foot forward.

But the salesman hadn't finished, and clearly wouldn't be giving up unless he had a deal in the bag. He spit out another balloon. "These here're twenty-dollar pills. You buy two, I give you one more, free."

I really had to stop myself from laughing at that one. They were unquestionably ten-dollar pills—thirty dollars' worth—that he wanted forty for, the extra ten going straight into Dopey's pocket. Maybe he wasn't so dopey after all.

"That one from the her-o-wine mine too?" I asked.

"Best shit in OKC. My personal guar-an-tee."

I shook myself, still trying to process the sales bullshit being tossed around the Cutlass. Time to go. "I'll go talk to Sleepy and if he can't match you, I'll be right back."

"Your money." Dopey backed out of the window and straightened up, popping his three ten-dollar pills back into his mouth. "But I tell you what. You go run down there, get yourself a nice twenty-dollar hot cocoa, then come back up here, get some a this stuff. Don't get any fresher outta the mine."

I said that sounded fair and pulled off down the block, easing myself into Sleepy's queue behind the white truck, seeing the quick spit of bright rubber into the palm, the money coming back and going into the hoodie pocket. Thinking I'd done very well to avoid wasting the government's money on heroin from a mine or high grass from a cane/cornfield, feeling a bit smug about the whole thing and far superior and much smarter than some idiot who actually allowed himself to be called "Dopey" and thought heroin came from underground, I rolled up to Sleepy.

A minute later, I had two pills in my pocket and another street dealer in the bag. A few days later, the Oklahoma State Bureau of Investigation crime lab confirmed that just as I'd said all along; those pills hadn't come from a her-o-wine mine, of course.

They'd come from a world-famous chocolate company. Buy about fifty more just like them and I could make myself a very weak cup of hot cocoa.

Just like a guy named Dopey had told me.

I'd learn over time, wouldn't make the same mistakes, wouldn't get suckered as often as I had in those earliest of days. I'd develop rules for dealing with people like Dopey, unwritten personal guidelines and procedures that hardened into iron laws preserving my cases and my safety. One of the biggest was never to reverse roles with the drug dealer. Giving dope to an informant or anybody else was a ticket to disaster. Nothing good could come of going to that dark place. Except maybe getting a kidnap victim back. Which is why I went to that place one afternoon in late summer in Frogville, Oklahoma.

CHAPTER 4

LOOKING AT YOU

FROGVILLE, OKLAHOMA
SEPTEMBER 1977
MORNING OF THE FIRST DAY

In the parked car at the paper mill, Pat handed me the topo map, folded to the section that showed Frogville and its environs. I held it up to T.W., who eyed it before planting a thick finger on a spot just east of where the little town used to be. Good news: the map showed a tiny brown building. Bad news: it was located fairly close to the Texas border, now on this side of the river. Not even a quarter mile off. If I was growing weed, I'd want it in that gray zone where the people who had legal authority also had a hard time exercising it. And taking somebody down to the river for a long, final, face-down float down to Shreveport would be a cinch.

"What about the weed? We go over there, we gonna find all this hanging pot?" I asked, giving the map to Lewis, who checked the spot T.W. had pointed out and nodded.

T.W., meanwhile, went all shifty, eyes flitting around the car, not lighting on me. "Maybe not. I'm thinkin' those McCoys and the wetbacks probably cleaned it all out. Figured you boys'll be down here lookin' for it."

"Or maybe you guys looted the place before you left. Which explains why a dozen or so pissed-off McCoys faced you down in the street in Fort Towson yesterday," Pat said.

T.W. didn't argue this point either, which said more than any excuses he might've made. We spent another half hour going back over the story and having our new informant mark down places on the map where we could expect to find marijuana fields or structures where somebody might keep a prisoner. Even T.W. didn't sound too positive on that score, only Tommy's parents holding out hope their boy might be coming home. T.W. wasn't real happy to be reminded that stealing all the McCoys' carefully cultivated marijuana wouldn't make them any friendlier toward their captive, or likelier to cut him loose if they still had him. That's when I had an idea.

"If we offer to trade the dope you stole for the kid, will the Hatfields go along with it?" I asked.

"Maybe," he said, looking puzzled. "But can you do that? Give weed to people? I thought it went the other way around. Ain't you always takin' people's shit away?" he said, not denying he and his friends had stolen it, you'll notice.

"Yeah, well, I might be willing to try anything at this point to get this kid back in one piece," I said.

"I can ask around. I ain't got any myself, or I'd do it," he said.

"You better be real persuasive asking. Maybe go tell Tommy's momma to talk some sense into everybody who was out there at that barn. She wants her boy back, she'll light a fire under their asses and get 'em to bring in that dope. How much are we talking about, anyway?"

"I dunno. Bagged up already, maybe fifty pounds. A hundred still on the plants hanging. Maybe two. It looked like they might've got most of their crop in."

"That's a lot of weed. Even for this place," I said. "Which is why you and Tommy were sneaking around out there in the first place." I waved off his objection. "Never mind. Let's see if we can get some or most of it back. Get the Hatfields to pull together, then we'll see what the McCoys have to say."

"And hope they haven't already pulled the trigger on your buddy," Pat said.

"Hey, I sure as hell ain't talkin' to those McCoys, riled up like they are," T.W. said, shaking his head vigorously for emphasis. "They all got guns, now they know we been lookin' for Tommy. Shoot me before I got near to the front door."

"Well, isn't that just swell?" I said. "Shoot first and listen later. Thanks, man. Now Pat and I have to go poking around in the fucking hornet's nest you two yahoos stirred up."

T.W. looked to Lewis for a little support but didn't get any.

"Too late now," Pat said. "You just make damn sure everybody on your side of this circus knows OHP's out here, looking. And we've got guns too. I don't care if they're Hatfields or McCoys; they shoot at a trooper and we'll rain hell down."

"Start rounding up that weed," I told him. "And make sure Lewis knows where to find you from now on. We don't want to have to hunt you up too."

Lewis took the still-protesting kid back to the patrol car and U-turned back toward the highway.

"So we going into the marijuana business now?" Pat grinned at me across the seat.

"Hey, I haven't seen any pot. It's all just fairy tales up till now. I'll bet the thought's occurred to the Hatfields already though."

"Maybe that's why they took it to begin with, wanted something to trade."

"That's the most likely possibility, I guess. Or door number two, they're all just a bunch of dumb, greedy, dope-dealing assholes who hate McCoys and saw a chance to stick it to them."

"Huh. It's a lead though. But looking at that map, I think we're gonna have to go to Texas. Maybe go and get back while the plane's still up."

"Let's do it. Where can I leave my car? Might as well just take one and you're wired in a lot better than I am. All those antennas you got, you could talk to the moon."

Pat laughed. "Let's leave it parked here in the company lot. We can let security know to keep an eye on it."

"I'll get my gear out in case we don't get back for a while."

In ten minutes, we were on the road to the only bridge across the Red River for miles. We jogged south at Fort Towson on State Road 109 to run by Eugene McCoy's place and see if we could find any Mexicans about and scope out our search area. No signs of life, but we'd be back, and looking for dancing Mexicans with rope burns on their necks.

That was to be my introduction and welcome to Frogville, America, a nothing little place where I'd work a crime that didn't concern me, trying to help people whom I'd rather lock up, and make a case that would never get anywhere near a courtroom. Something that nobody outside Frogville would ever hear about or maybe even remember. That wouldn't be true of everything that came my way over the years. Like my brief encounter with the biggest music star in the world.

Memphis, Tennessee
August 17, 1977
A month before

A light rain was falling on Memphis as another agent and I passed through on I-40, headed east for Florida. Thousands of other people flocked to the city that August afternoon, come to the river city to mourn. Drugs touch every part of our society, reaching down to the humble like Tommy Hatfield, Franklin, Brad, and Dopey, and up to those much higher in wealth and power. One of the very highest—in every sense of the word—was Elvis Presley, the King of Rock and Roll. On August 17, 1977, the King was dead, and admirers everywhere took the news hard. One of our administrative people at OBN was so distraught about it that she followed us down the interstate from Oklahoma City to Memphis to stand with thousands of others in a vigil at Graceland before the funeral. The coroner chalked the singer's demise up to "heart failure," and of course, that's what gets everybody, eventually, but he signed off on the death certificate only three days after the King passed, long before the toxicology reports came back. Those listed some unpublicized "contributing factors" in Presley's case, namely a ton of drugs.

I'm not throwing the word "ton" around loosely. Elvis Presley got more controlled drugs than any other single person I've ever met, seen, or even heard of. He was the King of Drug Abuse. And abuse it was, because although he had many health problems, undoubtedly legitimate, that pain killers, tranquilizers, and sleeping aids could relieve, Elvis voyaged far, far beyond medical use. When he died, pathologists found eleven different drugs in his system, several "in significant quantities." Although the medical examiner ultimately came up with a different decision, the pathologist said the drugs were enough to end Presley's journey through life at only age forty-two. One wrote in an official report, "Together, all this information points to a conclusion that, whatever tolerance the deceased may have acquired to the many drugs found in his system, the strong probability is that these drugs were the major contribution to his demise."

One chauffeur on Elvis' chemical trip was George Nichopoulos, M.D. Dr. "Nick," who signed the singer's death certificate, was a ranking member of the Elvis entourage and a pallbearer at the King's funeral. That last part is sadly ironic because, in my opinion, the DEA's, and the State of Tennessee's, Dr. Nick helped put Elvis in the box he so lovingly carried later.

I met the doctor indirectly while I was working on the trial of another M.D. after I left Oklahoma to work in Honolulu. Although I'd been buying prescriptions undercover in the investigation, an interesting assignment since the doctor was a gynecologist, my job at this point in the case was to coordinate the witnesses and have the batting lineup full so that the US attorney could keep the prosecution on schedule. These trials always relied on other doctors to testify as expert witnesses on their colleague's practices, the key issue being whether the prescriptions were written in "good faith" for a "legitimate medical purpose" (addiction and recreational drug use aren't "legitimate") and within the "normal scope" of the medical practice. My opinion and those of other cops on those issues didn't cut much ice in court. The jury had to hear from other doctors about what was "normal" and "legitimate" in the suspect's practice. And the experts gave an opinion on "good faith" too.

Being out in the middle of the Pacific, we usually found our expert witnesses on the island but not this time. This was a high-profile trial and the doctor defendant had made it abundantly clear that he planned to fight it until the last dog died. He started out by getting one of the most noted and high-powered lawyers in California for his defense, and we went to the West Coast too for our expert witness, engaging a highly regarded physician, someone at the very top of the field. Dr. Forest Tennant had a doctorate in public health, as well as his medical degree, and was recognized worldwide as an authority on drug abuse and treatment. He'd done the expert witness thing many times before and agreed to share his opinions about the case at our trial.

I spent some time with the doctor, going over his report, making sure he had all the facts, and keeping him advised on any issues that needed to be addressed in his testimony. As we waited for other witnesses to finish, Dr. Tennant and I sat on the benches outside the courtroom and chatted, talking about the transportation and hotel arrangements and his plans for the time in the islands when he wasn't at the courthouse. He didn't mind the wait, saying he was keeping busy, getting ready for another trial back in Tennessee. I'd heard about that; most of America had. It was the upcoming criminal case against George Nichopoulos, Elvis' personal physician. I assumed that Dr. Tennant would be testifying for the government; we'd paid him to come to Hawaii and his reports in our case showed he had little patience for doctors who abused their prescription privileges.

He'd testified for the prosecution in the case against Howard Hughes' physician, which was how we had found him in the first place. We talked at some length about that case because I'd looked into it when I'd visited the DEA office in Las Vegas. We wanted to hear what the agents there thought of their expert witness, so I got to see the case file and the trial records, the government's documentation of the many prescriptions for narcotics received by Hughes. The case was in some ways eerily similar to Dr. Nick's. Hughes' doctor had prescribed huge amounts of codeine, a Schedule II drug, over a long period of time, the same drug that the Tennessee coroner had found in massive quantities in Elvis' blood. Like Elvis, Hughes was getting some other controlled drugs, though not nearly on the King's scale. That the movie mogul, aviator, and billionaire was addicted to codeine didn't seem much in doubt, judging by the amount he fired up on a daily basis, even if, as Dr. Tennant told me, all those codeine injections hadn't caused Hughes' death. But the astronomically wealthy eccentric definitely had a drug problem, graphically illustrated for me, not just by the volume of prescriptions, but by the set of autopsy x-ray photos the DEA had as part of the case file. The pictures of his skinny little arms—he was 6'1" and weighed only ninety-three pounds when he died—were stunning. They were studded with hypodermic needles, broken off beneath the skin and embedded permanently in the flesh. It was silent, sobering, and compelling testimony to the supreme power of addiction: photographic proof of how drugs touched the richest man in the entire world.

Although Dr. Tennant had testified for the government against Hughes' doctor, he told me this time he'd signed up for Dr. Nick's defense. He didn't think Nichopoulos had been responsible for Presley's death either and proceeded to tell me why. He had a record of every prescription the doctor had ever written for the King. In 1977, there were two hundred of them just through the first half of August, and the list for the previous months and years held hundreds, thousands more. That was just the tip of the iceberg; everyone knew that Presley and his entourage got more delivered directly by Dr. Nick. The doctor traveled on tour with Elvis and took three suitcases full of prescription drugs with him on the trips. Everybody—from the King on down—stayed well medicated on the road.

And Presley did all right at home too, according to Dr. Tennant's papers, which he laid out for me. He had a massive file, one that included the autopsy report and the toxicology results, providing a detailed picture of Elvis' last minutes. The prescription records expanded that painting to the singer's last days, weeks, and months, and they were astounding. Seemingly endless columns, page after page, listing almost every controlled substance in the statute book. Narcotics, tranquilizers, amphetamines, barbiturates, sedatives, stimulants, uppers, downers, tens of thousands of them. The opioids alone would have been enough to thoroughly hook several, maybe even dozens of people. Dr. Nick was writing scripts for stimulants and depressants on the same form on the same day, over and over. The last script—written on August 15, 1977, the day before Presley's death—ordered six different controlled substances, all Schedule II, the most restricted under federal law. These were:

- Dilaudid: 4mg, 50 tablets, a narcotic, twice as powerful as heroin, used for intractable pain;
- Dilaudid: 2mg, 20cc injectable solution (Elvis was shooting up);
- Percodan: 100 tablets, another narcotic/opioid, containing the now-notorious oxycodone;
- Quaalude: 300mg, 150 tablets. This was a five-month supply of sleeping pills for a normal person taking one tablet per night to help get to sleep;
- Amytal: 3mg, 100 capsules. Amytal is a highly addictive barbiturate used for sleep, called "Blue Heavens" on the street, and favored by other dead celebrities Marilyn Monroe and Judy Garland. It can be deadly to take this drug with Quaalude, or Percodan or Dilaudid, for that matter;
- Amytal: 500mg, 12 ampoules. These were injectables also, so Elvis was shooting up more. He must've had tracks like the Illinois Central. That's three separate sleeping medications.

He needed those because of the
- Dexedrine: 5mg, 100 tablets. A potent amphetamine, though not as good as…
- Biphetamine: 20mg, 100 tablets. Known on the street as "Black Beauties," a very sought-after upper.

All that on a *single* script, enough controlled drugs for several months, maybe more, for a normal person, even one with multiple serious medical conditions. There were requests for six hundred different tablets and thirty-two injectable vials *on this one paper alone*. And Dr. Nick wrote prescriptions like this every week. Sometimes every day. I flipped through the catalog, which went on and on for years. It was a thick packet of paper, and I was amazed then, and still am, that Elvis lived as long as he had. The quantities here should have put down horses, much less the singer, even if he did weigh three hundred and fifty pounds.

I have to admit I was looking pretty askance at Dr. Tennant at that point. The doctor on trial in our courtroom had written thousands of prescriptions too, for methaqualone: almost sixty percent of all the Quaaludes prescribed in the state of Hawaii, and north of one percent of all of that medication prescribed in the whole country. One man. But he never wrote more than one prescription per paper, for more than thirty pills at a time, or more than one prescription per month per patient. He did have hundreds of patients he was treating for "sleep disorders," although as a gynecologist he didn't specialize in sleep, which was a factor in our prosecution. But sitting there, looking at page after page of virtually every controlled drug in the statute, Dr. Nick seemed an order of magnitude worse.

And somebody was dead too, just like in the Hughes case. Our doctor hadn't killed anybody that we knew of, least of all the King of Rock and Roll or one of the world's most well-known billionaires. While I made plans to pull the assistant US attorney aside at the next break in the proceedings and let him know about the problem, I asked Dr. Tennant what I thought were the logical questions. Like, what in all that evidence showed anything like "good faith" on Dr. Nick's part? And if Dr. Nick hadn't killed Elvis, what did?

Dr. Tennant explained. All those drugs hadn't actually caused the singer's death, although he was willing to concede that they turned him into a stone addict. In fact, of the drugs found in the King's system in the autopsy, only two had been on that last prescription: the drug in our trial, methaqualone (Quaalude), and barbiturates (Amytal). The others—Ethinamate (a Schedule IV sedative); codeine; meperidine (Demerol), another potent narcotic; morphine; and Valium, a tranquilizer; as well as a non-prescription antihistamine—were mostly present in small amounts. Elvis did have ten times the normal human dose of codeine in his system, but Dr. Tennant pointed out that Dr. Nick hadn't prescribed codeine in the last script or morphine. Despite the abundant prescriptions (including many previous ones for codeine), he said Elvis still didn't have enough of Dr. Nick's dope in his body to kill him.

That seemed altogether beside the point to me. Elvis might not have gotten it the day before, but I could point out fifty prescriptions Dr. Nick *had* written for codeine, just going back through the last couple of pages, and the Demerol, morphine, and Valium too. How did this ton of dope show good faith, especially when Dr. Nick knew that Elvis was getting drugs from other doctors when Dr. Nick wasn't available, and most probably was giving some of the pills to friends and other entourage members?

And Elvis certainly wasn't the first celebrity to go down this road. Marilyn Monroe's doctors had prescribed an almost identical cocktail of problematic—and very dangerous—substances. Although she'd gotten Nembutal, known on the street as "yellow jackets," a potent barbiturate sedative/sleeping pill, the empty bottle found on the bed stand next to her body, she also got scripts for Amytal, Seconal (which killed Judy Garland), and phenobarbital, plus Dexamyl, a combination of Amytal and amphetamine, all but the last potent sedatives. She poured these on top of the same highly addictive opiates Elvis got from Dr. Nick— morphine, codeine, and Percodan (oxycodone)—and lifted herself out of the sedation with Desoyxyn, Dexedrine, and

Benzedrine, the best amphetamine stimulants that money could buy.

One big difference between the two megastars' cases was that in 1962, when Marilyn washed down her Nembutal with a stiff shot of brandy, only the opiates were "controlled"—then called Class A narcotics. Amphetamines and barbiturates could only be dispensed on a doctor's prescription but there weren't nearly as many restrictions as when Elvis went into the bathroom that last time, fifteen years and two weeks later. By 1977, doctors had a much clearer understanding of the dangers of prescribing all these things together, especially the potentiation problem, which causes the drugs—especially barbiturates, narcotics, and alcohol—to become more powerful and potentially deadly when combined. Dr. Nick surely knew this, and I, being rather intimately acquainted with drug-related death certificates, and never having seen anything even close to as many substances on a single record, pushed Dr. Tennant hard on the point.

We had plenty of time to kill, all morning, so he gave me the same pitch he wound up for a Memphis jury a couple months later. Maybe I was his dress rehearsal for the trial. He told of how Dr. Nick had tried to get the singer off the meds, tried to substitute weaker doses for the stronger ones, even had special placebos made up to look like the real thing but had no dope at all in them. He'd been involved in detox and methadone treatment for the narcotic addiction and was immersed in Elvis' long, long catalog of very real health problems. The autopsy recorded almost twenty medical conditions as factors in the death, and that probably was just a snapshot. Dr. Nick, the expert said, was acting in good faith.

I'm no expert on the matter. Obviously, that's what we needed Dr. Tennant for. But it still didn't sound good or faithful to me, and the file, page after page of the most highly regulated substances in the country, didn't convince me of the rightness of Dr. Tennant's position either. I argued the conclusion with him, using the catalog of prescriptions and the same arguments that prosecutors would throw at him when he got to Memphis. I noted that his list didn't show a reduction in the number of prescriptions; on the contrary, Nichopoulos was writing just as fast at the end as he had been earlier. It also didn't include any fake-looking "placebos" or sugar pills, just thousands and thousands of genuine articles. I said it looked to me like Elvis might be sharing some of the take with his entourage or somebody else, seeing as how most of these drugs potentiated each other, and taking all of them together would be hazardous, to say the least. Likely to lead to severe medical conditions like, for example, sudden death in your bathroom. And aside from the amphetamines, most were sedatives or depressants. If he wasn't sharing, and was really taking all this stuff himself—half a bottle of sleeping pills *every night*—when was Elvis Presley actually awake, singing and conscious?

But Dr. Tennant was smooth, confident, and had an answer to all the objections, which is what made him so great in court. He was the expert, a decent, fair, and much more knowledgeable authority than I, who clearly called them as he saw them. The clerk came for him a few minutes after that. While I sat outside and sweated, he testified that our gynecologist hadn't shown much good faith at all. The jury agreed, coming back with a guilty verdict a few days later.

I got it on one level. Celebrities tend to get what they want from their entourage, and everybody *in* that entourage knows they'll be *out* of it if the celebrity doesn't get what he wants. The people in Michael Jackson's entourage knew it, and so did the ones in Marilyn Monroe's and Prince's. Maybe Whitney Houston's too. Dr. Nick knew it, and he stayed around, writing prescriptions, even after an adamant Presley shot at him once, wounding him slightly. What had made the King so annoyed with his doctor that he started blasting away at him with a handgun? The doctor claimed the shooting happened after he turned Elvis down on a prescription for narcotics. And Dr. Tennant told me that Dr. Nick kept right on writing after getting winged. In good faith.

With Dr. Tennant's help, Nichopoulos beat the rap on the over-prescribing charges in state court in Tennessee. The Tennessee Board of Medical Examiners didn't see things quite the same way, pulling his medical license for three months and giving him three years' probation in 1980. They yanked the ticket permanently in 1993 for over-prescribing to many other patients. Prosecutors said the doctor wrote prescriptions for over six *million* doses of controlled substances and dispensed or administered plenty more drugs directly to his many patients over the years.

"My patients, the ones I didn't kill, were very faithful," the man people called "Dr. Feelgood" told a reporter later. Well, sure they were, Dr. Nick.

"Faithful." What an interesting choice of word from the man Elvis Presley had trusted with his life for "good faith." Drugs touch everyone in society in some way. The prosecutors couldn't prove it in court, but I'd read the file and talked to the pro and knew how drugs touched the King.

Dr. Tennant had his opinion and he was the expert, but I had a different one about good faith and those patients Dr. Nick "didn't kill."

POSTSCRIPT

Time flies, and I didn't hear anything of Dr. Tennant for more than thirty years. In November 2017, the DEA executed a search warrant at the doctor's premises, The Tennant Foundation, in West Covina, California. The agents were looking for evidence the doctor had provided narcotic drugs, including fentanyl and oxycodone "prescribed and dispensed other than for a legitimate medical purpose." It wasn't Tennant's first run-in with the law; he'd been convicted in 2001 for fraudulently billing California's Medi-Cal program, and of course, he had been involved in many other drug-related criminal cases as an expert witness.

At the time the agents served the warrant, the doctor was out of state. He was in Montana for the trial of another physician who'd been charged with illegally dispensing the narcotics that led to the fatal overdose of a patient. Dr. Tennant was testifying for the defense.

POST-POSTSCRIPT

In July 2021, Dr. Tennant published a book, *The Strange Medical Saga of Elvis Presley*, a companion to *The Strange Medical Saga of Howard Hughes*, which he published the month before. In both books, he describes the circumstances surrounding the deaths of the two notables and the relationship of their drug use to their demise. He didn't mention me or our doctor but justified his conclusions and his testimony in both the Hughes and Elvis trials. Dr. Tennant clearly hasn't changed the opinions he offered in either of the two cases.

Neither have I.

CHAPTER 5

BABY DRIVER

We put a lot of miles on the Patrol cruiser that day, down and back from Frogville to Paris, Texas, over to Durant to meet the OHP pilot. Dirt roads down by the river. Hours with a map on my lap as Pat drove, marking down places the pilot said might be marijuana patches or buildings way off in the bushes.

We waited until late to go after the Mexicans at the McCoy place, figuring they'd be home from the fields at the end of the day. If they weren't hiding out somewhere. Or dead already. We found the McCoy place right where T.W. told us it would be, a two-story wood farmhouse, set back a ways but still visible from the road. We ignored this, heading up the long gravel driveway, right past the house into a backyard scattered with junked cars and rusting farm equipment, a swing set, and assorted castoffs. And a ratty-looking old trailer, just like T.W. said—built sometime in the fifties probably and not seeing a lot of good days since—hunched on a little rise behind the house. It was darkening out, still a glow in the western sky but the trees and brush around the place were already deep in shadow. The farmhouse was black too. Nobody home or people pretending not to be. Lights shone from the trailer and the strong smell of beans cooking wafted out through the open windows. If we were working off stereotypes, we'd found the right place.

Finding it, however, was just the first of our problems. Pat didn't speak any Spanish and I said, "Don't look at me. I took French in school. I know about ten words and most of them are from a movie."

Our plan was to grab all three Mexicans and take them down to Hugo, where we hoped to find somebody who could translate for us. All we had for probable cause was the statement of our unreliable informant that these three were illegal immigrants and were involved in the marijuana business. Which, looking at the trailer, sounded more credible every second. Still, it wasn't much of a plan.

We climbed out of the car, easing the doors shut. I got my shotgun. Pat had a large-frame revolver, and we eased up to the side of the trailer. The voices inside all stopped. My guess was they knew we were out there.

"*Policía! Policía!*" I jerked open the door and Pat vaulted past me up the steps and disappeared into the trailer. I followed a moment later, the interior steaming hot and reeking of a Mexican supper. Three young men—two shirtless and sitting at a flimsy dining table, one standing at the stove, wearing a white wife-beater—turned toward us, staring open-mouthed.

"*Manos arriba!*" I pointed the shotgun at each of them, making the point. Everybody quickly raised their hands, the communication seemed to be going well.

"*Siéntate! Siéntate!*" I motioned with the gun to the floor and the wife-beater sat down, the other two climbing down from their chairs, everybody with hands still in the air.

"That worked good," Pat said when everybody looked settled in on the floor. "What else have you got?"

"I don't think it's gonna help."

"Give it a shot."

"Okay, but you deal with the fallout. I'm gonna pretend this whole thing is your idea. *Donde está la caja? Abrela!*"

The attentive, eager-to-please looks on all three faces vanished in an instant, replaced by anxiety and confusion. The hands came down a fraction, and the mood in the room shifted, and not in a good direction.

Pat got it right away. "That didn't work. Try something else," he said quickly.

"Pat, all I've got is *siéntate*, and they're already sitting, and *manos arriba*. They got that too, and they know we're the *policía*." The hands did go a little higher at "*manos arriba*" and higher still at "*policía*." Everybody back on the same page, even if it was the only one in my

Spanish book.

"The hell with it. Gimme your handcuffs. You cover me while I hook 'em up. We'll search them outside." He holstered the revolver.

I'd brought two pairs of handcuffs and Pat had a pair, so that part went well. Nobody resisted and we chivvied them out through the door and onto the dirt outside, proning everybody flat on the ground. Pat searched them for weapons, coming up empty. All three did have distinct red circles around their necks, so T.W.'s story was sounding better—or at least more accurate—all the time.

"I'll go back in and get a couple shirts for these guys. Turn off the stove," I said.

There was some loose pot piled on the table and a few rolled reefers and a zip-lock. The loose stuff looked nice and green, fresh from the field. The Hatfields hadn't gotten all of it. I found a paper bag and scooped the weed into it, then got three shirts off one of the beds.

"We'll let 'em put the clothes on when we get to the sheriff. I don't want to unhook anybody out here. I expect it gets real dark down in this country," Pat said. "We'd never find him if one rabbited."

With all three belted in the back, we turned toward Hugo, leaving Frogville behind for the moment. We'd be back. I'd have bet the McCoy farm on that.

We were finally going to the sheriff's department and making our presence known and our case official, although both of us suspected the sheriff already knew. Word gets around fast in these small towns and sheriffs take pride in knowing everything that's going on in their counties, and we'd spent enough time that day talking to people in Choctaw County that we figured the word was out already.

We'd spent part of the afternoon with Tommy's mother, dropping by her weather-beaten farmhouse on the road between Fort Towson and Frogville. Mrs. Hatfield stood tall in her doorway, a big, rugged woman who filled the entrance to her home, projecting equal measures of determination and sullen desperation as hope she'd see her boy return through that door faded. I pitched the pot-for-hostage swap, saying, "We won't interfere if somebody returns that stuff your people came across. Call it lost and found. We'll talk to the McCoys and see they get the same message. Everybody comes away happy with something they want."

"Those folks hurt Tommy, we're gonna raise all kinds of hell. We seen 'em yesterday up in Fort Towson. They were pretty sassy then," she said.

"Hold off on the hellraising for another day or two. Let us see what we can do," Pat said. "In the meantime, pass our message along to your kinfolk. We won't interfere, but you can't interfere with us either. We've got a job to do and we're gonna do it. Anybody—McCoys or Hatfields—that gets in the way, the State of Oklahoma will land on them like an April twister."

She said she'd get the word out, that she had considerable pull in the family, especially now, a mom missing her son.

I wanted to remind her that her boy wouldn't be in this jam if he hadn't been out poaching other people's illegal operations, but that didn't seem necessary, and I didn't see determination on her face as she nodded, tight-lipped, just doubt about our prospects and the strain of hopelessness and despair.

Pat and I still had our own misgivings, questioning the reliability of our new informant, both wanting to know more about the possible involvement of the sheriff and any other local cops. Talk's cheap, but these were serious accusations getting thrown around, running all the way from selling drugs to being involved in the kidnapping. Actual evidence, of course, was lacking, but the animosity was crystal clear. These folks didn't like the sheriff or trust him, and since they freely admitted that, until recently, they'd been paying him not to mess with their marijuana operations, they felt more than a little betrayed. As things turned out, they had good reason to feel that way.

We pushed the question and she said, "Folks are pretty mad at him. He didn't do nothing when we told the deputy about Tommy, said he'd probably turn up. Ain't happened yet."

We said we'd do what we could, and headed back to the cruiser. A girl, maybe eighteen but probably a few years younger, edged around Mrs. Hatfield and came down the steps to our car. The polar opposite of the older woman, she had a pinched, unhappy face, and stood about five feet tall, carrying ninety or ninety-five pounds on a wiry frame. She didn't look like a Hatfield. I guessed she might be Tommy's girlfriend, at the house to maintain the vigil.

"I got a picture of him," she said, holding it out.

"Who are you?"

"Amber. Tommy's fiancée. We're gonna get married, you get him back."

"We'll try," I said. "Can't make any promises, but it'll help if everybody stops acting like a bunch of banditos, stealing shit and hanging people. Tell all his kinfolk, we can't be having that. It just gets everybody mad."

She nodded and turned away, walking back up to the porch where her future mother-in-law waited. I put the picture with the one Lewis had gotten earlier, wondering if we'd ever get to see the kid grinning slyly in his tuxedo, standing next to Amber in front of a red Camaro. On their way to the senior prom.

I could certainly empathize with the Hatfields and their situation. They were dope dealers and pot growers and Tommy probably wasn't the only one in the clan who'd thought about ripping off someone else's grow. But they had lost a family member, a son, brother, cousin, maybe for good. It was easy to be sympathetic with some people. I still ache for a girl named Violet. But I learned over the years that there's a time and a place to feel sorry for folks. I found that out the hard way with a couple of people, like the old lady in the Hoveround and the Man with No Legs.

HONOLULU, HAWAII
1980s

Right or wrong? I still agonize over this one, and it's been almost forty years. I was a young agent, pretty new to this job, and we got called to a pharmacy on an altered prescription for narcotics; I can't remember which one, but it was a big one. Dilaudid, maybe. Twice the power of morphine. Altering prescriptions is just a stupid crime, easily detected, easily proved, usually no other suspects, just dead bang. But it's a felony, and we always arrested anyone found at the scene. My partner and I got to the store, where a very sheepish pharmacist says he feels bad about this one. He says he doesn't want to press charges and he's talked to the doctor, who doesn't want to either. Well, that's not their option. They're not the victims in this crime, just witnesses to it. The prosecutor is the one who decides, and we tell him that. He just shrugs, looking sick.

The suspect is this young woman, Violet. She's in her early twenties but looks about twelve, very skinny, maybe eighty pounds. She's crying and her mother, who's her driver, is crying too. I explain she's under arrest for prescription fraud; the mother's begging me not to bust her, says her daughter's a terminal cancer patient, didn't know, in pain, needs narcotics, didn't understand, doesn't have long. Months, maybe. I'll make sure she doesn't do it again. Etc.

It's too late, the doctor knows the prescription's been altered, the pharmacist knows, we know, it's a felony, she's there at the scene, we've got to book her. That is the "proper procedure," though it's already making me sick. She's so little her hands go right through the handcuffs and they fall on the floor. The only time that ever happened to me. We let her ride in the back uncuffed. Book her at the station, the mother's outside, still pleading, we tell her we're releasing her pending further investigation, which means no bail or court appearance for now while we refer the case to the prosecutor. Meanwhile, I gave the suspect her property back, which includes a bag full of cancer medications—and I mean a bag *full*—that she'll be taking home with her. The bag does *not* include the narcotics. She has to go back to the doctor and get a valid prescription for those, but I told her I'd talked to him and he said he'd write her another script. Violet left the station with her mother, and that's the last time I saw her.

There's still some work to do on the case. We needed a written statement from the pharmacist, had to interview the doctor and get a statement from him, and had to write up the report and submit the whole thing to the prosecutor, who had to make the decision at his discretion to submit to a grand jury or not. That's the approved, standard procedure, the "by the book" routine in every case. Not this time. In this case, for the only time in my life, I disappeared that file. That's not my call to make. I should have gone to the prosecutor and talked them out of filing charges, and in later life—maybe a year or even six months later—I have no doubt I could have done just that, but I was young—only five months with the state at the time—and not yet confident enough in my ability to move the deputies one way or the other.

Should I have gone "by the book," played by the rules, followed SOP? There are two really good arguments for doing that: one practical, the other philosophical. On the practical side, an officer or agent will almost never get in trouble for sticking strictly to the book. Deviating from the manual, skipping an approved procedure, cutting a required corner, *that* can land you in serious hot water, especially if something bad happens. Defense—or even worse, personal injury—attorneys will make major hay out of lapses like that, however well-intentioned they may have been. Our manual said in black and white that if we responded to a pharmacy on a forged script call and found the suspect there or nearby, an arrest was mandatory. There was strong support, legal and practical, for that policy, but it "made the call" for us and gave the responding agent no discretion.

It's the right call for philosophical reasons too. We're a government of laws, not of men, and representatives of the criminal justice system shouldn't make decisions playing favorites based on people's circumstances or positions. That's why the statue of Lady Justice wears a blindfold.

That way, giving cops the discretion to arrest or not, to grant a favor or deny one, lies anarchy. What are the rules under that system? We pass a law but leave the option of how to enforce it, or even whether to enforce it at all, to people like me. Cancer patients get a pass. Okay, I'm cool with that, except in Walter White from *Breaking Bad's* case. What about cerebral palsy? I'm very sympathetic to those suffering from that condition too. What if their disease is "only" as advanced as R.J. Mitte's, also from *Breaking Bad*? What about people with phantom limb pain? Look it up, that's quite terrible, and I'm very sympathetic to that too. It wasn't my case, but I helped arrest somebody with that condition for the same offense as Violet. He was a Vietnam vet, amputee, a Purple Heart recipient, and should have been very deserving of a compassionate break. Except he was a jerk, a junkie, and someone who got off exposing himself to women and resisting arrest. So we only bust the phantom limb people who are jerks, but the okay/sick ones get a pass?

Who makes those calls? Now it's the prosecuting attorney who is supposed to use his options to seek justice, not convictions. Prosecutorial discretion extends to whether or not charges are filed, whether to plea bargain or dismiss those charges, whether a case should go to trial, and what sentence the government recommends to the court. The agent doesn't get to make any of those decisions. I don't *want* that authority because while I like to think I might be okay with it, sure as hell there are people out there who will use that power the wrong way.

I guess on the face of it I abused my authority by disappearing Violet's file, usurped the prosecutor's role in cutting her a break. (This, by the way, is *exactly* what FBI Director James Comey did by tanking Hillary Clinton's email case and look where it got him.) Was it the "right" thing to do? It still *feels* right to me but whenever I think about it, and I do fairly often, I wish like hell I could turn the clock back four decades, dispense with "proper procedure," and cut her loose at the front door of that pharmacy. I'm sorry, Violet.

I met some other people over the years, some in Violet's same situation, that didn't deserve an ounce of sympathy and didn't get it. Some were just straight-up junkies; it was almost their defining characteristic, their career. They were drug abusers, out for themselves, chasing the rush that the drugs provide or just trying to sustain their addiction. For many, the objective is to get high, stay high, and repeat for as long as they can keep the party going. Others are messed up physically or psychologically and come to drugs without really meaning to. Once they're there, though, some of these people, many with very real, severe, even chronic medical conditions, lust just as hard and go to the same, mostly illegal, lengths to chase that rush. I did feel sorry for those people, sympathy for the troubles that brought them to the new lows they reached while they pursued the highs. I think Elvis lived in that zone before he went into his Graceland bathroom that last time. But looking back, it's awfully hard to summon up any pity for the lady in the Hoveround power wheelchair.

She was a decrepit sixty, damaged somehow by disease or maybe just age, weight, and whatever condition ailed her that had confined her to a Hoveround, one of those electric mobility scooters. She was getting narcotics on prescriptions from a couple of doctors, had come up on the office radar screen before for altering a prescription, and the word on her was out at the pharmacies.

Nobody was surprised when she tried to pass another altered prescription for narcotics at a big local drug store, the pharmacist calling with the news. Like I said, altering scripts is about the dumbest crime you can commit. It's like signing your name on your bank robbery note or having the kidnap ransom dropped at your home address. This is especially true when your description—sixty-year-old white female, grossly overweight, confined to a pink power mobility scooter—is as distinctive as hers.

She'd dropped bad scripts before, hit a number of doctors and quite a few drug stores. We'd already alerted the pharmacies in town about her; the scooter kept her in the downtown Honolulu area where she had about ten or twelve possible choices, not counting the big hospitals where she got the prescriptions she altered. So the pharmacist who called that day had a description of her posted by the counter and recognized her right away. He said she'd been ambitious, changing her doctor's order from ten Percodan to a hundred Percodan, reaching up from the scooter to lay the now bogus script on the counter.

The pharmacist looked at it, thought, "Uh huh," called the doctor, verified the original amount, then called us. It's a short drive and two of us got down there in a few minutes, walking to the pharmacy counter at the back of the store where there's a commotion going on.

Right up against the counter was this hefty old lady on a scooter, raising all kinds of hell about why her prescription was taking so long. We stood back and I caught the eye of the relieved-looking pharmacist and gave him the nod. He went ahead and gave her the bottle with the hundred pills, completing the fraud, and I went over and badged her. All hell busted loose.

She had an awful lot of energy for somebody bound to a Hoveround, and she lit all of it off at once, going fully berserk as I started to tell her she was under arrest, refusing to hand over the pills, clutching the bag to her ample bosom. Meanwhile, she's screeching, "Keep your hands off me!" and "Help!" jamming the Hoveround into reverse. The getaway was on.

We both opened fire. No, that didn't happen. We tried to stop her, grabbing onto the seat and the handlebars as she ran into one of the pharmacy shelves. Boxes and bottles flew everywhere. She tried to ditch the pills in the confusion, backed up into my legs, knocked over a rack of reading glasses, then floored the scooter for the exit while I was hobbling along beside her, trying to figure out how to shut the damn thing off. *There's got to be a freakin' switch or a key...*

We called in the pursuit on the radio. No, that didn't happen either. Who'd admit to a thing like that? But it is a pursuit, slow-speed, slower than O.J.'s, down the aisle through dental care and laundry soap, one of us on each side of her as she crossed a busy intersection and charged into candies. Now, she's yelling that she's being robbed. "Help, police!"

Shoppers skipped out of the way and mothers were grabbing their children as we trundled toward the front door. She's slapping my hand away every time I reached for the controls, which threw off her steering and she grazed some shelves, spilling candy everywhere. I open fire. No, damn it, that still didn't happen, although I was seriously considering it by now.

Now think about how this looks to the casual observer. Two scraggly-looking younger guys in street clothes, wrestling with this elderly handicapped woman on her motorized wheelchair as she screams about rape and robbery, a trail of destruction in their wake. At this point, I'd almost like to be able to say, "Fine, take the freaking ninety extra Percodan and get the hell out of here. Just shut up and go. Ride like the wind, Outlaw Queen." But what I did was grab her by the neck and shoulders and pull her off the cart and onto the floor.

The driverless Hoveround swerved into another shelf and stopped just short of the cash register aisle. She'd almost pulled off the full Steve McQueen *Great Escape* to the exit, but we got her. Now, we rolled her over with a little difficulty and got a pair of handcuffs on those thick wrists. It's Miller time.

Maybe not quite yet. She's still screaming and complaining, but now that we have her, we've got another problem. How do we get her to the car and then down to the receiving desk to book her? Transporting her and the Hoveround in our car was going to be difficult, maybe impossible. I had no idea what her medical issues were and I was starting to think the best way to handle this was to get all her personal information and release her (despite what the manual says) and then get a warrant and let somebody like the sheriff repeat the whole lovely Hoveround chase scene.

Then she saved us, saying the magic words. "I've got chest pains."

Thank you, ma'am! Call an ambulance. Let those guys deal with her. Although she refused to say anything useful to me (the language got quite salty), I got her info from the purse in the basket on the handlebars. She was on welfare and Medicaid. It turned out she was driving the taxpayers' Hoveround. We forfeited it to the government. No, even that didn't happen; both of us just wanted to forget the whole thing ever occurred and I left the abandoned Hoveround and the rest of the debacle in my rearview mirror.

Maybe not quite yet... Still had to write the ridiculous arrest report, carefully leaving out any mention of difficulties, resistance, and *especially* Hoverounds. Or injuries. I could have used a couple of those Percodans that night, dealing with some leftover aches and pains. Drugs touch everybody and she'd touched me. In fact, she'd barked both of my shins and ran over my foot with the damn scooter. Those things are heavier than they look.

That touch, of course, includes tens of millions in America who never actually use, sell, or even possess the stuff themselves. You can't work in the field, fight in the war, without seeing these people too, all the time. Many of them are young, the children of drug abusers or dealers, caught up in the frequently miserable, sometimes dangerous, and occasionally deadly drug world, whether they want to be or not. It's hard seeing dope as a "victimless crime" under these circumstances. I certainly saw people like Violet and Elvis Presley as victims, and their families too.

I've arranged to take a number of kids out of homes on account of unfit parents. That was always sad because the kids wanted to stay with mom. One mom was taking her daughter, six or seven years old, with her to score heroin, which she shot up in the car, buying on credit and not paying back, and using the kid as a kind of a shield, hoping the dealer wouldn't kick her ass in front of the kid. Call CPS. The little girl was pleading not to be taken to foster care, asking me and the social worker, "Who's gonna protect Mom if I'm not there?"

Had another mom, who was a hype-heroin addict and fought it off, got herself mostly clean. Married a good guy, had a couple of little boys, stayed straight for maybe eight to ten years. Her husband had a solid job, upper-middle class, paying for everything so she didn't have to work. She's driving a Jaguar and living in a beautiful country home, vacationing in Europe and Africa. All she had to do was just take care of the boys; it's all turning out like a picture-perfect family and a great redemption story. But she's still got the yen, and one day she does some crystal meth, falling right out of her good life into the deep end. Disappears into the meth culture, which is in many ways worse than the heroin one. She just abandoned her family without any explanation, vanishing from it like it had never existed. The boys don't know what's happened and the husband's devastated and can't explain it to them.

Now she's on the big slide, got a maggot boyfriend who dies from an OD, she's stealing stuff from her parents' house and her old, straight friends, who learn fast to cut her out. She used to be very attractive but meth fixes that for you, and before long, she doesn't care and looks like it. With her moving from shadow to deeper shadow, she finally vanished into the darkness. I'd lost track of her and suspect she's probably dead now. That's where she was headed, having it all and trading it for some rocks and a glass pipe. Drugs touched her hard, and they nailed everybody around her in a wide circle of pain, her little boys at the epicenter of that disaster. One of them grew up to be a hardcore heroin addict and heavy cocaine user. It can always get worse.

Maybe not always. I met another little girl who got touched even harder, her life shaded in a truly awful way. I didn't meet her through my job but knew her story. I think my son was in the third grade at the time, going into a new school and making friends with this girl called Kacey. One day, he asked if we could give her a ride home. I said okay and tried talking to her on the way. I couldn't get much out of her, basically her first name, that she lived with her grandmother. and she'd moved to Honolulu recently. Other than that, she was dead quiet. My son said later that she just didn't talk around grownups, but she was okay with kids. We gave her a few more rides over the following weeks and after we dropped her off one afternoon, my son said her mom had been murdered. He told me her last name and where it happened, and I remembered the case.

Kacey's mom had been into some drug thing, meth again. Crystal methamphetamine or "batu," had blasted Hawaii, wrecking entire communities and destroying lives by the bushel. Meth users caused more problems for themselves and everybody else than ten of the other kind. Kacey's mom had ripped off her cousin, who was locked up on a drug charge at the time, and she'd been snitching for the police at the time, though apparently not very effectively.

In other people's worlds, this might have been nothing more than a family quarrel, a little spat that some talk and some reason might work out, mostly to everyone's satisfaction. With batu involved, it turned into one of those "disputes" that happen all too frequently in the drug culture, petty conflicts that accelerate at the speed of meth, spinning out of control and into something far more critical. The cousin got out of jail and she and her husband decided in a batu-fueled fury that they'd had enough, and found Kacey's mom at her house. Although her four housemates were present at the time—caring, compassionate souls who watched the scene play out—nobody said a word as the couple tied Kacey's mom up and gagged her so tightly they deformed her face. Then they beat and tortured her for two hours, at one point supergluing her nose and mouth, the cousin saying, "You're never going to be able to talk again." Not yet finished, they wrapped her in a blanket and threw her into their car, Kacey's mom still pleading incoherently for mercy from behind her tape and glue gag in the back seat.

None of the housemates objected or interfered, and nobody called the cops until they finally told someone who had an actual functioning conscience and by then it was way too late for Kacey's mom. Police found the body the next day, buried in a shallow grave, a plastic bag taped over her head. Cause of death was suffocation.

Both of the killers got life sentences despite the cousin's plea that the "meth made her do it." Drugs touch everyone in society today, somehow, some way. They'd touched Kacey, so now she didn't talk much around grownups and I asked my son to be as good a friend to her as he could be.

I sure felt sorry for her.

***

And I did for Kevin too. But not for long. "You felt sorry for him? Sorry? What the hell?" Jimmy Birdsong wasn't happy, staring at me like I was crazy, waiting for an answer. Maybe I was, maybe he had a point, but I still felt sorry for Kevin.

Kevin didn't seem like a bad dude, although Jimmy's informant said he was selling cocaine, so something needed to be done. As usual, that meant me, working him undercover. I'd made one buy from him, a quarter ounce with the informant present, and since Jimmy didn't want to waste a lot more time and money, he decided I'd go alone for the next one and make that a buy-bust.

We'd done the first one at Kevin's house, a very nice, well-kept place on Oklahoma City's southwest side, close to but just over the line into Cleveland County. That was important because there was a judge in that county at the time who thought drugs should be legal and consequently dismissed or otherwise ditched any of those matters brought before him. He didn't like undercover agents either. As a result, OBN took any cases made south of 89th Street to federal court, but these had to involve substantial quantities. For our buy-bust, we planned to get a couple of ounces, normally not enough to get to federal court, but sufficient to meet the US attorney's special Cleveland County minimum.

That amounted to about four thousand dollars' worth of coke, but unlike in a "buy-walk" scenario, this money wasn't strolling off with the crook. He, the coke, and the cash were all getting seized together as soon as he handed over the dope. As in Brad and Shep's case, this meant doing the deal at the seller's house; still a bad idea, but Kevin seemed like a mellow sort. He'd never even left his easy chair for the first deal, sitting and chatting easily in his well-appointed living room, producing the packet and taking the money, right on cue. I told Jimmy that's pretty much how I expected the second deal would go too.

It didn't.

Just about everything went wrong, starting on arrival, where I discovered a party going on, or at least a social gathering. Kevin and his buddies outnumbered me 5-1: bad odds if things went any further south. I had backup outside, four agents in two cars, but they couldn't see me and were dependent on the wire I was wearing to keep up on the situation inside.

We called this the "Kel," named for one of the original manufacturers of the equipment. It was about the size of a modern iPhone, but a little thicker, with one long lead for a microphone and another for the antenna. It all had to be taped to your body, and I used a lot of tape to make sure nothing came loose at a bad moment. Getting patted down for a wire in those days would immediately create one of those bad moments, and we had an agent get into a fatal (for the crook) shootout when the bad guy detected the wire.

Even when it was taped on and working, it could be trouble. I had one heat up to the point where it started melting the tape and scorching skin. That can cause a bad moment, like when the crook sniffs around and says, "What's that smell?" and your response is, "Nothing to worry about, just me, cooking..." If either of the leads came loose, it stopped transmitting, and there was no way for the backup people to let you know that you were now on your own. And on the rare occasions when it worked as advertised, the quality sucked and the range depended on where you were, the weather, and even if someone got between you and the receiver. Because it was so unreliable, we didn't use the Kel to preserve the conversation; for that, I kept a cassette recorder in my boot or taped somewhere else on my body. So I was loaded with all this electronic gear when I got to Kevin's place.

Once again, he was comfortably seated in his chair, and he had the two ounces right at hand. I got the dope and handed over the buy money, mostly twenty-dollar bills because I wanted him to take time counting it since I'd just given the bust signal over the transmitter. This was a standard word or phrase, one everybody but the crook would recognize. "This looks like really good stuff" was a personal favorite, something unobjectionable that let the backups know I had the dope in hand, the sale complete. "Count the money" worked too because there was a strict rule about not "fronting," or advancing, the cash before getting the product. We also had a "rip" signal, something for emergencies if the guy tried a rip-off/robbery. I never used the word "gun" on the wire unless I wanted the backup in the room *right now*, and I was letting them know that somebody had a weapon and to be ready for it.

That didn't happen much, and it didn't with Kevin either, but things could still go bad, and they were at that very moment. Although I had no way of knowing it at the time, the transmitter started cutting in and out shortly after I arrived, and nobody heard the bust signal. I figured this out fairly quickly, as Kevin got finished counting the cash and looked at me, everybody wondering why I was still hanging around. You can only give the signal so many times before things get weird.

"This looks like really good stuff..." Awkward silence. "Yep, *really* good stuff." Raised eyebrows, questioning glances. "Really *good* stuff..."

Aw, the hell with this. I got out my car keys and dropped them, bending for the gun on the ankle that didn't have a cassette recorder taped to it. "Police! Everybody get on the floor!" I loudly repeated the message a couple times, and everybody got it.

The other partygoers hit the deck promptly. Kevin, though, was taking his time, and moved awkwardly, looking like he wasn't trying very hard. I yelled at him again to hurry up and get on the ground, now. Outside, I heard doors slamming and people coming, so I gathered that the transmitter had finally broadcast at least *this* bit of the conversation.

Deciding to hurry Kevin up before any of his buddies got any ideas about noncompliance, I grabbed his shirt collar and jerked him out of the chair and toward the floor just as the door opened and Jimmy and the others came through, yelling, "Police."

Something felt strange about Kevin. He went down easy, too easy, lighter than I expected, in a disordered jumble of arms and legs and a clatter of metal. It hadn't been pretty, but he was definitely prone on the floor, finally, and the whole situation under control. One of the other agents handcuffed Kevin behind his back and I went to attend to my two mandatory priorities: checking him for weapons and getting my buy money back. This led to a startling discovery.

I patted him down, starting with his waistband and moving south, and immediately found metal on one leg. "What the hell is this?" I said, pulling up the pants.

Kevin had no leg. It was completely gone well above the knee, replaced by a prosthetic device made of steel tubes, a plastic foot with a shoe, and a cap over the stump. This surprising revelation was quickly followed by a second one; Kevin didn't have the other leg either. This explained why he'd gone down so easily and so awkwardly. He was all head and torso, almost no weight below the waist. I already felt bad about that, but it was fixing to get worse.

Making sure he didn't have any weapons on what was left of his body, and feeling pretty rotten, I helped him back up and into his chair.

"What happened to you, man?" I asked, and he came up with a sad story, which he'd clearly told more than once before.

"There was an accident. I was driving down in Wichita Falls, Texas, and somebody wrecked. It was raining and I pulled over to see if I could help. I was standing behind the guy's car and this state trooper comes up over the hill, going way too fast, couldn't stop in the rain, and hit me and the car. Took both legs off. I'm lucky to be here, really."

Lucky. Boy, I don't know if that's the word I'd have used. I'm thinking that basically, one state cop is now busting this guy who's permanently minus two legs and a lot of his future life only because another state cop took them. Now I felt worse and told him I was sorry to hear it. He shrugged. "That stuff happens. What can you do? I got a big settlement and insurance and bought this place." Maybe letting us know the nice house hadn't been purchased with drug money.

I had to fill Jimmy in on the deal and the involvement of the other four people, so I turned away and we ran through the story. To get a little privacy, we both stepped outside the front door and started putting together the probable cause for a search warrant for the house.

After a couple of minutes, we went back inside to separate the other people for a little chat and I looked over at Kevin, who was curled up in the chair, almost in a fetal position, mostly face down, his head in one corner. It was a big chair but he still looked very uncomfortable. I hadn't thought I'd thrown him down hard enough to really hurt him, but he was apparently writhing in pain. Of course, I felt even worse. Jimmy brought me around.

"Where's the buy money?" he said.

I'd completely forgotten it, what with the whole no-legs distraction. "What? Oh, he put it in his pants pocket. I'll get it."

I went over and reached into the pocket, finding... nothing. No four thousand dollars. No money at all. Thinking I might have gotten the wrong pocket, I checked the other one. Nothing. What the hell?

"Hey, buddy, where's my money?" I poked Kevin on the shoulder. He didn't answer and didn't turn face up, just squirmed a little more, so I pulled him over.

It was immediately apparent where my money was. Kevin's cheeks bulged like a chipmunk with a mouthful of nuts in a very red face and he was frantically chewing as fast as the thick wad of bills would allow.

"God damn it," I said, grabbing him by the throat, yelling at him to spit it out. He didn't, locking his jaw. There's a pressure point you can use to get somebody's mouth open when they're seizing up, and we used it frequently on the Eastside, where people often resisted "coughing it up." Kevin and I had a short struggle, which ended painfully for him and with me holding a gob of wet, gooey bills. I went into the kitchen, washed them off, muttering, and counted them. He'd chewed up a few but they were all there. He'd gotten maybe a thousand bucks into his mouth; the rest was still on the seat. If he'd taken it in smaller bites, he'd have gotten some of it down, which would have caused me all kinds of problems. Money is not supposed to just disappear in a buy-bust and I don't know how I would have explained it.

But I'd felt sorry for him and left him alone, which Jimmy told me right there and in no uncertain terms was "dumber than that guy is. Did you check the chair to see if he had a gun stashed in it?"

I hadn't, being distracted by (clearly misplaced) sympathy and general dumbness.

"Check it now," Jimmy said.

I did, and sure enough, there was a 9mm pistol, a Browning Hi-Power, loaded and ready to go, tucked into the cushions, right about where Kevin's handcuffed hands were when I sat him back down in his chair.

"We're all lucky he didn't start shooting," Jimmy said, saying out loud the same thing I was thinking.

You might think a guy handcuffed behind the back couldn't pull something like that off. We were under no illusions on that score. Only a year before, DEA Special Agent Frank Quintal and his partner, Larry Wallace, arrested a drug dealer on Guam and put him into the back seat of the DEA car. Wallace had been working the guy undercover and when he found out where the heroin was stashed, he gave the bust signal and Frank came in with the Guam police and grabbed the dealer. Although they patted him down and handcuffed him, he had a pistol in his waistband that they'd missed in the initial search and he got it, opening fire and putting three bullets into Frank. One of them went through his arm and hit Wallace in the head, killing him. Frank then shot and subdued the suspect, which I expect didn't much console Wallace's wife and three small children.

I got to know Frank, a hometown Honolulu agent quite well over the years, but never had the chance to meet Larry Wallace. Jimmy and I both knew all about him though. Although he died seven thousand miles away on Guam, he was originally from Oklahoma City and his family brought him home to be buried at Chapel Hill Memorial Cemetery. About a mile from my apartment.

"You felt sorry for him? Sorry? What the hell?" Jimmy said. "Sorry'll get you killed. *Never* feel sorry for these sorry sons of bitches."

I can't say I never felt sorry for anyone I arrested again. Some people deserved sympathy for any number of good reasons. But I never again made the mistake of letting that get in the way of the job. "Sorry" is just one more diversion that can turn you into a dead undercover. And there's a time and place for everything, even sympathy. There had been a time for it back in southeastern Oklahoma once, and that time came for me when we got our prisoners to the Choctaw County Sheriff's Office. And turned the clock back to 1900.

CHAPTER 6

APRIL (FOOL) COME SHE WILL

HUGO, OKLAHOMA
SEPTEMBER 1977
EVENING OF THE FIRST DAY

Hugo's courthouse was dark and silent, a blocky, brick building squatting on a neat lawn with shading trees, another of those stolid edifices built early in Oklahoma's statehood to remind everybody that law and order had come to replace the rough and ready. I'd been in a lot of these places, from one end of the state to the other. I'd usually been invited in by the local law, and always warmly received, but I had my doubts about this visit.

Hugo isn't a big place, maybe six or seven thousand people, one of those towns that closes up and goes to sleep early, streets empty, all quiet and peaceful. Just like the courthouse and the jail. The night deputy came out and checked our IDs and our prisoners, then waved us inside. We parked the prisoners on a bench and explained what we needed, somebody who spoke enough Spanish to translate questions and answers. The deputy said he was going to call the sheriff and let him know what was going on. Meanwhile, he wanted to know where we'd picked up the Mexicans, a little surprised to hear it was Frogville.

"Don't get that too much. Not many beaners out in the county. More of 'em here in Hugo or over in Valliant."

"Who've you got around here who does the Spanish translations in court?"

The deputy shifted the toothpick he was working. "That'd be Loretta. Married to a preacher. I got her number here somewhere."

"Let's give her a call."

"Okay. But what am I gonna tell her when she asks who's paying for this deal?"

I had official funds, the cash the state gave me for buying dope and paying informants. Maybe Loretta fell into the informant category or could be pushed there. I said I'd take care of it and the deputy made the call, and another one to his boss.

The sheriff got there before Loretta, and we had to go through why we were there at his jail with three prisoners, and how we were looking for a witness, Tommy Hatfield, who might be missing in action. We didn't share most of it, which felt weird to me, having relied so many times on local sheriffs and their deputies to back me up undercover in dark and lonely places. We didn't say anything about any payoffs for protection or crooked cops, but I believe he'd already heard most of that story and could fill in the missing parts on his own. He sure didn't seem very upset or even particularly surprised to hear about the things going on in his county, but he offered us whatever help we needed, then left us with our translator and the three amigos.

We took them one at a time, getting the same basic story: a horrific tale of torture and lynching, each rubbing at his raw neck as he recalled the events of two days earlier. A couple of them had used a few words of English but it had been far too inadequate to deal with the Hatfields' demands. They all agreed that they'd been at the barn when the McCoys confronted the two Hatfields, one of them escaping, but said they hadn't seen what happened to Tommy. Never saw him or his car again although they said T.W. had come back with friends, guns, and a rope. They were really clear on that part, what it felt like to have your head in a noose and dancing like your life depended on it.

"Supposed to be nice and peaceful here in the country, but there's sure some bad people out there," Loretta said while Pat was fetching the next Mexican.

"Yeah, and it's getting kind of hard to figure out who's who down here," I said.

"Good luck. I'm married to a minister and I haven't got it yet."

"I wouldn't go saying anything about the sheriff thing," I said. "That could be total bullshit as far as we know."

"Don't worry. We hear things all the time at church. Folks do like to gossip, but you shouldn't put much credit in it. It must make your job harder though."

We'd asked the Mexicans if they wanted to press charges against the people who lynched them; not encouraging it but giving them the option. That suggestion hadn't flown very high, all three saying they didn't want any trouble, probably knowing deportation loomed. But the first two had mentioned they didn't have much confidence in American law, since "*Señor* Gene" enjoyed a cozy relationship with one American "*jefe de policía*." They said he'd been out to the place, although they didn't see him in the barn or actually with any marijuana. Still, it was one more piece of information that backed up Terrell's statement. We didn't have a photo lineup or anything to show the witnesses for some kind of ID of the suspect, but Pat and I were fairly confident we had the right person.

After two hours of back and forth, Loretta in the middle, Pat and I leaned back and looked at each other, the string run out for the time being.

"The kidnapping's pretty solid. They lock this Eugene McCoy guy in on that part. And I think we can make weed cases on everybody. We need to hold onto these guys," I said.

"They're our only witnesses unless you count that T.W. jackass. And you're right; their boss 'Señor Gene' has to be the prime suspect, even if they didn't see anything happen to the kid."

"So what do we do with them now?"

"Better talk to the deputy. We ought to keep them locked up for something."

"Like what? I got a little pot out of the trailer, but that's probably a misdemeanor. And the search might not hold up," I said.

"Let's ask the deputy," Pat said.

He heard us out. "You ain't gonna charge 'em?" he asked.

"No, we got nothing on them. We might need them for witnesses."

"They're still illegal though. You can call Border Patrol."

"Where are they?"

"Tulsa or Dallas." He looked at his watch. "I doubt you'll get anybody tonight. And they ain't gonna come down here to pick up three guys anyhow."

"What are we supposed to do with them, then?"

"We'll take care of it. We got the 10-5 drill down pretty good."

"10-5? What's that?" 10-5 was the radio code for "relay," and was usually used for a message, information, papers, or other items being passed from one unit to another. There was another 10-code for "prisoner transfer," although I hadn't used it and didn't know what it was. I'd never heard of a 10-5 for people, much less prisoners, and judging from the expression on Pat's face, he hadn't either. Turned out, it was exactly what it sounded like.

"Relay. We'll 10-5 them down to Lamar County over in Texas. They'll 10-5 them to the next county south. Sooner or later, if they don't get sick or die, or run off somewhere, they make it back to the border." The deputy didn't seem to find anything unusual in this arrangement.

"Really?" I said. "Texas has a couple hundred counties…"

"There are a bunch of 'em," the deputy agreed amiably. "Probably not more than twenty or thirty in a straight line south though."

"How long does it take to get them back to Mexico?"

"I got no idea. We'll probably hold 'em for a few days, but once we give 'em up, they ain't our problem anymore. Those Texas sheriffs, they might keep 'em longer than that, get a little work out of 'em before they do their 10-5."

I shook my head, thinking the whole thing was bizarre, especially the nonchalant way the deputy described an obviously well-established and very comfortable process. But then, this same day had also seen lynching and torture and terrorism portrayed almost matter-of-factly. I could see that my partner was having almost as hard a time with this as I was.

"Hold off a second," I said. "Let me and Pat talk it over."

We went out into the reception area, both of us shaking our heads. "What do you think, Pat? Is this 10-5 thing for real or what?"

"I never heard of it," he said. "We'll take prisoners from one county to another sometimes, but that's usually when they're wanted somewhere else. Just passing them on... All the way to Mexico. Or even just to Dallas. It doesn't sound right."

"I'll tell you what it sounds like. A bad joke. If the sheriff's in with the McCoys like T.W. says, he'll probably just send them back to the trailer. Or after we're gone, just cut them loose."

"Maybe," Pat said. "But the sheriff won't be happy to hear these birds are in here singing to us if he knows they've seen him hanging out at *Señor* Gene's."

Yeah, that did turn the heat up on the Mexicans, and leaving them in the sheriff's custody, even long enough to get the 10-5 train underway, seemed like a bad option. I still couldn't quite wrap my head around that concept, which sounded like it came from another century or someplace like Mexico. I was still pretty new at this job. People pulled my leg all the time, enough so that I got fairly suspicious of unreal-sounding proposals like this one.

And almost anything coming from James Michael Birdsong.

OKLAHOMA CITY, OKLAHOMA
A YEAR EARLIER

I said Jimmy was a practical joker, liked putting a good prank over on somebody, and he took that hobby seriously, working elaborate routines on anyone—crooks, cops, and citizens—he thought would be good for a laugh. By luck, mostly, I frustrated him on this score, not falling for either of his first two scams, though they were beautifully set up and perfectly executed. He didn't give up easily, and he got me with the last one. I'd brag that the tables got turned on him in the last prank, arguably giving me the last laugh, but it turned out there was nothing but sadness to commemorate and no rejoicing or room for laughing or bragging for anyone.

How did I get over on Jimmy's first two tricks? Just like I made it through a lot of my earlier undercover deals, on pure luck and coincidence; because I wasn't smarter than his usual victims or more clever than the master mischief maker. He was perfectly capable of setting up his prey over days, even weeks, prepping the landscape and the sucker for the perfect moment to—in one case, literally—spring his trap. But chance—nothing but sheer, dumb luck—favored me on his first effort.

"What the hell is that thing?" I said, pointing at the wooden box in the back seat of Jimmy's state car, a maroon Oldsmobile Cutlass that was reportedly the fastest in the fleet.

"Dead animal. Well, probably dead. The mad ones, they can play possum on you. I'm taking it to the state vet for a rabies test."

"How come you've got it?"

"Midwest City cops gave it to me 'cause they knew I know the veterinary board people. Some fool's wife turned it in at the PD after it attacked her husband." He climbed into the driver's seat.

"What kind is it?" The Olds was a two-door, and as I got in on the passenger side, I swiveled around and checked out the box, which was about three feet long with a wire mesh screen on the one end I could see. It had DANGER: WILD ANIMAL stenciled in red on the top and side, and took up almost the whole back seat.

"Mongoose. Mean little bastards. Glad it's dead." He put the car in gear, and we rolled out of the state office building parking lot.

"Mongoose? Huh... I didn't think there were any mongooses in Oklahoma." I looked over at Jimmy and back at the box. I hadn't been living in the state for long, but I believed I'd have heard if there were mongooses roaming the wide-open prairies and rolling hills of central and western Oklahoma. Or Midwest City, a middle-class suburb of OKC. Midwest City had Tinker Air Force Base, lots of B-52 bombers, tanker planes, and the AWACS early warning aircraft coming and going, and plenty of Air Force people, but I was fairly confident both the city and the airbase were mongoose-free zones.

"Looks like there was one, anyway. Some idiot, keeping it for a pet." He snorted. "Like you could ever tame one of these things. They're the ones go after those snakes—killer cobras, ten, twelve feet long. Mongoose is so fast, snakes can't kill 'em, and they got teeth like needles."

"Uh huh," I said. "Yeah, I heard about the snake thing. Rudyard Kipling and all. Maybe the dude was trying to train him to go after rattlesnakes. There could be rattlers in Midwest City. Those'd probably be easy meat for a mongoose after cobras."

"How the hell you gonna train something wild like that?" he said. "Probably ten times more vicious once they get the rabies too. Poor bastard who turned him in, cops said his face was all tore up; mongoose goes for the eyes. Maybe gonna lose 'em. And now he's gotta find out if he's got rabies; hope it's not too late for the shots."

It was a grim, terrible, frightening picture he painted, all right. There were just two problems with it. First, unlike Jimmy Birdsong, who'd grown up maybe visiting his state's only mongoose at the world-famous Oklahoma City Zoo, I'd seen thousands of them. I'd been raised in Hawaii, where the petite, weasel-like animals—known as *manakuke* (mah-nah-coo-kay) —are as common as house cats. Like he said, they *are* fast, but they're shy little critters, wary of people, hustling off quickly in the other direction if you try to get too close. Almost everybody in Hawaii likes mongooses on some level; they've got a charm that's hard to resist, their cute little faces, stubby legs comically working a mile a minute, that bottle-brush tail, and a mongoose mother frequently escorting one or two even cuter babies across a road or along a stream bank all make endearing images. But everybody also knows they're invasive pests with a liking for the eggs of endangered birds (and the birds too), as well as insects, frogs, lizards, and grubs. Since Hawaii is snake-free, they have to do without cobras or anything else that's slithering on its belly. If you're not paying attention, they'll eat the sandwich off your golf cart when you make the turn at the ninth hole snack bar, so some will do snatch-and-grab crimes, for sure. Assault with intent to blind? Possible, I suppose, but not likely. Not in my experience.

The second hitch in Jimmy's scheme was even more problematic for him, though he obviously didn't know it. I'd seen this mongoose-in-a-box scam before. I knew the punch line, although I had to admit that Jimmy's setup was, as always, masterful. And he was finally ready to flip the switch as we pulled in behind another state office building off Lincoln Boulevard.

"Here we are. You can give me a hand with this thing," he said, climbing out of the car. "Let's take it out on your side. More room."

I tilted the seat forward and checked the box again, watching Jimmy grab his end.

"You see it through the screen? Is it moving?" he asked.

"Nope, some fur, but it's not moving," I said, getting ready.

"Good. Don't get your hands too close to the wire, just in case." He pushed the box toward me.

The end with the wire screen opened with a vicious snap, an explosion of gray fur erupting out of the shadow and whipping across my face. I'd been expecting it, but I'll confess it was still a shock, and I jerked away. Jimmy was already laughing, but that faded off as I pulled the box out of the car and set it on the ground, saying, "We'd better put this back inside. Reset it for the next guy."

It was a strip of raccoon or rabbit skin, tied to the cage door with a bit of fishing line so that when it flipped open, the fur arced out and directly into the victim's face. If they'd been properly prepped, and Jimmy saw to that, anybody would think the rabid mongoose would be going for their eyes, just like he'd predicted. It should have worked with anybody else and sure as heck would have with me if I hadn't been prepared.

Then I had to explain about mongooses in Hawaii and how I'd seen this gimmick before.

"Well, you're no damn fun" was the main reaction, but I could see right then that I'd thrown down a challenge and Jimmy wouldn't be satisfied with losing just this round.

He did say he'd worked the stunt on several other cops and they'd all "freaked," and I assured him it was a great scam and he'd done a beautiful job selling it. However, flattery wasn't going to get me anywhere. Jimmy would try again; I'd bet big to that.

His second effort was just as beautiful, one he'd spent at least a week preparing for and playing perfectly on a real fear I'd been foolish enough to express openly in the office. Spotting the weakness, this time he thought he had me.

I don't like heights. I avoid cliffs and the lanais of tall condominiums. Anything over about four floors gives me the willies, and western and central Oklahoma, which is flat and almost totally without tall buildings with open lanais, is a perfect place for people like me. And I especially don't like anything to do with parachutes. There is no way in hell that I would ever go skydiving, and I'd let everybody in the office know it.

The subject came up because several of the agents had taken up the hobby, going out on the weekends and jumping out of perfectly functional airplanes "for fun." They'd tried to convince me to go, and did persuade my partner, but I was having none of it, expressing my firm belief that they were all crazy, stupid, or both, proclaiming it would snow in hell and Honolulu before anybody got me to strap on a parachute. Jimmy noticed.

He wasn't a skydiver himself. I don't know if they even make parachutes for people that big, but he'd recently obtained his private pilot's license and spent his weekends building up flying hours in a single-engine airplane. Oklahoma is great country for small aircraft, with dozens, maybe hundreds of airports, former military airfields, and dirt- and grass-landing strips dotted all over the state. He'd taken a real interest in air smuggling and had gotten a big case with a DC-4 four-engine cargo plane and a smaller aircraft, plus seventeen thousand pounds of marijuana. We'll talk more about this in a little bit. His flying hobby brought him into contact with the operators at a lot of the airports, and, he hoped, leads to the next big smuggling case.

He'd carefully tracked my issues with heights and parachutes and guessed (wrongly) that I also had a fear of flying, probably, especially, in small planes. But again, I grew up in Hawaii, where you have to fly long hours to get anywhere on the mainland, and shorter distances to hop between the islands. At that point in my life, I undoubtedly had many, many more hours in airplanes than he did. Probably more than everybody else in the office combined. And I'd been in little planes before too, on inter-island flights, helicopters, a seaplane, and even a glider. I'd been up with a DEA pilot on a marijuana case, and in a leased Cessna with tracking gear on a clandestine lab investigation, and flown with my uncle, who had his own Beechcraft in California. I liked flying just fine, and for whatever reason, the height up in a plane didn't bother me a bit, so Jimmy may have been taken aback when he asked me and my partner if we wanted to go flying with him one weekend, and I said, "Sure, why not?" And once again, coincidence and a bit of useful previous experience were going to spoil a very well-laid plan.

We met Jimmy and his instructor pilot at the Downtown Airpark, a private, one runway strip just east of the stockyards on Oklahoma City's southwest side. Jimmy was upgrading his license, either going for his instrument rating or the commercial ticket, I don't remember which. He got both not long after, so he was pretty competent, but for this flight, there'd be an instructor pilot in the right-hand seat, and I'd already checked with a couple other guys who'd flown with him before and heard Jimmy was a good, careful flyer himself.

So it was somewhat surprising when Jimmy's safety briefing included the unexpected newsflash that he'd put parachutes aboard, under the seats, "just in case something goes wrong and we need to bail out."

This didn't fit with my flying experience. I'd never been in any plane, large or small, that carried parachutes for emergencies. Life vests and rafts, sure. Hawaii's surrounded by a couple thousand miles of water and chances are good that if you need to land urgently, you're going to get wet. Every pilot I'd ever flown with expected to ride the plane down and hope for the best. Parachutes didn't factor into it. And Jimmy, knowing how I felt about "hitting the silk," undoubtedly also knew that this news would be less than reassuring, especially since we were already on our taxi to the runway and it was too late to "bail out" now. Something was up.

In a minute, it was the four of us, and we rose into a beautiful, clear, blue Oklahoma morning as I forgot any misgivings or sudden suspicions. In another minute, we'd turned back and crossed the North Canadian River, angling up and over the vast, empty state fairgrounds, starting a wide, climbing arc around the north side of downtown OKC, the tall buildings gleaming in the warm sunshine. Oklahoma being as flat as it is, you've got a big view from up there, and this morning, I felt like I could see clear to Kansas up north and Texas far to the west. That early in the day, the air hadn't heated enough to create the bumps that make flying a little plane at relatively low altitude less enjoyable, and Oklahoma City's famous winds were calm. It was a nice, smooth, effortless ride.

We got over the northeast side, where I spent so much time on the streets and Jimmy spent even more. It all looked so peaceful from three or four thousand feet, no bangers with guns or guys slinging rubber pills of heroin visible on this Saturday morning. We were too far up to see anyone hanging on the corners, though I'm sure they were there and loaded for the early weekend business. I looked for houses we'd hit, places where we knew we could always find drug action. A barber shop, a shoeshine parlor, a place next door to the KFC which served as a shooting gallery for people scoring on NE 23rd Street. But everything was bright and clean and shiny, dark green trees shading lawns that all looked neat and well-trimmed, golfers and their carts on the public courses at Lincoln Park, and cars full of children, pulling into the parking lot at the Oklahoma City Zoo.

And then the engine quit. That gets your heart pumping faster and focuses you on things much closer than hypothetical drug dealers on the ground below. It concentrates the mind wonderfully. Losing the engine doesn't make the plane go dead silent; there's still plenty of sound as you start gliding at one hundred and twenty miles an hour, but it gets a whole lot quieter, enough that you can hear yourself thinking and easily hear people talking, even without the headsets we were all wearing. I could hear Jimmy clearly enough.

"Lost the engine. We're going down. Grab your parachute."

This was the point where I was supposed to panic and start scrambling around the cabin for my parachute. This is the moment when your life flashes before your eyes, but I didn't get to see the whole movie. I just got the two scenes that were eerily identical to the one playing at that moment. I'd been in a plane with no engine before. Not just in the sailplane my dad rented for my eighteenth birthday and flew completely unpowered for almost an hour. I'd gone up in that one expecting total silence and now recalled the fairly noisy and familiar rush of the wind as it charged under our wings at two miles per minute. That's the sound of the sky, holding you aloft until you can find a nice, flat place to set down. Unlike Hawaii—where the flattest thing around is probably made of water—Oklahoma, as previously noted, is full of such nice, flat, hard earth places. Sailplanes can glide a long way, much farther than a high-winged Cessna with a dead propeller, but there were two more reasons why I wasn't ready to panic yet.

The first was the reassuring sight of Tinker Air Force Base, just off the right side of the airplane. Two long runways, four miles of wide concrete, both pointed roughly in our direction. I'd also been up in my uncle's plane when he suddenly switched off our motor. We were near an airport that time too, in case the standard drill—one that pilots practice a lot—for restarting the engine didn't work out as planned.

The second thing I noticed was that neither of our two pilots was reaching for *his* parachute (assuming there even was one under the seats as advertised). Nor were they making a request for an emergency landing or doing any other talking on the radio, which I had access to on the headphones. Maybe if they didn't think it was a big enough crisis to leap into space or tell somebody outside the plane, neither should I.

"I don't know, Jimmy," I said. "Maybe we should try an engine restart before we jump. That's what my uncle did when I flew with him and he cut the prop. Or we could land at Tinker. It's right there."

The instructor pilot looked over at Jimmy and shrugged. "Engine restart," he said, and watched as Jimmy went through the procedure, flipping switches and pulling knobs. It took a minute, but the engine turned over, caught, and held, revving back up to full power as the prop spun a silver circle in front of us.

I couldn't catch any more conversation in the plane, thanks to the reassuring drone of the Cessna's motor, but I could clearly hear Jimmy's voice on the plane's intercom.

"Man, you are no fun at all."

But I knew that wasn't some admission of defeat. Jimmy Birdsong didn't make those. It was a challenge.

For his final stunt, Jimmy skipped all the preliminaries and cut straight to the punchline. I definitely hadn't seen this one before, so it worked just like he planned.

OBN issued us this "bulletproof" gear and these consisted of Kevlar panels to be worn under a shirt or jacket. This wasn't called body armor at the time; that would have been far too grand a pretension. These were nothing like the reassuringly heavy, thick, armored vests of today, with their ceramic plates and tremendous stopping power. Our protection covered most of the torso, though not the sides, with panels about the thickness of a bath towel in front and back. They're heavier than a towel, a couple of pounds, but easily concealed, and wearable in almost any situation where you needed to be low-key, although I never wore one undercover.

Mine was white, looking like a wifebeater or a tank top, if a little bulkier when it was under the shirt. It didn't amount to much though, and you needed to wear a good deal of faith along with the Kevlar to be comfortable in it. That was blind faith because nobody I knew had ever been shot in the vest, and I certainly hadn't.

Jimmy changed that.

On this particular day, a warm one in early spring, we were suiting up for a search warrant, getting our gear together in the parking lot of the Jim Thorpe Building, a short distance from the State Capitol. I'd gotten the vest on and was holding off putting my shirt over it, knowing about the heat that the whole ensemble generated. Birdsong was so immense that the XXXL vest he wore looked like a kid's dining bib, reaching halfway down his stomach. He covered it with a shirt, then turned to me.

"Do you think these things really work? Let's find out," he said.

He pulled out his backup gun, a little .38 Chief's Special, just like mine, and like a child's toy in his massive hand.

And exactly like Jack Ruby nailing Lee Harvey Oswald, he shot me with it.

It didn't hurt nearly as bad as I thought it would; that was my instant reaction. We'd been told that the vest would stop a .38 round, keep it from penetrating, but all that energy has to go somewhere, so you'd still get a wicked punch, and maybe some broken ribs or other damage. He got me just below the ribs, a little left of the solar plexus. I felt the punch, but it was more like a tap, really. The most painful part was getting tattooed on my left arm with the burnt powder and the hot gas from the muzzle flash. That stung. Maybe the big punch and more pain took a few seconds to kick in? Maybe I was already in shock? My ears were ringing a bit.

My second reaction was disbelief, and the third, a flash behind the first two, was to pull my own gun.

But Jimmy jumped away, light on his feet and moving fast for a big man, laughing madly. "Whoa! Whoa! It's just a blank. You ain't really shot."

Sorry, but I wasn't seeing the distinction clearly at that moment, or the humor in the situation either. I looked down to see if he was right, registering the powder burn, a ragged black scar on the fabric. It looked like the cloth carrier had burned through to the Kevlar.

A minute or two of incoherent cursing and wild threats followed. Unimpressed by either, Jimmy kept up the triumphant chortling, this practical joke an unqualified success. He absolutely refused to let me "test out" his vest though, especially after I told him I didn't have any blanks and would just use whatever was in my .357, which was a 158-grain jacketed hollow point.

"You got that fat lard belly, you'll probably never even feel it," I grumbled, aiming for his pride since I apparently wouldn't be hitting anything else.

"Wooooh. Man, you are sure sensitive, heh, heh, heh," he chortled. "Nah, I ain't gonna let you shoot me. I've seen you shoot. You'd probably miss the damn vest, even from a foot or two." The conversation went downhill from there.

I finally let it go, not having much choice in the matter; you could boil Jimmy in meth oil before he'd ever admit he'd been wrong or foolish. He'd had his triumph, finally. But I got another chance, this one on a desolate day with no victory or satisfaction anywhere in it, to poke him a little before leaving it completely behind.

Not even a month later, on April 19, 1977, a man we both knew, Sergeant Terry Glenn Lawson of the Oklahoma City Police Department's Training Division, was conducting felony car stop exercises with a group of police academy recruits. One of them shot him with a .357 revolver from inches away. Although the staff got Terry to a local hospital, he died two days later, the victim of an accident, terrible and pointless.

He'd been killed with a blank .38-caliber cartridge, the muzzle of the gun hard up against his right side, right where the gap in the panels of a bulletproof vest like mine would have been, the hot gases and burnt powder exploding through his clothes into his chest. Even without a bullet, the near-contact shot devastated his lungs, liver, and kidneys, and the doctors couldn't save him as the damaged internal organs failed.

The accident came as a terrific shock to OCPD and every other agency that used blanks in training. It affirmatively proved, if anyone had doubted before, that these were dangerous tools that shouldn't be taken lightly. I figured I'd emphasize the point to somebody who'd very recently shot someone in almost exactly the same way and made extra sure to get to the office before Jimmy the next day.

"You see the paper this morning?" I asked him when he came into the squad bay.

"Yeah, I got it right here," he said. He didn't meet my eyes as he threaded his way to his corner.

"Me too." I waved the *Daily Oklahoman* at him. "So you heard about Terry Lawson?"

"Huh." That might have been a yes. Probably was.

"'Died Thursday as a result of being shot in the chest at point-blank range with a police gun,'" I read from the article.

"Hmm. Yeah, that's what I heard. Training accident," Jimmy muttered, unfolding his newspaper and disappearing behind it.

"It happened on Tuesday. Larry Upchurch told me yesterday. They're all tore up about it down there at the PD, trying to figure out how it could have happened. You know why?"

Jimmy didn't answer, just rattled the pages.

"Mostly because it didn't go down at the range like I first thought. It happened at the fairgrounds by the academy. And the gun was loaded with blanks. See, it says so right here. 'Lawson was handcuffed and pulled a small handgun he had hidden on his body. At that point, the trainee shot him twice at point-*blank* range with the *blank*-loaded pistol.'"

Jimmy didn't say anything, rattling his papers a little louder.

"'The *blanks* punctured Lawson's lung and grazed internal organs,'" I read, putting as much emphasis as I could on the keyword in the article, then put the paper down.

The low rumble barely reached me, the words almost inaudible, even in the silent room. "I wish it hadn't have happened," he said.

I'm pretty sure he was talking about Terry Lawson. Probably was. But I didn't care anymore, folding up the paper and turning to the phone. I wished it "hadn't have happened" too, but there was no going back and no point pounding on it.

OCPD stopped using blanks in that sort of training, and so did every other law enforcement agency I knew of. One officer dead was enough. The recruits Lawson was training were scheduled to graduate that very morning; this had been one of their final academy training exercises. The rookie involved was twenty-three years old. My age exactly.

I expect the memory haunts him on occasion. Mine still does.

And that was that, as far as Jimmy Birdsong pranking me. He moved on to other games and other victims, and I guessed I'd passed whatever test he'd been giving. Until word got around to everybody to be extra careful about inspecting any crates Birdsong marked DANGER: WILD ANIMAL, he even used me as an accomplice in the mongoose box gag, introducing me as the "guy from Hawaii, where they've got all kinds of mongooses." I played along and backed him up on that one. But I never flew with him again or fooled around with blank cartridges.

And I was sadly right about parachuting and the whole heights thing too. A couple of months after our flight over the Eastside, a member of the skydiving club the other agents joined had a chute malfunction and fatally pancaked into a field. All the jumpers in the office got themselves new hobbies.

Mainly golf, as I recall.

CHAPTER 7

SOMEWHERE THEY CAN'T FIND ME

FROGVILLE, OKLAHOMA
SEPTEMBER 1977
EVENING OF THE FIRST DAY

"We can't just spring these folks. If the kid turns up dead, this is a murder case and they're living at the prime suspect's place," I said.

"No. They're material witnesses. To the kidnapping for sure, so we can't just let them go. They disappear off to Mexico or even some sheriff's office down in Texas, we'll never find them again," Pat said.

The two of us were standing outside the sheriff's office in the Choctaw County Courthouse, trying to work out the next move in a case that wasn't getting any simpler.

"We don't even know for sure who these guys are," I said. "None of 'em had any ID. We can book them and fingerprint them on the pot charge but they'll get out tomorrow unless we go to the court and lay it out that they're witnesses."

Neither of us thought that was a good idea. Telling everybody in open court in Hugo that these people were key witnesses in a major crime seemed like a sure way to get them intimidated, hurt, and maybe killed. Again. Word travels fast, and if the sheriff didn't tell them, somebody else would notify the McCoys about their Mexican problem. And maybe they'd join Tommy on the river journey.

"We could take them up to Oklahoma City. Tell 'em it's for their own safety. But I don't think we can legally hold them if they don't want to do it," Pat said. "Or Tulsa; take them to the Immigration people up there. We'd be liable to lose them, though, if those guys ship them out to Mexico."

"Maybe the Texas thing would work if we could keep track of them. They'd be somewhere the McCoys or the Hatfields couldn't reach."

"Or the sheriff. We know they're not going to testify that they've seen the sheriff out at the McCoy place, but McCoy and the sheriff don't know that. He'd be pretty upset if he found out they were talking about him at all," Pat said.

"Jeez. What a mess," I said.

"I dunno. Those poor bastards have been through some hell already..." Pat said. "Sending them south sounds like more slave labor to me."

"I know, I keep getting this picture of some Texas sheriff keeping them locked up for a month while they clean the courthouse or pick cotton. And then the next 10-5 does the same thing. They could be two years getting back to Mexico."

Pat laughed uncomfortably. "I didn't think it could get much worse than getting strung up from a barn rafter."

"It makes living in that shithole trailer and going to work in the weed field every day look like a Florida vacation."

"We can't do this to them. It's not right."

There it was, and I was glad to hear him say what I was thinking. "I'm with you. But even if we don't go to court, everybody in the county's gonna know tomorrow that we've got them."

"That's okay. We'll be busy all day tomorrow out in the fields. Everybody's gonna know that too and they'll be more interested in what we're finding than in these guys. I hope."

"Probably, but do we want to leave them here?"

"No. But I don't want to send them back to McCoy's either. That's not safe," Pat said.

We pondered that one for a minute. Finally, I said, "I've got some more state cash. I can spend it on informants, which they sort of are now. Let's put them up in a motel tonight and figure something more permanent tomorrow."

We told the deputy we'd take care of the three prisoners and got Loretta to tell them they couldn't go back to the trailer tonight. "Tell them they can stay here locked up or we'll get a motel room for them. Maybe tomorrow they can go home," I said.

The Mexicans took the motel option, nodding at Loretta's translated instructions that they sit still, shut up, and above all, not tell anyone where they were until we got back to them the next day. Then we drove them to a place in Hugo that had a vacancy sign. It wasn't much, but the Mexicans seemed glad to be there, piling out of the car with lots of "*gracias, señores*" and big smiles as I gave them enough money for the dinners they hadn't gotten to eat back in the trailer.

Feeling a little more comfortable, especially postponing the 10-5 thing, maybe permanently, we hadn't even left the parking lot before Pat outed the question that must have been on his mind for a while.

"So I've got to ask you. What was that thing you said to those boys, got 'em all jumpy for a second there back in the trailer?"

"What? '*Dónde está la caja? Abrela!*'?"

"I guess, yeah."

"Oh, that's 'where's the safe? Open it,'" I said.

"'Where's the safe, open it?' That's it?" He shot me an incredulous look as he turned out onto the highway.

"Hey, I told you, I got it out of a movie and I said it wouldn't work."

"Holy cow. We're lucky to be alive. And those poor bastards probably figured they were getting robbed and shot and maybe lynched for the second time in two days."

Yeah, that's just about how I'd read it too.

***

I'd never been lynched but I had been assaulted, robbed, and, thanks to Jimmy, shot. Undercover work was far more dangerous back in those days. Sooner or later, you were going to run into bad people with bad ideas. Undercovers went looking for those people, after all. You just hoped none of them came together at the same time to turn it into a really bad day.

Those can happen suddenly and without any warning. You tried to avoid that by planning and preparing, which law enforcement agencies do much more intensely today. However, some things you just can't avoid. There were two scenarios I dreaded more than anything else. In both, you have very little, if any, control over the outcome, which all too often comes down to luck.

The first scary scenario was getting burned. There was always the chance that somebody would recognize me and know I wasn't who I was pretending to be. Maybe they saw me in court, maybe they were present at an arrest or a search warrant. As Kevin said, stuff happens, and I had no control over that stuff except to work areas where I hadn't done anything official. Even there, the heat could still flash up, and "getting burned" could be as fatal as if the flames were real. We had an agent who had to shoot his way out of a burn when the crook found the wire on the informant and drew down. I got burned a couple of times and had to fight my way out once, but they could've gone the other way in a second or two. One played out in a public but fairly intimate setting. The other happened in front of God and everybody.

"Oh man! I knew you were a narc!"

I heard that one quite frequently after we arrested the seller. I usually laughed, but Jimmy heard it once and said, as he was putting the handcuffs on, "Well, you big dummy, if you knew he was a narc, why'd you go ahead and sell to him, then?"

I was just meeting with an informant, but those were always clandestine affairs, undercover for all intents and purposes. It happened on a slow afternoon in a bar on Oklahoma City's northwest side and it had been quiet in the place, the exact opposite of a Saturday night disco or a bustling country-western saloon, both of which I tried to avoid because your chances of getting burned went up dramatically with the number of people around to see you. This day, only a smattering of customers sat at the bar or at tables, no loud music cutting through the smoke. A swell place for a discreet chat, and we had a high-sided booth that gave us pretty good privacy.

Standard procedure for undercovers (and everyone else in these troubled times): sit with your back to the wall so you can keep an eye on everything happening in the place. I followed this rule faithfully, and it paid off this time. I saw him from across the room, the recognition flaring, trying to put a name to the mop of whitish-blond hair and pink face. He was a big, burly guy in his thirties, well-dressed, and by himself. I knew I knew him and was still trying to figure out how when he got up, paid up, and walked out. Watching him leave, I got it. He was a defense attorney and we'd met in a couple of cases.

I hated defense attorneys generally. There are only three possible defenses for an undercover sale case: one, alibi/ mistaken identification, when the crook says, "It wasn't me, I was somewhere else;" two, entrapment, when the crook says, "Yeah, I did it, but the undercover offered improper or illegal enticements that would have caused an otherwise innocent person to do the same thing;" or three the dope wasn't dope, where the defense attorney challenges the lab analysis.

Note that two of the only available defenses rely on attacking the main, and sometimes only, witness, the person standing between the defense attorney's client and the state penitentiary. Me. It's part of the job, taking that crap from the lawyers. I got that, but that didn't mean I had to like it. I had several attorneys come up to me after court over the years and say, "It's nothing personal" after they'd just spent an hour or two ripping on me in front of the judge or twelve strangers.

I had a stock response. "Yeah? Screw you. Not to you, maybe, but it's personal to me." This comeback always seemed to shock them for some reason, probably because they were used to their prosecutor buddies taking the same detached and impersonal response toward their clients, however scummy those people might be. Having spent time with their clients undercover and thinking I knew exactly what kind of folks they were, I took their lawbreaking more personally. Anyway, I wasn't real popular with the defense bar, and vice versa, and I was glad to see that member of it leaving. I wouldn't be happy for long.

About ten minutes later, the bartender takes a phone call and looks around, puzzled, settling on me. He comes over to the booth and says, "That's the cops on the phone. They said you're robbing the place and you should come out with your hands up. They got your description."

"Robbery? What are you talking about?" I said, thinking it was some kind of gag.

He repeated the message, adding, "I told them nobody was robbing anybody but they don't believe me."

This information took a moment to process, trying to work out how a quiet conversation had turned into a hostage situation with SWAT rifles and shotguns right outside. I went to the phone and talked to the OCPD sergeant, explaining who we were and what was going on inside. He probably believed me but there's still a protocol for these situations, one that includes the "robbers" walking out backwards with their hands up and lying in the parking lot in handcuffs until SWAT sorted everything out. And that's *if* somebody didn't get jumpier than they already were and started shooting.

It didn't come to that. I got the office to call the police and we only spent a few tense moments at gunpoint until IDs could be verified. Then, I went after that defense attorney, telling the cops whose voice I thought was on their 911 recording. We could never prove it, of course. I listened to the tape myself and couldn't identify the clearly disguised voice. But I knew the son of a bitch had burned me, then tried to get us killed, or at least mess us up. Plus, he used other law enforcement people to do it since he didn't have guts enough of his own. I took that kind of personally too.

Avoiding burn jobs: one more reason to stay away from bars, and another to hate defense lawyers.

And of course, you don't need help getting burned; you always do it to yourself in every undercover case, setting aside the persona, by making the arrest, perhaps even testifying in court. That guy you bought from definitely knows who you are now. Do any of them do anything about it? My work never came back on me like that, but another undercover agent showed how real the risks could be, and the whole thing hit way too close to home.

In the early morning hours of October 22, 1987, somebody lit up Honolulu Police Officer Troy Barboza, shooting him three times through the window of his home with a 12-gauge shotgun. Barboza was killed instantly and his murderer vanished unseen into the night.

The killing threw Honolulu into an uproar. This was a cold-blooded assassination of a police officer, the murder going down in a place where everyone is supposed to feel safe. HPD went after the killer with everything it had, detectives working the crime scene for a couple of days, and for a week, officers stopped everyone driving on Barboza's once-quiet street, asking if they'd seen or heard anything useful on the night of the slaying.

None of it worked. The killer had gotten away clean, something that could not be tolerated if the Thin Blue Line were to remain intact. Once people got the idea that they could kill off-duty police officers in their homes and get away with it, that line would be broken forever. HPD brought the hammer down. Somebody, somewhere, knew something about the crime. They just had to be persuaded to tell the cops about it, so HPD put the heat on every criminal on the island. Sex workers, gamblers, and drug dealers down to below street level found themselves in jail for an astonishing array of charges from jaywalking and trespassing to major drug sales. Business as usual was over until somebody handed over a killer.

The case started to crack, with a suspect, Tony Williams, identified at last. Williams, a Los Angeles gangbanger from the notorious Crips street gang, had been in Honolulu selling cocaine. He sold some to Troy Barboza in an undercover deal and got arrested and released on bail to await trial. While he was out, he correctly concluded that Officer Barboza was the only person standing between him and Oahu Prison, and decided he'd eliminate that problem.

Williams found Barboza's home address, bought a shotgun and three shells, then laid in wait by the window until he saw the officer, firing all three and screaming "like a girl" in triumph. He took off for L.A., anticipating the charges would be dismissed now that the key—and only— witness against him was dead.

He got greedy, though, and lured by an informant, returned to Honolulu to do another dope deal. HPD arrested him, tried him, and convicted him for Murder 1, a mandatory sentence of life without parole. It wasn't a happy ending; there's no real joy or even justice in the death of a fine young man and police officer, a son, and a brother, nothing that will bring him back.

Why did this case hit so close to home for me? Because it *was* home, or almost. My family lived on a quiet street full of peaceful 1920s homes in a fine old Honolulu neighborhood. One of the city's police chiefs grew up in the house across the street from ours, and on the night he was murdered, Troy Barboza lived—and died—across the street and a block or so down.

***

The worst part about getting burned was the danger, obviously, that in the heat of the fiery discovery, the crook acts on a violent impulse. The other bad part was not seeing it coming. I could make a mistake, say something or do something that would cause that light to go off in the crook's head. The more I worked undercover, the fewer those mistakes happened, as my confidence and security built. But there's nothing you can do to prevent a random encounter, some fluke, or just a moment of bad luck. When those things happen, the undercover, formerly the hunter, may become the hunted, and worse, not know it as the crook works out the best way to deal with the new reality before they can.

In those situations, conditions can turn to hell in a flash, as the undercover's carefully hoarded control vanishes and if there's one thing worse than getting burned one-on-one in a bar or some drug dealer's crappy living room, it's taking the hit in front of about ten thousand people. All of them know you're a cop now. That's exactly what happened to me at a two-day outdoor festival at Wolf Mountain, just west of Poteau, Oklahoma, and the Arkansas state line on America's bicentennial weekend in 1976. The concert featured country-western artists mostly, and faced strong opposition from the community, which remembered Woodstock, only a few years earlier, and all the drugs, sex, and rock and roll that had gone on there. The organizers actually had to get a court order recognizing their right to assemble freely on America's two hundredth birthday.

Those organizers were certainly hoping for Woodstock-style success, charging ten dollars admission for the weekend and to assure the community that they didn't approve of Woodstock levels of drugs, sex, and other anathemas in Oklahoma—a pretty strait-laced state—they asked for an "undercover law enforcement presence," which the Bureau of Narcotics agreed to provide. That presence consisted of three agents, me included, and all of us agreed before we got anywhere near Poteau that we were going to get good seats, enjoy the music, and not spoil the weekend by doing anything stupid like making drug cases.

This worked out well for a few hours until the party right in front of us opened up for business, selling small quantities of marijuana and the white tablets billed as "meth tabs" but almost never were. Pretty soon, word had gotten around the festival grounds and customers were coming and going in a steady stream, money and drugs changing hands like somebody had legalized the business while we'd been driving down. We figured we couldn't just ignore it, so I bought some weed and a little meth from the head cashier, a long-haired, ferret-faced tweaker called Wilson.

To keep from burning me, the other two agents waited until Wilson went down the hill to the food concession trucks, on the presumption that he and his buddies wouldn't connect me with his sudden disappearance into the LeFlore County criminal justice system. It should have worked. There were, after all, dozens of other potential customers who could have been responsible for Wilson's unexpected absence from the concert.

Well, it didn't work. I found out the hard way that I'd been burned when one of Wilson's pals came up to where I was sitting on the grass, something like "you fuckin' narc," and started pounding on me. It took a minute, during which I took a few good shots, but I eventually turned things around and returned the favor with considerable enthusiasm. I had a pair of handcuffs on me and managed to get them on him, by which time everybody in the place, all ten thousand of them, was looking at us. Me, in particular, since I was sitting on top of Wilson's friend, his face in the dirt. Everyone could see *my* face clearly enough, including the band, which was Asleep at the Wheel, and in case there was anyone on Wolf Mountain who *hadn't* gotten a good look at the only undercover agent on the premises, one of the band members pointed out the two people fighting.

Obviously, that was the end of that, me being burned right down to my shoelaces. Sheriff's deputies came up and got the new prisoner and we all went down to the courthouse, so I missed Hoyt Axton and Crystal Gayle, damn it, and Jerry Jeff Walker ("Up Against the Wall Red Neck Mother"), which always got a country crowd going. But our concert-going days were over, and the people who wanted a "presence" got it. The guy who assaulted me got two years to think that over, and Wilson got two more.

Neither of us had managed to do much damage to the other in the scuffle, so getting burned was probably the worst part of the whole experience. But we should have waited until the end of Day Two to collect Wilson. Freddy Fender was coming!

I got a little shaky after the festival burn, thinking about all the things that could have made it worse, but luckily didn't. That happened a lot, and looking back now, with the wisdom of forty years of life experience, I marvel sometimes that I survived at all. That's okay; those doubts and reflections are fine after the fact, and essential for learning, but there is no time for fear undercover. Like feeling sorry for someone you're trying to put in prison, it's a distraction you can't afford. I might have gotten those shakes afterward but you can't lose focus in the moment.

When I started out in the mid-70s, the expectation for state and federal narcotics agents—and a high percentage of city and county narcs too—was that you *were* going undercover. Almost everybody went under. We didn't have specialists like they do today. Where I worked, the case agent (the person in charge of the investigation), whoever held the case number, got first dibs on the undercover role and first pick of the UC if he declined. We had agents at OBN who were undercover machines. Turn them loose, they were coming back with a head on a plaque for the wall. We had others who talked a good game but didn't have the gift and couldn't work undercover on their best day. One or two had done their time under and burned out, or in at least one case, had a deal end very, very badly and just couldn't go back down again. And we had a couple who were too scared to try UC at all. Most case agents, I was happy to be asked to work UC on their cases. The scared ones I resented deeply because they were "poking me out front" when they were too chicken to go there themselves.

My goal undercover was to keep everybody in the mindset that this is just another normal, routine, ordinary dope deal. These were people—many of them professional criminals—who'd been in the situation hundreds, maybe thousands of times before. What I wanted was for this meeting, thirty seconds or eight hours, to be just like every other one—regular, typical, accustomed—everything under control. I was totally tuned into the vibe of it, trying to see and hear everything going on, feel whether anything was wrong or off. That meant keeping track of everybody in the room, anyone coming or going, constantly monitoring the informant, always watching for any of what the shrinks call "leakage"—nonverbal communications, body language mostly—that differed even the slightest from the words I was seeing or hearing. I read books on nonverbal communications, body language, lying, influence, and sales techniques, and practiced those so I could "leak" the right signs and read the wrong ones. I think I got so into this that I actually developed an Alarm, a form of ESP, a weird, unexplainable phenomenon which I'll describe later and came in very handy a few times.

Control was always ideal, but in reality, the UC is almost never in complete control. You can't make people do things or behave the way you want them to, and often times you can't even control who these people are. I'd compare it to whitewater rafting on a river you've never seen before. You know from experience how to read the river signs, you can see some of the obstacles ahead, and you have the tools to deal with them, but ultimately, you're going to be going with the flow and you don't know if there's a big rock or a waterfall around the next bend or a nice stretch of flat, calm, safe water. You only have so much control. Just like whitewater rafting, this is a huge rush, but it's emotionally and even physically draining. I had a great time working undercover, very satisfying, matching wits with people, even the dumb ones. But I couldn't have done it forever, couldn't handle the continuous stress, tension, and the need to constantly be "switched on."

It was a helluva ride, but I didn't miss it when I moved into calmer waters after the rapids. Procedurally, it's all different now anyway: more clinical, a thicket of rules and procedures designed to make the process much safer and more effective. The rush is gone; they took all of the fun out of it.

The rules protect you; though, in fairness, most of them are in place to protect the bosses and the politicians. Pat Grimes and I had already bent a couple of little rules the first day of our kidnapping case. We'd be stomping all over a couple of big ones, starting in the morning, and as the night wore on, our chances of finding Tommy Hatfield alive and in one piece seemed thinner and thinner.

CHAPTER 8

WEDNESDAY MORNING

3 A.M.
FROGVILLE, OKLAHOMA
SEPTEMBER 1977
SECOND DAY

The next day dawned clear and hot. It was going to be as scorching and muggy as the day before, probably pushing a hundred, but well into the nineties for sure. The difference was, yesterday we'd spent most of the day in nice cold cars or air-conditioned buildings. Today, we'd be outside, in the woods and fields, with the mosquitos, ticks, the heat, the marijuana, and maybe the killers of an eighteen-year-old kid.

Aside from their vivid and memorable descriptions of what lynching was like from the lynchee's perspective, the Mexicans were a bust for us, no more help in locating the missing Hatfield in translated English than they had been to the bad guys in Spanish a couple of days before. They'd seen the two boys, and identified Tommy from the family photo, but said he'd run off and never came back. They said the Hatfield posse had cleaned out all the marijuana, just like we'd thought, piling it into their pickups before hauling ass. They'd gotten some more plants out of some nearby patches too, something T.W. had failed to mention.

None of that had been much good, but it was enough that by the time we got too far from the motel the night before, Pat and I had a plan. We'd talked to the Hatfields and the Mexicans. Tomorrow, we were going to talk to the McCoys.

With our prime suspect in the kidnapping, Eugene McCoy, short at least one hundred and fifty pounds of weed, I thought the Pot-For-Hostage swap might be an even better bet, assuming McCoy hadn't given up on reason and already perforated Tommy. We had another edge too and hit him with that as soon as we got back to Frogville.

McCoy met us at the door, matching the Mexicans' description of "*Señor* Gene," a bushy gray beard under the white, windblown hair that Bernie Sanders would make popular a few decades later, bib overalls, chewing tobacco. The only thing missing was a shotgun and "Dueling Banjos" playing somewhere in the darkness. He didn't look surprised to see the badges or particularly impressed by them either. And of course, he hadn't been keeping up on any of the local news.

"Don't know nothin' about that," he said when I told him we'd arrested his three illegal-immigrant farmhands.

"Right. And you definitely don't know anything about this kid, who was last seen the day before yesterday at your barn," Pat said, showing the Hatfield photo.

"Hatfield boy. Nope. Ain't seen him for a while. Maybe a month or two."

"His folks are real worried about him. His friend says he was hunting hogs with him in this neighborhood and he hasn't seen him since," I said.

"Hogs. Yeah, those're some dangerous critters. Got some down in the bottoms that'll go two hundred pounds. Supposed to be a couple of 'em, might could be five.

Pigs that big could kill a person. Eat him. Been known to happen."

"Uh huh. Well, we all better hope they didn't kill Tommy," I said. "Because we're down here from Oklahoma City looking for him and we're not leaving until he turns up."

Pat pushed the point, showing our edge. "It's just us right now, but if we don't find him, alive or dead, we're calling for help. Troopers, airplanes, dogs, boats on the river, helicopters, we'll turn this place inside out. We may be a month or two. Hell, we might be here till spring."

"That's likely gonna piss some folks off," Gene said.

"You think so?" I said. "Almost harvest time. We may not find Tommy, but I'll bet there's still plenty of work for the Oklahoma Bureau of *Narcotics*. We usually only have one plane up for eradication, but I'll bet with three or four we can find every last marijuana leaf between here and Hugo. Plus, you don't have your Mexicans to get the crop in or help with the rest of it. We got 'em. You McCoys will have to do all the work yourself. And here's the best part: no more fooling around in Choctaw County Court. The hell with all that good ol' boy shit. Anybody we find in a patch is going to see the federal judge in Muskogee." Showing him the other edge, which was probably a stretch, but I wanted to let him know that having the sheriff—or a local judge— in his pocket wasn't going to be much help in this situation.

"All that's the bad news," I went on. "The good news is, we heard some people might've found some… stuff that belonged to you. We've been asking around, and it seems these folks maybe want to put it back wherever it was they found it. They don't want any trouble with you, and they don't want any with us either."

"Don't know nothin' about that."

"Of course not. But maybe you know somebody who does, so pass the message along, okay?" I said.

Gene grunted, not a yes or a no.

"Dead or alive," I said. "I ain't gonna lie to you, Gene. Dead will be bad. Dead, there'll be a ton of agents down here: OBN, OSBI, FBI, maybe even Texas Rangers. Hell, we'll drag Immigration up here, see what they think. Dead means there'll be some hot times for a while. I don't think any of your local lawmen are gonna be able to fade that much heat."

"That's a lot of trouble, all for some punk kid out poaching other folks'... hogs," Gene said.

"That's why alive is much better," Pat said. "Kid *comes* home, we *go* home, you and everybody else in Frogville can run right back to doing whatever you do. Everybody's happy."

"Mmm. And y'all just goin' away, just like that..."

"Hell yes," I said. "No offense, but I got better things to do with my time than chase after pissant pot growers and illegal Mexicans in freakin' Frogville, USA. I'll hit the road so fast, you won't see anything but a blue streak. And before I go, I'll cut those Mexicans loose. They can do whatever they want, maybe come back and live in that shitty trailer you gave 'em."

"Offer expires at five this afternoon," Pat said. "After that, we bring the bloodhounds and a couple hundred more police."

Gene shrugged. "I don't know what you boys are talkin' about," he said and pulled the door closed between us.

We'd passed the message along, had to hope somebody was listening and would act on it. In the meantime, it was time to "go out in the weeds," as we called it. The high grass, as it were. A few years later, Hollywood made a movie from the story in the 1960s television series, *The Fugitive*. It featured Tommy Lee Jones as the relentless Deputy US Marshal Samuel Gerard, and he got to give a short, inspirational speech to his fellow manhunters. "What I want from each and every one of you is a hard-target search of every gas station, residence, warehouse, farmhouse, henhouse, outhouse, and doghouse in that area. Checkpoints go up at fifteen miles." When I heard it, I thought back to a late-summer day in Frogville, Oklahoma, where that was exactly what we'd done on our second morning down by the muddy river. Only we didn't have an army of lawmen, dogs, or helicopters, just two guys, poking their noses and shotguns where they weren't wanted.

OTHER TIMES AND PLACES

Search and seizure is bread and butter for narcotics work. It's a big game of hide and seek; most people in the drug business don't leave the really interesting stuff—their stash, their cash, their dope dealer accessories—out in the open where cops or rip-off artists might see them. So they hid it and we tried to find it, and we had a few tools to assist in the seeking part. Dogs could be a big help, although I found that in a drug house, our pooch pals tended to alert on everything.

Search warrants changed over the years, and the way we executed them changed even more drastically. It had never been a quiet, risk-free, "routine" operation; people got killed during search warrants. It's no surprise that people who deal drugs frequently arm themselves. It's a tough business and a dangerous world; we encountered guns so often in drug houses that we usually included a paragraph in the affidavit saying why we expected to find them in the place we wanted to search. I'd guess we found weapons in at least half of the homes and a sizable percentage of the businesses we searched.

Nobody ever resisted one of my warrants with deadly force, but we usually didn't give them much opportunity. Nowadays, the people inside have even less chance to fight off a raid, as SWAT teams or their tactics are standard operating procedure for most drug warrants, precisely because so many of them end up with the recovery of weapons. Now, the "no-knock" raid is very much in vogue. Under the old standard, those executing the warrant had to knock loudly, announce their presence and intent (to serve a warrant), and wait for admittance. The wait time varied by the size of the premises and other circumstances, but the general rule was you were supposed to stand by long enough for a person to come from the other end of the residence to open the door. That rule (figuratively) went out the window if you detected any sign that the occupant didn't plan to cooperate. This included such things as "furtive movements," attempting to flee out the back door, or flinging dope non-figuratively out the window.

A no-knock warrant needed to be specifically authorized by the judge who issued it, and you were supposed to provide him or her with facts justifying it. That we were looking for drugs, which could be easily disposed of down a toilet was one factor, and the information that we found weapons in a very high percentage of the premises we hit was another. But even with these considerations, I never sought the no-knock authority.

With a no-knock warrant, the occupant first discovers that the police would like to come in when their door comes crashing down and five officers swarm into the place. This sort of "dynamic entry" is thrilling for the officers, and more so for the occupants. It's arguably safer for us and perhaps everyone else because there is little or no opportunity for resistance. There's even less if the entry team uses shotgun breaching rounds to take down the door and flashbang grenades to immobilize everybody inside. I've seen a Los Angeles Police Department SWAT team execute a search warrant and clear a small house in well under thirty seconds. Those guys are like a perfectly tuned piece of machinery. Resistance to such a machine is likely to be brief, ineffective, painful, and possibly fatal.

We didn't always use SWAT teams or "special" tactics to gain entry. In fact, on many of my warrants, we didn't use force at all. I very much preferred to use stealth and trickery rather than energy and violence. It's very important to note that you cannot use "stealth and trickery" to do an illegal search or even to make entry under false pretenses. You can, however, use a ruse to get the person to open the door. Long before websites advertised "weird tricks" on the Internet, I used a few to serve my warrants.

Which weird trick frequently depended on the type of property. For motels, which often have very heavy doors set in steel frames and didn't belong to the person occupying the room, we wanted to avoid expensive ram or sledgehammer damage. Plus, some of those motel doors are stout enough to resist painfully long minutes of hammering, during which the person inside could easily flush every piece of incriminating evidence and still have time to take a shower and rent a movie. So getting the occupant to open the door on his own gave us a huge advantage. This led us to the "my insurance will cover it" weird trick.

Almost everybody who checks into a motel has a car, which they park in the motel lot. They usually give the license number or description when they check-in, and sometimes pay for parking. And almost everybody loves their car, especially drug dealers, who had to take a lot of risks and do a lot of deals to buy the thing. A call from the front desk, or even a knock at the door by a sorrowful guest, announcing that he's (actually, having a female agent make the call usually worked even better because of the negative stereotypes about women drivers, I guess) just backed into the suspect's parked car. "Gee, I'm really, really sorry but I'm almost positive my insurance will cover everything... Probably. Maybe... If my boyfriend paid the premium..."

Have a couple of people standing next to the room door, because this news invariably got the occupant out of the room, often at very high speed. Whoa, there, fella. Got some good news and some bad news. The good news is, your car's fine…

This ploy would work on apartments too, but I liked another trick: the old "you're raining on my parade" scam. You need a bucket of water for this one to be really effective. Start by going upstairs (you can obviously only work this on apartments above the first floor). Find your suspect's place and slosh a little water under the front door. It doesn't take a lot, but you'd like him to get his feet wet when he answers the knock. I've had people open the door before the knock just to find out where the water's coming from. In that case, your job is done. But if not, no worries. Just knock and give the explanation. "I'm in an apartment downstairs and I think you've got a pipe leak. It's coming through the ceiling." Set the bucket aside because he's going to open the door. At which time you say, "I've got good news and bad news. The good news is, there's no leak…"

For houses (and every other place where there are people who don't like annoying people, which is, like, everywhere) you can take Warren. With this one, you get to knock (the more, the better) and announce your identity, presence, and purpose (again, multiple times is great), and *still* get them to open the door on their own, sometimes quite heatedly. Let me explain, but you'll have to help me out here because Warren is more of an auditory phenomenon.

Say "police" out loud. But now, draw it out so it sounds a lot like "puh-leaze." Or just "please" because it's nice to be polite. You need to make it as whiny and irritating as possible. Good. Now, say "warrant" in the same tone and with the same whiny inflection. Maybe de-emphasize the "t" a little. Put them together a few times. "Puh-leaze, Warren." No, make it more whiny, shrill, and annoying. Excellent.

Now, go to the crook's door, preferably with another agent standing on one side, just out of sight. Knock loudly, and say in your most wheedling, whiny, grating voice, "Police, warrant, open the door." It probably *sounds* a lot like, "Please, Warren, open the door," but that is the point, after all.

Keep at it and change it up. "Warrant? Warrant? Open the door. Warrant." "Why won't you open the door. Warrant? Police? Police." You can throw in a real "please" now and then because you *are* asking politely. Make it sound as irritating as possible. Knock some more. You're clearly not going away until you see Warren, er, Warrant.

After several increasingly bothersome iterations, he'll probably try to tell you through the door that there's nobody named "Warren" there. Don't be discouraged. If you keep knocking and asking nicely, he'll open up eventually. "Warrant? Is that you? Open the door. Warrant, I need to talk to you. Police?" I went through twenty-six versions once, counted them all, before the occupant, red-faced and smoking hot, yanked open the door, screaming, "There's no fuckin' Warren here!"

"Ah," you respond in your normal voice. "But there *is* a warrant here."

We worked one routine once where I was "Serge" and looking for "Warren." That let me say, "Hey, warrant? It's (a) search, warrant. Police, open the door" about ten times before the guy opened up and said he didn't know any Serge or a Warren.

I got good news and bad news. The good news is… well, no. There is no good news, Warren.

CHAPTER 9

THE BIG BRIGHT GREEN PLEASURE MACHINE

FROGVILLE, OKLAHOMA
SEPTEMBER 1977
MORNING OF THE SECOND DAY

We had no search warrants down in Choctaw County that September, just a map with some possible marijuana plots marked and a countryside full of riled-up Frog-villains. On the morning of my second day, Pat and I headed back down toward the Red River, seeing if we could stir things up some more. After delivering the message to Eugene McCoy, we wanted to reinforce it by demonstrating that the heat was on and wouldn't be coming off until we got some word on Tommy.

We grabbed an early breakfast and stopped back in at the Hatfields' place to make sure they understood that the heat radiated both ways. Nothing on our map told us which plots the pilot had located belonged to McCoys, which were the Hatfields', and which might belong to some other ambitious grower in the area. Mrs. Hatfield and Amber had a crowd around the place that morning, four or five kinsmen, all wearing overalls or jeans and t-shirts. Some of these were in camouflage patterns with matching ballcaps, which made us wonder whether they planned to be doing any woodland exploring of their own that day. Nobody had any visible weapons but we both guessed they had a stash of those nearby. Pat made it real clear to Tommy's parents and their currently unarmed family members that in case they had any ideas about hiking around Frogville that day, we would take any resistance to our hike around lower Choctaw County very seriously.

"You think it's hot now? Wait and see what happens after somebody takes a shot at us. Tell everybody we said so. No point anybody getting dead over a few plants," he said, although, of course, that was probably exactly what had happened to their boy.

We got a lot of noncommittal responses and more shifty looks, but they said they understood.

It was time for me to bring up our hostage swap proposal again. "Good," I said. "Now, like I told Mrs. Hatfield yesterday, we heard some of you folks came into some pot that didn't belong to you. Maybe by accident, maybe not. It doesn't matter at this point. We're not here to mess with you over it. You got something they want back and they got something you want back. Maybe we can get everybody together and work this thing out."

They didn't say yes, they didn't say no, but confirmed that T.W. and Mrs. Hatfield had passed along the same message the day before. So they were thinking about it, even if they wouldn't say so to us. Good enough for now, and we headed down the road to Frogville.

We may not have hit the hen- and doghouses, but we stopped in at every house, mobile home, and barn, starting with the McCoys. Nobody shot at us but we didn't make any friends. We found a few pot patches, the high grass taller than either of us, and budded out, ready for harvesting soon. We didn't touch any of it, just announced loudly that we weren't there for the weed and were leaving, and if anybody could hear us, they should send Tommy Hatfield back to his folks. It was nerve-racking at first, walking down a gravel road or a dirt path to a falling-down structure full of silence and menace, hearing your voice echo in the shadows, feeling crosshairs on your back. A day would come when I'd be shot at doing exactly this, but all of our visits on this day ended tensely but quietly. After the first ten places, it wasn't tense anymore, just hot, sweaty, and tiring, with ticks and other biting critters making the whole experience even more fun. After twenty, and a half-dozen terse conversations on enemy porches, it was hot, sweaty, tiring, and fruitless. We turned up no red Camaros, no dead bodies, and no sign that Tommy Hatfield had ever been in these parts.

SHAWNEE, OKLAHOMA
1978
SOME MONTHS LATER

Marijuana's everywhere. We lost the pot battle in the War on Drugs before I even got out of high school, with people all across America buying, selling, growing, and using weed as if the laws against those things never existed. 420 is 24/7, and "everybody does it" is the marijuana motto. That's not far from the truth, from Bill Clinton and Barack Obama on down.

With those facts firmly in place, the whole country is taking a different line on pot, and it's going to be legal everywhere soon. It's already gone legit in seven or eight and Hawaii won't be far behind. Oklahoma, the "Buckle of the Bible Belt," will probably take a little longer, although they've already legalized the medicinal kind. That battle in the war's over and weed won.

I knew that as far back as 1977, seldom wasting time or energy making cases on a substance nobody cared enough to fight over. There were a couple of exceptions. One, of course, was for Tommy Hatfield and Company. Another might have been the largest marijuana seizure in American history. Neither of them worked out well.

MARIJUANA, MURDER, AND THE CASE OF THE CENTURY

"This is a great deal. Why is this guy being so nice to us?" I was puzzled and the informant sounded just as mystified.

"I dunno. On account of it's supposed to be contaminated or something, I guess. He's got a lot of it though." he said, skeptical along with me about why we were getting such a great deal on the pound of weed up for sale. It sounded too good to be true, and if you dig far enough, there's almost always a good explanation for that. Contamination might do it.

Paraquat. That's the first thing that came to mind when anybody in 1978 was talking about contaminated marijuana. The American government was providing the herbicide and aerial spraying equipment to Mexico to eradicate marijuana and opium poppies and had destroyed over thirty thousand acres of both (mostly poppies) only the year before. In late 1977, scientists reported that they'd found that the marijuana Americans were smoking was thoroughly polluted with herbicides, including paraquat, and there was concern this would cause lung problems, cancer, poisoning, and even death. The levels were usually low, but downstream in the business, neither dealers nor consumers in the US could know whether their pot was tainted. That this guy might—and lowered his price accordingly—meant OBN should do something to stop him. Nobody wanted hazardous substances on the street, and we'd want to go as high as we could on the chain above him to cut off supplies to other dealers.

I got the information on Jeffrey, the man who had the pot for sale, and the CI made arrangements for the introduction. Although Jeffrey was from Seminole, in the southeastern part of the state, I wanted to meet him in Shawnee, one county over, and in the western district of Oklahoma, in case the investigation got big enough for federal court.

That was highly unlikely, as the US attorney wanted at least a hundred pounds before he'd take a look, but after Ardmore, everybody at OBN was leery about taking pot cases to state courts. In a career full of big busts and major investigations, Ardmore had been Jimmy Birdsong's most notable case by far, his seizure in December 1976 of a DC-4 airplane and seventeen thousand pounds of Colombian marijuana. It was the largest seizure in OBN history at the time and may still hold the state record. In fact, it was one of, if not, the top marijuana hauls ever in the whole country.

You need a big plane to haul that kind of weight, and a DC-4 fits the bill. With propellers on four engines, it had been a military workhorse since World War II and the Berlin Airlift, and airlines used it all over the world before jets took over. A DC-4 could carry a lot of people or the equivalent weight in cargo; in this case, 276 plastic- and burlap-wrapped bales, sixty pounds each. The seizure, at the Ardmore Airpark in southern Oklahoma, wasn't only significant because of the size, but because the ring operating that plane, and a smaller Cessna 310 escort that Jimmy also grabbed, was one of the biggest marijuana smuggling operations in the country, maybe the whole world.

Run by El Paso businessman Jamiel "Jimmy" Alexander Chagra, it consisted not only of the men busted that night, but also a network that extended from Las Vegas to El Paso and Miami and on to Mexico, Colombia, and the Caribbean. Chagra wasn't in Ardmore and didn't get arrested with the ten pilots, truck drivers, and other members of the offload crew rounded up by local police, OBN, and the highway patrol. Maybe he was in Las Vegas, where he was well-known as a "whale," a mega gambler and high roller who could lose a million dollars in a single night. Marijuana money had made Chagra a legend in Sin City, where, short on cash one night due to some lucky baccarat players, one Strip casino borrowed five million dollars from the huge stash of currency Chagra kept on deposit in the casino cage. He made the casino sign a marker for the money, which is a switch, but the infusion let the casino keep its doors open until morning. Everybody knew where that money came from, and it was common knowledge that the big-money El Paso gambler and smuggler was behind the Ardmore DC-4 load, a multi-million-dollar loss for Chagra and his group. With seventeen thousand pounds of Chagra's dope and at least some crooks in hand, Birdsong set out to prove it.

Although I would eventually get to see Jimmy Chagra's marijuana three times, I'd missed the whole show in Ardmore. On leave back home in Hawaii when the planes arrived and the arrests went down, I got my first look at all that weed when OBN assigned me to guard the seizure. When I got back from the islands, I spent a few nights at a National Guard armory, watching those bales before we moved them to a more secure facility, one of twenty-five hundred bunkers at the US Naval Ammunition Depot outside McAlester. There they would stay until nobody needed them for court, and since I didn't have anything to do with the case, I figured I'd seen the last of that pot when the truck pulled away from the armory. But I was wrong; I'd be seeing it again. Right after Jimmy's big case went into the toilet.

The thing looked like a lock, at least to me, a somewhat detached observer. After all, the Customs Service had tracked the DC-4, which was using a false identity and callsign on the northbound trip from Colombia, then watched on radar as it descended into Ardmore. It wasn't a mere coincidence that Chagra had his offload crew standing by at that small, unattended airport, or that they quickly and efficiently loaded their trucks up with eight and a half tons of weed before speeding off into the night. And everybody there except the pilots had been caught in those vans and trucks, each stuffed with bales of marijuana. Based on all that, I expected I'd hear about some guilty pleas, but there were holes, and in a trial in Ardmore in July, all ten people arrested that night took their chances with an Oklahoma jury, pinning their hopes on the lawyers they'd brought with them from Texas. The lead attorney for the case was Jamiel Chagra's brother, Lee.

Flamboyant, colorful, extremely smart, and as we would discover, very, very good with a jury, Lee Chagra had an El Paso law practice concentrating on criminal defense, especially drug trafficking. Being as it was El Paso and right on the Mexican border, he got a lot of business. It didn't hurt that, like his brother, Lee was also totally immersed in the drug trade, from his thousand-dollar custom-made ostrich cowboy boots right up to the top of his trademark black five-hundred-dollar Stetson hat. He spent thousands more on a massive cocaine habit and was trafficking the drug with high-ranking members of at least two different Mafia families. People in the drug world—and in the courthouse—knew him as a major player.

A third Chagra brother, Joseph, was also an attorney and law partner with Lee, but Lee was the star of the Ardmore show. He flew into town on a private Learjet, driving a white Cadillac back and forth to court every day. He had bling before bling was a thing, wore about a pound of gold jewelry, carried an ebony cane with a solid gold handle, and partied heartily with a large and enthusiastic entourage in the normally quiet and staid farming community. He was the tiger shark in an Oklahoma goldfish bowl, and the folks in Carter County took to the smooth-talking Texas pettifogger like he was long-lost kin. The first jury liked Lee enough that eight of them voted for acquittal, the jury hanging 8-4 after two days of deliberation. One of the jurors, an attractive young lady, took up with the DC-4 pilot after the judge called the mistrial. The court set the second round for two months later, but the writing was already on the wall, and Lee Chagra would be coming back to Ardmore to make sure the jury read it loud and clear.

That had been some months earlier, and although the memories at OBN were still raw, none of them were on my mind that afternoon in Shawnee.

"So how is it I'm getting this great deal, man?" I asked.

The informant and I met Jeffrey Howard at a truck stop off I-40. Jeffrey was a good ol' boy, about twenty-five, lanky, long-haired, sporting prison tattoos, and a brown paper grocery bag with a pound of loose pot inside. Looked like marijuana. Smelled like it too, maybe with a hint of truck. But we *were* at a truck stop, with semis coming and going all around us.

"I got another load coming and I need the cash. It's good stuff. Colombian," Jeffrey said.

I checked the bag again. It didn't look great, but there was about a pound of it, so we had our felony. "If it's good, I'll want some more. How much can you do?"

"Hey, fire it up right here. You won't be sorry. I got another fifty, sixty pounds where that come from," Jeffrey said, not worried about critics' opinions.

"And this is really Colombian? That's usually more expensive than the stuff we get around here, not cheaper," I said. "I'm not complaining, just wondering how come."

"Guaranteed Colombian, just like the coffee. Santa Marta Gold. Roll one up. Nobody's lookin'."

"Let me see," the informant said, hearing his cue. I held out the bag and let him look inside. He was supposed to play the bad guy in our little one-act drama, the skeptic whose qualms might skew the deal. "I don't know," he said doubtfully. "It looks a little dried out and moldy. What's that white fuzzy stuff?" (He was supposed to ask about anything unusual, letting me be the good guy, coming in to "rescue" the sale.)

"That's just the T, man. (tetrahydrocannabinol: THC, marijuana's active ingredient, often claimed, seldom actually seen) Colombian always has a little shine on it from the T. It's quality."

"Okay. I'll try it. The price is right, even if we do have to come clear down here. *If* it checks out and *if* I want some more, I'm not doing all this driving for less than ten pounds. You sure you can do that much?"

"Hell yeah. Easy. I get you fifty, you want that much. All quality. I'm tellin' you, check it out right here, you'll see."

"Nah, man, I gotta go back to OKC with this shit. I don't want some trooper smelling smoke and jacking my ass up. How much do I owe you?"

There was no point haggling over the price, which was already below rock bottom, even for the locally grown or Mexican weed that filled almost one hundred percent of the Oklahoma market. Real Colombian pot was fairly rare and the exotic stuff from Hawaii or Northern California or Thailand was almost mythical. Jimmy Chagra's trucks, packed to the roofs with real Colombian weed, had all been screeching out of the Ardmore Airpark en route for other states and bigger markets as fast as they could drive. I'd gone undercover to buy that half-ton of Colombian the year before but had to go all the way to Florida to get it.

I passed over the cash and got Jeffrey's phone number, saying I'd be in touch, then watched him climb back into a white pickup and head toward Seminole. We went the other direction, down I-40 to Oklahoma City, the OSBI crime lab, and though I didn't know it, into the Chagra case. Which, as I drove westward, was officially dead as hell.

It got that way because, like I said, the Ardmore thing had some holes. Almost every case has a couple, but they're usually not big enough to let out any of the facts or let in even a little thing like reasonable doubt. That's true unless the defense attorney is somebody like Lee Chagra. He could make those holes big enough that he could fly a DC-4 through them. That's just what he did in Ardmore. By the time he'd finished his closing argument in the second trial, he had the case in the bag. The jury deliberated briefly, then came back with not guilty verdicts for all ten defendants. Then everybody—at least some of the jurors included—went out to party. Many of the partygoers—at least some of the jurors included—were seen wearing the Chagra entourage's custom t-shirts the Chagra clan had made up that read FREE THE ARDMORE 10.

That wasn't the end, of course. Everybody, winners and losers, went back to work, all of them doing exactly what they'd been doing before. Jimmy Birdsong continued chasing airplane smugglers, his current interest, although he still had time to work the heroin dealers with me on Oklahoma City's northeast side. The smugglers returned to running marijuana and coke, Lee and Jimmy Chagra both having plenty of gambling debt and their whale and major player reputations to uphold. They made a decision to not quit while they were ahead in Oklahoma, and this led directly to murder, attempted murder, assassination, a "case of the century," and lifetimes in prison.

Meanwhile, we didn't need all that weed—all eight and a half tons of it—now taking up space in the ammunition bunker, nothing but a nuisance. The feds down in Texas were still working a conspiracy investigation on the Chagra organization, and the Ardmore seizure would eventually be one of the overt acts charged in that case, but the prosecutor said he didn't need the physical evidence for trial; samples and photographs would do. That meant the 276 bales, each weighing the standard sixty pounds, compacted into tight cubes and wrapped in plastic and burlap, could all be destroyed.

Nobody had any experience in 1978 with the destruction of that much pot. As these big seizures got more common, law enforcement would figure out efficient ways of getting rid of tons of vegetable material. Burning it in power plants was one solution. In that year, we were winging it, and the answer someone came up with was original, well-prepared, and executed perfectly. Up to a point. After that point, it was a complete fiasco.

It gave me a chance to get my second look at Jimmy Chagra's dope, this time as it was all going up in smoke. It took much of the morning to load the truck at the bunker, the day warming up as we stacked bales almost to the ceiling. The weed gave off a rank stench, old and moldy. It was dry inside the bunker but the moisture inside the plastic-wrapped bales and the heat from decay set some of the pot rotting. After an hour of loading, we were all covered in the residue and smelled as bad as the bales.

The truck took a meandering route on county roads off the base and out into Pittsburg County, finally stopping at some anonymous ditch in a nameless clearing. Now we had help emptying the truck, some sheriff's deputies and a half dozen "trusties" from the Pittsburg County Jail. It still took forever to get all the bales out and then a couple of us and the trusties started busting up the bales with axes until we had a big, loose pile in the ditch. Threw the plastic garbage bag and burlap wrappings in there too. Then a tanker truck sprayed the whole thing with diesel and somebody lit it off.

The heat was ferocious, a real inferno, and a thick cloud of white smoke began piling up over us. To encourage the flames, which looked to me like they were doing just fine on their own, the diesel man shot some more onto the pyre every now and then, the smoke changing to black and then graying as the fuel cooked away. Marijuana burns really hot and it got harder to get close, so we were chucking more weed on from farther and farther back.

Bust up more bales and tossed those in. Repeat, over and over. About half an hour in, somebody noticed all the trusties were clustered downwind of the fire and not doing any work. We couldn't even really see them; the smoke was so thick. A couple of us and the deputies had to go into the smoke and drag those asshats out of there. Toss in more bales, shoot in more diesel. Go drag the trusties out of the smoke again.

After about an hour, people got tired of busting up the bales and started tossing big chunks, five or ten pounds at a time into the fire, which crackled and popped merrily as we fought our way through the smoke to haul the trusties out. After an hour and a half, Jimmy told the sheriff to take all the prisoners back to the county jail because none of them could see straight or stand up and he was afraid they were going to fall into the fire. By that time, half and even whole bales were going in. I left shortly after that, before the burn was finished, and about half the load was still on the truck or sitting on the ground outside it. It was an all-day job, for sure, maybe two. I heard they had to keep somebody at the site overnight to make sure the fire didn't get out of control, and that it finally went out.

Obviously, that hadn't been thought out very well beforehand. And clearly, those trusties couldn't be trusted. Because they may have been stoned out of their minds, and *ever* so grateful to the Oklahoma Bureau of Narcotics for The Very Best Prison Work Detail of All Time, but they weren't so stoned or stupid that they forgot where they'd been. And that ditch? Yeah, it was dry streambed. When the rain came, it spread primo Colombian seeds for about twenty miles. Next year, the sheriff had ten times the eradication problem he'd had before. Not exactly law enforcement's finest moment.

Freeing the Ardmore 10 *had* been Lee Chagra's finest moment, a triumph in the biggest marijuana case in American history, but he and his mega-smuggler brother had no idea about quitting while they were ahead. And though neither of them knew it, even as the seventeen thousand pounds of pot was going up in smoke down in McAlester, so was the Chagras' world. Committed by their lifestyles to staying in the marijuana and cocaine business, Jamiel and Lee both roared back from Ardmore, determined to make up losses, climb back to the top, and stay there. Only it didn't work out. The feds were getting indictments together. The DEA and Customs didn't have a planeload of dope this time, but they had a number of excellent witnesses from inside the Chagra organization. The pressure was relentless. Jamiel decided on drastic steps to relieve it.

The roof starting to cave in, Jimmy Chagra took his situation from bad to worse in an effort to get out from under the rubble. He contracted for a hit on the prosecutor in his case, a longtime foe, Assistant United States Attorney James Kerr. In November 1978, gunmen shot up Kerr's car with a .30-caliber rifle and a shotgun, but the prosecutor escaped without major injury. The Chagras were obvious suspects and the FBI poured people and resources into an investigation that only promised to get bigger until they found whoever was responsible. Jamiel would be facing all that heat alone. A month after the Kerr hit, Lee was found shot dead in his law office, victim of an apparent rip-off of $450,000 in drug money.

This left Jimmy without the Lee Chagra legal magic when the feds indicted him for a major trafficking conspiracy. Facing thirty years to life in prison was bad, but it got worse; the case was scheduled in front of Federal District Judge John H. Wood Jr. in San Antonio. John Wood didn't like drug dealers, and frequently demonstrated this at sentencing. He'd come by his forbidding nickname legitimately, and Chagra knew he'd get no breaks nor see any slack cut in the courtroom of "Maximum John."

Once again, Chagra turned away from legal defenses and went straight at what he perceived as the heart of his problem. He supposedly offered a ten-million-dollar bribe to the judge, and when that didn't work, he definitely paid a hit man $250,000 to kill Wood. On May 29, 1979, hired killer Charles Harrelson, father of future television and Hollywood star Woody Harrelson, shot the judge in the back as he was leaving his San Antonio home. The assassination of a sitting federal judge was unprecedented; none had been killed before in the twentieth century and nobody could remember one before that. It was a very big deal, a direct attack on the federal criminal justice system, and nothing could have brought more heat onto Jamiel Chagra or his case. The FBI made the matter its top priority in the entire country and multiplied the effort from the Kerr assassination attempt by about fifty. One writer called it the FBI's most important case and a "Crime of the Century."

If Chagra expected the killing to change the outcome of his trial, he was disappointed. A jury convicted him in August and the new judge gave him thirty years (although he probably would have gotten life without parole from Wood, so...). He tried running, jumping his $400,000 bail and becoming a fugitive, but he had far too high a profile to be very successful at the whole Richard Kimble game. The feds caught him six months later—in Las Vegas—and off to prison he went.

The Wood killing blew apart the rest of the Chagra family and utterly destroyed the drug empire Jimmy had built up. Jimmy's wife Elizabeth got thirty years for delivering Harrelson's fee to the hitman. She died in prison in 1997. Brother Joe Chagra was convicted of obstruction of justice in the case and received ten years in exchange for his testimony against the other defendants. Charles Harrelson dodged the death penalty but got two life terms without any possibility of parole. He died in the Bureau of Prisons' "supermax" facility in Florence, Colorado, twenty-eight years later. Harrelson's wife was convicted and got twenty years for buying the murder weapon and conspiracy.

The murder bullet missed Jimmy Chagra, acquitted when his brother Joe refused to testify against him. The jury did convict him of obstruction of justice in the case, the sentence added to the thirty years he received for the drug trafficking conspiracy. Although he later admitted his role in the assassination, flipping to get his wife released (a ploy that didn't work), he served twenty-three years of the original sentence. Released for health reasons in 2003, he died in 2008, a shadow of his former, larger-than-life self. That ended Jamiel Chagra's drug trafficking saga. My bit part in the drama, one he never knew or even suspected I played, was over much earlier.

It actually ended almost the minute I got back to the office to process my pound of pot. I put the bag under a light for a closer look. Except for a small amount for the field test kit, we never took evidence out of its original packaging. Defense attorneys would grill you all day over that. This batch didn't look great but it was definitely pot, and it turned the test chemicals purple, so we had a winner.

"Weird, though. Check this out," I said to one of the other agents.

He got up and came over. "He sold it to you in a paper sack?"

"Yeah. Like a brown bag lunch. But smell it. What's it smell like to you?"

He gave a couple of whiffs and came back for another. "Diesel," he said. "Uh oh. Where's this guy from?"

"Seminole, I think."

"That's not that far from Mac…"

"That's what I was thinking. That'd be a helluva coincidence. He's saying it's Colombian too. 'Santa Marta Gold.'"

"Maybe McAlester ditch weed. Our ditch."

"It stinks like it. That's probably why he's selling it in paper bags instead of plastic. It hides the diesel smell."

"Well that sucks," he said. "End of the line."

That's just what it was. Operating narcotics undercover means working "up the ladder," buying drugs from somebody on a lower rung and then climbing up to that dealer's source, then repeating until, in theory, you reached the top. It almost never turned out that way. People like Lee and Jimmy Chagra at the top had the money and power to keep folks like me from getting close enough to really threaten them on their perches. Sometimes they threatened or intimidated, or even killed, informants. Sometimes they went so far as to try to murder prosecutors and assassinate federal judges. Although you could get close, even tantalizingly close, high enough that you could see the prize, in most cases, you usually ended your ascent on some lower—mostly much lower—step, the last bit a reach too far.

I had a paper sack with a pound of Jamiel Chagra's marijuana and knew right where to go for fifty or sixty or a hundred more just like it. All of them would look like they'd aged well past their sell date and reek slightly of diesel. The sale of any of them to me would have been a felony in every county in the state, and every single pound was linked directly to the biggest marijuana trafficker in the whole country. But although I could see the man above me on the highest rung clearly enough, knew his name and all of the details about his bag of pot and how it got to a parking lot in Shawnee, Oklahoma, that case was going nowhere. I'd climbed all the way to the top of the ladder, gotten to the source and found out it was... us.

Jeffrey hadn't been one of the trusties out on the burn with us that day, but he had been locked up with them in the Pittsburg County Jail when they came back, babbling about the wonders they'd seen. He probably wasn't the only one to find that ditch in the clearing and mine it for some Santa Marta Gold. But neither he nor anybody else was ever going to pay for that violation. Case closed without arrest or prosecution. Send the evidence out for destruction. Burn it. Again. It happens that way sometimes. Some investigations, there's no satisfactory ending. But at least now I knew the answer to my original question. Why *was* I getting such a great deal on that pound of weed?

Because Jeffrey was having a fire sale.

CHAPTER 10

OVERS

No sign of Tommy. The day wore on with nothing to show for it but ticks and scratches. We didn't smell anything like a dead body anywhere we went, even following some circling buzzards once but they didn't know where Tommy was either.

Whenever we got back to the car, Pat would check in with Lewis to see if there was any news. We broke for a late lunch, driving back to the Hatfield house, ready to turn up the heat on the pot-victim exchange, see if the Hatfields were having any luck rounding up all that dope. The whole family turned cagey when the subject of weed came up, understandable under the circumstances. Here we were, two state cops, one with a Bureau of Narcotics badge, essentially encouraging people to distribute an eighth of a ton of marijuana. In a county where the local law was, by their lights, itching to lock them all up for whatever charge he could muster up, I'd have been twitchy too.

We checked on the Mexicans too, forking over enough investigative funds to cover another night in the motel and something for food. That was something of a concern because we ordinarily made this type of expenditure in connection with an actual, documented, ongoing criminal case. I wasn't supposed to spend the state's money on matters unlikely to result in a prosecution. As the second day wound down, this prospect, already dim from the get-go, faded away almost completely. Nobody's head would be going on the wall in this case.

This wasn't the first time, nor would it be the last, when I failed to reach that finish line. Sometimes I didn't try very hard for one reason or another. Violet's story is a good example. In other investigations, the evidence just didn't add up, the case getting sidetracked or shut down before it could reach the prosecutor. This didn't happen much in undercover cases, and I made a lot of those. We did charge the guy who made office deliveries but I passed on the Waikiki sniper. And never arrested anybody at all on Anzac Day.

OTHER PLACES, OTHER TIMES

We called it "getting over." Once the deal had been done, once the crook had gone hand to hand and sealed his fate, we'd gotten over the obstacles in the way of a successful case. And put one over on the seller. Some of the deals were quick and easy, some long and hard, some perilous or filled with unexpected wrinkles. Every one was different and the variety kept the whole undercover process from getting jejune and the agent on his or her game.

Some of the experiences keep you entertained from start to finish, though maybe, looking back, most were only funny after we'd gotten over. A few were bust-out-laughing situations in the moment.

We got bored once with actually driving out to make buys and decided to liven things up by seeing how close to the office we could get the deal to go down. We did one down the block, and another one in the big parking lot next to the state office building. I figured, there's lots of dumb crooks out there, let's see if one will come right to the office. I got one on the hook and told him I worked at the state arts and humanities council, which had their offices across the hall from ours. Gave him the room number and told him I'd be waiting. I didn't make any changes to the office lobby, just removed the sign that said OKLAHOMA BUREAU OF NARCOTICS AND DANGEROUS DRUGS CONTROL, leaving the arts people's sign the only one visible when you got out of the elevator. I'd given him the room number, which opened into the Enforcement squad bay, a big space with ten or twelve desks. There were about five other agents sitting around, waiting to see what happened. Guy shows up, comes in, comments on all the drug-related stuff: posters, triple beam scales, diplomas that said "DEA" or "Bureau of Narcotics," my graduation certificate from the state law enforcement academy, etc. I said, "Oh, we're doing an exhibit on drugs for the schools." He was fine with that, handed over the methadone, and got busted on the spot. Lest you think this was an aberration, that nobody could be this stupid, I repeated the whole thing in a Quaalude case a couple of years later, and that guy had a dental degree.

I was working undercover one night at the Diamond Head end of Waikiki Beach, the area known locally as the Gold Coast. Very expensive condos, apartments, and some regular (and some really expensive) houses. The informant and I go up to the crook's apartment, a low floor if I remember it right. The guy let us in and we're ready for business but he's not. The lights are all off and there's some other people there, just shadows mostly, although there's some light coming in from apartments in the building across the way, which aren't far off; the buildings are set pretty close together, at least these two were. Fifteen yards at the most.

The guy tells us to hush up, don't make any noise. So, quietly, I asked him what's going on and he says there's a pervert in the apartment across the way who waits in the dark for women and girls in our building to come to the lanai or a window, whereupon he turns the lights on and voila! He's naked and ready for action. After the surprise reveal, he actually does go into action, if you catch my drift. He did it with his glass sliding door open because he evidently especially liked to hear the reactions.

The guy (who, remember, is the drug trafficking law violator we've come to see about some Quaaludes) says in this outraged tone, "There's families with little girls over here. They can't even go out on their own lanais!" I asked him how little, and he said one was five. I think she was in the unit one floor up. He said they'd called the police but they were told that the man was in his own apartment and had a right to... well, perform "normal" functions in his own place. He's not forcing people to watch and they couldn't make him draw the drapes or turn out the lights. I don't know if the police actually told anybody that, but that's what he said, and he was pretty worked up about it too. Then he says, "We're gonna fix that, right now."

I said, "What are you going to do, take his picture?"

He said, "Hell no. We're gonna shoot his ass." Uh oh.

The apartment had two rooms facing the apartment in question, one's the living/dining area where we were, and the bedroom. They've got a girl in the bedroom, maybe the crook's girlfriend; I don't know, I never really saw her. When they're sure the perv is ready, she's going to go out on the balcony and wait for the lights to come on across the way. With the target fully... exposed, the designated marksman would take a shot through the open sliding glass door off the living room. Now that I looked more carefully, I could make out this gentleman, prone on the floor under the dining table, and bench resting a scoped rifle pointed next door. And there were a couple other people standing around, "spotting" or whatever. Maybe they're just a cheering section, but there were too many of them for me. I had a Model 60 revolver .38 with five rounds in an ankle holster, and a recorder running but no transmitter, so nobody outside knew this was happening. Who else had guns? How many? I didn't know, but I figured I ought to step in before these people assassinated somebody, no matter how badly he might need it. I was also wondering if—when—they finally came to their senses, they'd not be real friendly toward perfect strangers (like me) who just witnessed their homicide. My position seemed to be rather shaky and getting more precarious by the minute.

Normally, it's the undercover agent's job to witness a criminal act, then go to court and testify about what he saw and heard. The UC isn't there to create the crime or persuade people—especially innocent ones—to join in. That's called "entrapment," a legal defense and a major undercover no-no, but it definitely didn't appear to be an issue in this case. There was no entrapping this group of very determined and highly motivated criminals. They had their course mapped out by the time I got there and were, as the courts liked to say, "predisposed to commit the offense." Very predisposed. Downright enthusiastic about it, in fact.

Also, crimes of violence—murder being right at the top of the list—were bright red lines for the undercover. You couldn't let people cross those and then go to court later and tell everybody what you saw. You're supposed to intervene, summon help, warn the potential victim, do *something* to prevent someone from getting assaulted, robbed, raped, or killed. As you might guess from the circumstances in this situation, finding a path through that minefield can be a little tricky, and likely to end with a loud boom. Or two. With no way to get outside help or to alert the intended target, I decided to try and talk the killers off their charted course.

I said, "You can't just kill this guy, you'll all go down for murder."

The crook says, "Kill him? Nah, it's just a pellet gun. We're not gonna kill him, but he won't be yanking that thing for a while." (This explained why they needed a scoped rifle for a fifteen-yard shot. Much, much, much smaller target. I still wince at the thought.)

Relieved to hear that we weren't talking about a final solution to the flashing problem, I made another try at deterring the vigilante justice plotters. "I don't know, man. You don't want to get busted. This place has got a security guard."

The crook gestured at the rifleman. "He *is* the security guard. He's had enough of this shit too."

I said something like, "You all seem really busy right now, we'll come back later," and grabbed the informant. I told my backup we'd missed the connection but could go back later, but I don't think I ever did. So I never needed to use the tape, since there was no court case. I hadn't witnessed any crimes taking place. The informant told me later that the issue with the neighbor had been resolved satisfactorily. Never really wanted to go into the details with him, but I certainly sympathized with those folks.

Very, Very Short-term Undercover Operations

Things aren't always so tense or grim and there were many more light moments. It would rarely happen today, but once upon a time, an undercover operation would materialize on the spur of the moment, the agent overtaken by events. A couple of times, it happened to me by accident. On one memorable occasion, my partner and I were on surveillance down in Waikiki, heart of Honolulu's tourist district. Surrounded by high-rise hotels and condominiums, we had set up in a restaurant parking lot where we could see the condo where the undercover agent was meeting the crook. It was supposed to be a buy-bust, so the objective was to get close enough to provide effective backup but not be burned as surveillance. You don't want some crooked associate of the target walking in on the undercover deal and saying something like, "Hey, there's a bunch of cops sitting around outside." That kind of thing can spoil the undercover agent's whole day.

The government made this harder for us by issuing me a Ford LTD Crown Victoria four-door sedan. One that looked exactly like the most popular law enforcement vehicle in the entire country, and a model driven by most of the Honolulu Police Department at the time. Making it look less like a plainclothes police car posed real challenges, but I'd compensated a little by getting an authentic magnetized rooftop taxi sign. That helped because a lot of taxi operators used the Crown Vic too. With the sign on the roof and the motor running the AC, the two of us felt like we could pass as cabbies waiting on a fare, although we'd been stopped there for quite a while and were thoroughly bored.

All of a sudden, the back door opened up and this big, sunburned guy climbed into the back seat. Shorts, aloha shirt, rubber slippers. "Take me over to the Hilton, mate," he says in a strong Australian accent and a blast of beer fumes.

My partner and I looked at each other. I'm thinking, *what the hell, it's time to change positions and we can see the Hilton Hawaiian Village hotel from where we're sitting.* In fact, it's right next door to the place where the deal's supposed to go. Maybe dropping off a drunk tourist will add a little verisimilitude. It's a bad idea to have some big dispute with a drunk tourist about why you're not really a taxi cab when you're trying to be low-key and undercover.

"No problem, sir," I said, putting the car in gear.

We tootle over and stop under the Hilton's massive portico to let him out and he started trying to pay us, apparently not noticing we had no taxi meter. "No, no, this is our public service. Just don't try to drive anywhere," I said.

He said that was nice of us, but he thought he should at least give us a tip, even though it had only been about a two-minute ride.

"Not necessary," I said. "Part of the aloha spirit. And of course, it's Anzac Day, so we're letting Aussies and Kiwis ride for free."

This set him back for a moment, mulling this over through the beery haze. "Mate, Anzac Day's in April. The twenty-fifth. This is bloody October," he said finally.

"Ah, yes. Well, that's how you do things down under in the Southern Hemisphere. You're in the Northern Hemisphere now. Up here, we celebrate it in October. Have a nice Anzac Day."

"But, but…" Left him staring at us in the hotel driveway, the most confused Aussie in Honolulu at the moment.

I always wondered if he tried later that day for another free cab ride on Northern Hemisphere Anzac Day.

CHAPTER 11

THE DANGLING CONVERSATION

HUGO, OKLAHOMA
SEPTEMBER 1977
AFTERNOON OF THE SECOND DAY

Pat and I finished getting the Mexicans settled for another night and then found a Sonic drive-in (I practically lived on Sonic in my ramblings around the state; that and Dairy Queen) to wait for the 5 p.m. deadline. Neither of us was too sure about what needed to happen if the McCoys didn't cough up the kid.

"We'll have to do something though," I said. "Can't let these people call our bluff."

"Probably have to get OSBI into this thing. That might get a little touchy," Pat said.

I knew what he meant. By law, OSBI has "original jurisdiction" over only certain specified crimes—auto and oil field thefts, crimes involving the state government, a few others. For anything else, like the kidnapping and murder investigations they had a lot of experience with, somebody had to call them into case, give them an invitation. Usually, the county sheriff or a local police chief made that call. I didn't think that OBN could do that and the state was very sensitive about not stepping on other law enforcement toes.

Nobody was going to be too comfortable circling around the local lawmen. And I didn't think we were going to get much help from the Choctaw County sheriff on that score.

"FBI, maybe. It could be interstate; Texas being as close to Frogville as it is," I said.

"Either way, I figure we'll be out of it altogether in about," Pat looked at his watch, "fifteen minutes. I'll check in with Lewis again." He headed out to the car.

He came back grinning. "Tommy's home. Call off the hunt. Lewis says he made it back there about a half hour ago."

"Alive and well?"

"I guess. Alive anyhow."

"I don't suppose he's gonna want to file a kidnapping complaint," I said.

Pat laughed. "I doubt that he's thinking along those lines right this minute."

"Well, if he is, or his folks are, I expect they've got the sheriff's phone number. Like you said, we're out of it."

"That we are. I'd say our work here is done."

"I'm almost tempted to keep your map and come back with a plane and a bunch of agents and get all the dope we found, just to have something to show for this whole thing," I said.

"They'll have it all cleaned out by the time you could get back," Pat said. "And you've got something to show, now that Tommy's back and nobody got killed over all this. No dead bodies, that's pretty good."

We had gotten Tommy home to his folks, which is what OBN sent me to do, so even with no defendants to take to court, there were, like Pat said, no dead bodies, so it counted as a victory. It wasn't a complete win, felt more like a tie—a bunch of criminals on both sides getting away with everything, all that marijuana back on the market, and life in Choctaw County going on exactly as before. It was as if Pat and I had never been to Frogville at all.

We were done for good with Tommy Hatfield, that was certain. I could go back to working drug cases undercover, which felt much more like home than Frogville. I left Oklahoma to go to a new job in Hawaii a year later. Before I went, I'd shoot a man, make an arrest for a double homicide, and get a look at my own grave, reminders of how chancy life was undercover. And I'd find out that Pat had been wrong about one thing, something that would turn out to be tragically, heartbreakingly important.

There would be a lot of dead bodies before I put Oklahoma behind me.

***

Most accounts written by former undercover agents tell about deep-cover operations into major criminal organizations, or big cases involving millions of dollars and piles of illegal drugs or other crimes. Those are hugely stressful, very hazardous operations, hard on the undercover agent because players at that level use violence routinely, have a lot to lose, and have the resources and the intelligence to make any police investigation difficult.

The thing is, you can get just as dead trying to buy a quarter ounce of cocaine as somebody who's trying to bust a Pablo Escobar, El Chapo, or Manuel Noriega. Undercover is a dangerous game, and the people who play it know the risks, whether they're at the $2 table or off in the high rollers' suite.

Undercovers live (and sometimes die) by their rap. As long as you're talking, you've got a chance to keep the deal (and maybe yourself) alive. Once in a while though, you just plain run out of things to say, enough time to say them, or somebody willing to listen to you. When that happens, you're praying your backup will get there in time, or maybe start that fight for your life. Sometimes, there is no time even for that. Sometimes, the Reaper calls without warning.

I said before that there were two undercover scenarios that scared me, situations where the undercover has little or no control over the proceedings and may not discover that uncomfortable (and possibly fatal) fact until it's too late to do anything about it. Getting burned is one of those, and the other, even scarier one is the "straight rip."

Those are spooky words for an undercover, who never actually hears them as the Reaper murmurs to the crook. The straight rip kills, and it killed Paul Seema, a DEA agent in Los Angeles, when an undercover deal went as bad as it could go. I'd met Paul, who worked in L.A.'s DEA Group 4, the Asian heroin specialists. On the day he was killed, he was undercover, trying to buy a couple pounds of China White for eighty thousand dollars from some Taiwanese smugglers. These guys, however, had no intention of delivering anything but death.

Seema, born and raised in Thailand, spoke English as a second language and wished the DEA would let him go home. Instead, killers took him at age fifty-one from his wife and eight-year-old son. I didn't know his partner, George Montoya, who had only been out of the DEA academy for a month and two days when he died; or the third agent, Jose Martinez, who was severely wounded in the shooting. Their deal went bad when they "flashed" the eighty thousand in cash, confirming for the crooks that the buyers had the money to do the deal. The crook in the back seat of the UC car saw it and told them to pull up in front of a house, then started shooting, joined by a couple of buddies who had been following in another car. DEA agents and Monterey Park cops killed two of the robbers and wounded the third, who got life without parole, none of which would bring Paul back to his wife and son, or George back to his parents.

I dreaded the straight rip beyond any other undercover risk. Because there's no talking, no negotiating, no pleas or patter that's going to stop the guy who's heard the Reaper's lures and come to kill you for your buy money. It's the bitterest of ironies, but the undercover dies in this situation because he did his job perfectly; he's been so convincing in the role that the crooks believe they're killing another drug dealer, somebody no one will miss or make much fuss about. Just another "drug-related homicide." Paul and George were good and it got them killed. Straight rip. It can happen anytime undercover, and you won't see it coming until it does. When it happened to me, I got a chance to see the bottom of my own grave. Unlike Paul and George, the Reaper let me walk away.

I had made a buy from Daryl before. This time was supposed to be the big one, the buy-bust, when he got arrested after the sale. The informant set the deal up at the guy's house, a little box on Oklahoma City's southwest side, just around the corner from the stockyards, which I could smell in the fetid summer air as we got out of the car.

Thanks to Brad, Shep, Kevin, and other examples from bitter experience, I hated doing deals on the crook's home turf. The UC always wants as much control as possible, trying to surf the tsunami to a safe landing, but doing the buy in the crook's house gave control to him. The informant who set the deal up was even shadier than the normal CI, untrusted and unwilling or unable to follow instructions. I thought about canceling, mulled it over and finally decided to take another agent with me. Ordinarily I'd go alone, even for buy-busts, counting on the people outside to back me up when I called. My partner wasn't available that night, working somewhere else, so I looked around the office to see who might fit in.

I passed over Jimmy Birdsong, the memories of the Great German Shepherd Caper still fresh in my mind. Like that one, this deal was going down in southwest Oklahoma City, where, even though Birdsong wasn't nearly so well known as on the northeast side, he had still ended up undercover with a guy he'd already busted only a year earlier. Eventually, the boss made the decision for me: Jimmy was going. The theory was good. Hopefully his size—all six and a half feet of him—and his experience would give us an edge.

We got everything organized, had backup units on the street outside, waiting for the pre-arranged code words from the transmitter to come in for the arrest. A phone call had confirmed the time, and everything seemed to be going smoothly. This didn't last. When we arrived at the house, there were three people already there: Daryl; some other guy, an acne-faced tweaker, sitting next to the crook on the couch in the living room; and the informant. Both the tweaker and the CI were unpleasant surprises.

Seeing the informant pissed me off, though, of course, I couldn't show that. A real crook would be happy to have an old friend on hand. But I'd told the informant several times, including earlier that same night, *not* to be there. We didn't need him as a witness and his company was a distraction. We didn't need the tweaker either, since his presence evened the odds. I'd brought a friend and Daryl countered with one of his own. A poor start. At least there were no German shepherds anywhere in sight.

We talked for a minute in the living room, and I was getting nothing but bad vibrations, little tremors shaking at whatever control I had over the proceedings. But Daryl finally says he's got the meth right now, back in the bedroom, and he says he'll take us there. This all seemed eerily familiar after my last trip with Jimmy and a dealer to the back of a house, but I shook the feeling off, distracted by being so close to the finish line. Daryl quickly brought me back to reality. Before he stood up, I saw him slide a pistol from under his right leg across to the tweaker's left leg. Uh oh.

Because I'd been in the way, Jimmy hadn't seen it, and I didn't have a way to tell him as we walked to the bedroom. There, Daryl opened up a dresser and pulled out the dope—a half pound of methamphetamine—handing it to me. I checked it out, edging around so I can see the door to the hallway, expecting to see the tweaker come through, his gun popping. But it stayed empty as Daryl asked about the money.

I looked up at Jimmy, seeing the big grin building up on his face, knowing what was coming. "Well, you know what? We didn't exactly have that much in cash. But do you take gold? 'Cause we did bring some of that," he said, starting his chuckle.

The confusion on Daryl's face fled, replaced by instant understanding as soon as Jimmy showed him the golden OBN badge. He slumped over and Jimmy was too busy enjoying himself to do it, so I told Daryl not to say a word. I held off giving the bust signal because I didn't know for sure where the armed tweaker was anymore and didn't want our backup coming in with us in another part of the house. I told Jimmy, who was still laughing, "Be quiet, damn it; his buddy out there has a pistol. I'll go get it."

I walked down the hallway, yelling back over my shoulder, "I'll run out and fetch the money."

When I got to the living room, the tweaker was in the same spot, his right hand now under his right leg, his eyes following me like a cat tracking a canary.

"I'm just gonna get the cash out of the car," I said, walking behind the couch toward the front door.

He tried to keep me in sight as I walked behind him but couldn't, and as he turned his head, I yoked him around the neck and stuck my gun in his ear, telling him to bring his hand out slow and empty. He did, so I didn't have to shoot him, dragging him over the back of the couch and away from the gun, which sat on the sofa cushion, a shiny nickel .380. The informant looked back and forth between me and the pistol like he was thinking about going for it. I unscrewed my gun out of the tweaker's ear long enough to point it at the informant and told him to go outside and "get my friends." A minute later, the cavalry arrived and everything was back under control as I started thinking about the search warrant we'd need to take the place apart. But the informant wanted to talk.

"Psst," he hissed. "Come here, I wanna show you something." Okay.

He led me through the kitchen and out through the back door into a narrow yard with a high board fence around it. Another board, a sheet of plywood, lay on the ground in one corner. He lifted it off and pushed it aside; it was covering a hole about two or three feet deep.

He asked, "You know what that is?"

I said, "Looks like a hole."

He said, "That's your grave, man. They were never gonna sell you the dope. They were just gonna take the money and kill you and put you in the hole."

Huh. That's a pretty big proposition to get handed to you in such a casual fashion and put the hole in a different light. I contemplated the pit for a minute.

"That hole's not big enough for me and Jimmy both," I noted.

"I know. They didn't know he was coming. That's what threw 'em off. I think they'd have still done it though." He sounded a little wistful, like he wished he could have seen out that might have worked out for the two rippers. "Maybe they would have made it a little bigger..."

I shoved him into the hole, knocking him off balance and watching him drop to the bottom, arms and legs splayed, looking up at me in surprise, starting to whine.

"You stay down there until I get back, motherfucker," I told him. "Don't you climb out of that hole." I went to fetch Jimmy.

The two of us stood over the hole as I told Jimmy about Daryl's plan, the informant still protesting from inside the pit.

"Tough shit," Jimmy told him. "That's what you get for not giving us any kind of warning. You're damn lucky you work for him. Was me, I'd be shoveling dirt in on top of you right now."

That shut the informant up.

We eventually let him climb out, leaving with our prize and our prisoners. Before I got in the car, I went back one more time to the boarded yard with its bare dirt and its shallow digging for a last look. It's not everybody who can say they saw the bottom of their own grave and walked away from it. It's mostly a good feeling but you don't make a clean getaway. You can't walk off without leaving something behind yet taking something away too. No one leaves that place unscathed, and a little of the undercover's assurance is stripped away and left there in the hole.

It would be easy to lose everything in that hole, even if he himself wasn't lying there forever. You need supreme confidence to play the undercover game, the belief in yourself that you can talk your way in, and talk your way back out of any situation that comes up, that you can handle it, whatever *it* is, and handle them, whoever *they* are.

But what if you come face to face with a hole like that one? Dark and empty and stinking vaguely of cow shit? A lot could fit in that hole, even if it wasn't roomy enough for me and Jimmy both. It was plenty big enough to hold all my confidence, all of the undercover composure and self-assurance I needed to be able to walk into the next house, the next meet, the next possible straight rip. All that stuff could all be buried miles down in a grave only a couple of feet deep, and when I finally walked away, some of mine was.

That's what I left; what did I take away from the empty hole? The memory, of course, and the image of a body lying there, fitting perfectly, waiting to be covered over and forgotten forever. And something else, a little voice, a rasping whisper, that would play somewhere in the background every other time I went back undercover.

"Take his money and take his life. He'll never see it coming," the Reaper murmurs. "Straight rip."

The straight rip is just one reason why undercover is a dying art. A few years before I retired, I was on surveillance with a young DEA agent in Los Angeles and we got to talking about my old days working undercover. He listened to a war story or two (not the one featuring a grave and a conspiracy to commit murder) and then said, "I've only been working for a few years but I hope I get the chance to work undercover before I retire."

I was stunned, because for much of my career, almost every DEA agent worked UC at some point, and some did all the time. It was like breathing. Not anymore. DEA, FBI, and other federal agencies have decided UC work is just too dangerous to be routine, and it's been scrapped in favor of very tightly controlled programs that use carefully selected and monitored undercover agents for special, approved cases. They'll still put an informant into a hazardous "undercover" situation, buying dope or gathering evidence, but nobody wants to be the one to go explain to a colleague's widow why her husband won't be coming home anymore. Especially if he got killed trying to buy a kilo of coke or an ounce of meth when there are millions more just like those out on the street every day. It took a while, decades in fact, but people eventually arrived at the right conclusion. Everybody finally got it. The risks are too great for the rewards.

CHAPTER 12

FAKIN' IT

I never met Tommy Hatfield. Once the word came down that we didn't need to keep looking, neither Pat nor I was inclined to go talk to the kid who started the whole kerfuffle. I was happy to let Tommy go back to his family and for the whole bunch of them to plow on ahead among the possibly mythical Frogville frogs. Never saw any of them either. The rumor that Tommy been shot and dumped in the Red River even before Pat and I got to Choctaw County was obviously false, but I was pleased enough that the turtles and the frogs, and further down toward Arkansas and Louisiana, the alligators, hadn't gotten him.

With no reason to hang around any longer, I asked Pat to drive me over to my motel, climbing out of the car and retrieving my shotgun and all the other gear, setting it on the pavement next to his open window.

"That ought to be it," I said. "Unless Tommy's as dumb as his buddy T.W. and goes back to robbing other people's patches."

"He'll know what to expect anyhow," Pat said. "Can't count on being that lucky twice in a row."

"We'll see. Let's hope he learned his lesson." And we said our goodbyes, reaching through the window, shaking hands.

"I never asked you. What was the name of that film?" he said.

"What film?"

"The one you say you got all that helpful Spanish from…"

"Oh that. Yeah. That was *Butch Cassidy and the Sundance Kid*."

He stared at me, a big, friendly grin forming. "'Where's the safe? Open it?' I don't know. Maybe I'm just the suspicious type, but you look like somebody who's used that line before. I'm gonna be keeping my eye on you," he said.

I laughed. "I can't believe I'm saying this to somebody from Internal Affairs, but I think that'll be just fine by me."

Pat Grimes grinned, waved, and drove off. I'd see him again just the one time.

***

What seems like a good idea at the time frequently turns out to be anything but. That's true of almost any criminal act really, like ripping off marijuana patches that belong to people who hate you already. It works that way for prescription forgers too, who see an "easy" chance to get some pharmaceutical dope and take it. Most forged prescription cases are very routine and unimaginative. They certainly don't require any great investigative skills to solve. The perpetrators don't put a lot of thought into this crime. If they did, they wouldn't do it in the first place, but since they're mostly drug addicts—all of them drug seekers, for sure—they allow their somewhat hazy focus on the immediate goal (getting dope) to override whatever good judgment would ordinarily tell them to slow down. Pharmacies, and all those goodies within, make people a little bit crazy, so that little voice saying, "Hold up a second, this might not be the best idea you've had this week," gets ignored by the louder one saying, "Look at all that dope in there!"

So script passers aren't exactly criminal masterminds, not unlike Tommy Hatfield and his buddy, and typically leave a freeway-sized trail of clues. In many cases, including almost all of the ones when prescriptions were altered, they left their names, addresses, and phone numbers (and fingerprints) on the altered script. Not real hard to track those folks down.

The typical prescription forger was a female; it seems to be mostly a woman's game, although plenty of men tried it. They stole the blanks or made photocopies and connived somehow to get the doctor's DEA number, which you need to get the pharmacy to hand over a controlled substance. Considering how crappy they write, forging a doctor's signature isn't exactly complex or difficult. The key is to get a bad prescription past an alert pharmacist, and here was where the cons with talent and technique distinguished themselves.

Any schmuck could alter a valid prescription for "four" Percodan to try for "fourty," but most pharmacists (and most readers) are going to catch that one pretty quickly. We got two or three of those calls (or the even more ambitious "six" to "sixty" or the wildly optimistic "ten" to "one hundred") every month. A real pro created her prescription from a blank piece of paper and a true artist made a con game out of the whole process.

Take Becky. She wanted Dilaudid, a painkiller several times more potent than morphine and one beloved by many script chasers. Dilaudid is a Schedule II, just like morphine and cocaine, and Becky knew doctors don't just give Dilaudid away for stubbed toes or toothaches; they saved it for serious and really painful conditions. And even worse, she knew that pharmacists tend to take a hard look at any Dilaudid papers coming over the counter, calling to check with the author if there was any doubt about the prescription's validity.

She didn't want to be standing around in the pharmacy while one of those calls went out, so Becky planned her con much more thoroughly than the average script passer, and she started by doing some homework, researching a painful form of cancer, finding out which doctor treated it, getting his prescription and his DEA number. But she didn't stop there. She went to the library and read up on "her" new cancer, identifying two other drugs prescribed for the chemotherapy that accompanied treatment by that doctor. These drugs plus Dilaudid would be a very normal combination for someone with this condition, and something that a pharmacist would expect to see. With all this information in hand, Becky wrote the prescriptions, and the game was on.

A "game," because this wasn't just a simple forgery; it was a confidence game, one that relied on Becky's personal flair and a very carefully laid story to scam the mark; in this case, the pharmacist, the person she had to fool.

Druggists are a mixed bag when it comes to prescription fraud. Some of them don't really care that much, don't pay much attention, get sloppy or inattentive, and occasionally fail to follow the laws or regulations when they're filling prescriptions. Word gets out on these places at light speed. The junkie grapevine is extremely efficient and an "easy pharmacy" will have a line of script passers out the door before the pharmacist gets back from his lunch break. Word also travels to the narcotics agents, and not too much slower. We'll be by for an inspection or surveillance to see if we can nail a couple of passers at the counter, then start asking hard questions of the staff.

Most pharmacists know a bad script when they see one and can confirm a suspicion with a fast phone call before the passer knows the heat is on. Experienced passers watch for signs that their game is up and take off before the cops get there, but a high percentage of the pros—and all of the amateurs—are needy, desperate, or just hopeful enough to hang around, even though their prescription is taking forever to get filled.

Becky was a smart one, or at least very experienced at this business. She didn't plan on waiting around. The chemotherapy drugs she included in her scam were very unusual; most drug stores didn't stock them because very few patients needed them. Only a few hospital pharmacies in town had these rare and special medications. Becky knew this and factored it into her scam. Those pills were also extremely expensive, something else Becky knew. Dilaudid, invented in 1924, has been out of patent for decades, and costs next to nothing at a pharmacy. (On the street, it's a whole different story.) Becky built this into her scam too.

When she showed up at the hospital pharmacy's counter, it was right at the end of the normal business day, quitting time for most of the offices in the hospital, and just after office hours at the cancer clinic where she'd supposedly gotten her prescriptions. (This made it hard for the pharmacist to call and check with the doctor since the office was closed.) She handed over the three prescriptions and asked how much filling all three would cost.

$950. Wow… Gee… That much? No, she didn't have drug coverage on her insurance and she didn't have that kind of money on her. Maybe she could do a partial fill? She and the pharmacist talked for a little while about different options. Becky built rapport; the pharmacist was very sympathetic. After all, she's a cancer patient with real problems, medical and now financial.

Up until now, Becky hadn't made the actual ask, hadn't passed her Dilaudid script, just talked about options with the pharmacist, killing time, building her credibility, and establishing herself as a genuine patient. Everything was going exactly according to plan.

Most script passers don't have a plan, or if they do, it's a half-assed one. It boils down to this: one, write the prescription for as many pills as you think you can get away with; two, give the script to the pharmacy clerk; and three, hope for the best. A lot of these things are spur of the moment, crimes of opportunity. A doctor leaves a prescription pad in an examination room and a junkie patient sees a chance to rip off a few sheets or the whole thing. Or there's enough room on a handwritten prescription for a little alteration, and presto, "six" turns into "sixty," which is what the patient thinks she deserved in the first place.

Becky's con worked. She got her 120 Dilaudid. Walked away from the pharmacy clean. She and the pharmacist agreed she'd take the Dilaudid that evening, since she could pay for that one, and she'd be back in the morning with more money to split the two other scripts if the doctor would okay it. No phone calls to the doctor that evening. Mission accomplished.

Although those 8mg tablets sold on the street for up to twenty bucks each, making Becky's haul worth over two thousand dollars, she hadn't pulled off the perfect crime by any stretch. The pharmacist helpfully filled the two chemo scripts, halving the order like they'd talked about. Even more helpfully, he phoned the doctor for Becky the next morning to make the arrangements for the partial fill on those when the patient came back.

They do say the road to hell is paved with good intentions, and Becky's road to jail sure was. Of course, the doctor didn't recognize the patient's name when the pharmacist called, and the whole thing came apart. Our investigation took about six more hours to complete, and Becky made it easy for us.

She hadn't used her real name at the pharmacy or on the script, but the doctor's staff remembered somebody who fit the general description—a Medicaid patient named Becky with full ID who had seen another doctor in the office. Becky had a rap sheet already. In fact, she was on parole, and as I was about to find out, a career criminal with more than one illegal scheme underway at that very moment.

Her parole officer gave me a recent mug shot and I headed down to the police department where we got similar-looking mug photos from the robbery detail. I needed five more people who looked like Becky to fill out the six-pack photo spread. The robbery detectives, who were constantly making up photo spreads for their own cases, had the best files, separated by race, sex, and age. There was only one detective in the office that afternoon and he waved me over to the file cabinets and I started going through the photos, Becky's mug on the table.

"Becky," the detective said, seeing the photo. "What have you got on her?"

"Prescription fraud," I said. "She's getting Dilaudid. You know her, huh?"

"Oh yeah." The detective laughed. "In fact, that six-pack you're making will be the second we've put together on her today. We're looking for her right now. That's where everybody else is."

Maybe Dilaudid affects you like cheap beer on a Saturday night, wrecking your judgment and making you do stupid things in a cascade of dumber and dumber decisions. In Becky's case, that chain started earlier that afternoon with a decision to rob a savings and loan. This completely lacked the subtlety and finesse of the prescription scam. She invested none of the flair or the research or the preparation. She had just marched in and laid her note demanding cash down on the counter.

Here are two important pro tips for anybody thinking about robbing a bank. First: don't leave evidence—

especially your demand note—at the scene. It contains your DNA, fingerprints, handwriting, and other information the police find useful when they try to put you in prison. Second: don't write that demand note on the back of the appointment reminder for your next date with your parole officer. This tends to narrow the suspect population considerably, like all the way down to one. Becky made both mistakes, and the robbery dicks were all over it.

Even before I got back to the office from the pharmacy, where the druggist easily picked out Becky's picture from the spread, the police and the FBI, not to mention the paroling authority, were also looking for their robber and parole violator. Given the relative seriousness of the offenses, I opted to get some popcorn and take a back seat. She'd gone to another island but the detectives got her that night.

Becky's scam, despite the clown car robbery ending, was still five or six cuts above the average "fraudulent obtaining controlled substance" scheme. But even Becky's case wasn't very hard to clear. Most were even easier. I was startled once to be talking with a pharmacist about a forger when another one, somebody who was on an alert for having stolen a pad of prescription blanks, came in and dropped a bad script from the pad. The pharmacist never even called the doctor to confirm it, just looked up at the passer, over at me, and shrugged.

Even Paranoid Forgers Can Have Real Enemas

You don't get much opportunity to go undercover in forged prescription cases. It's not that kind of crime. But I did in a few, and one was my shortest-ever undercover role. In it, I played a doctor. Since I obviously never went to medical school and didn't even watch doctor shows on TV, it's a good thing my turn on stage only lasted for about one minute, start to finish. I thought I was pretty convincing, but

I still wouldn't recommend me as your family physician. It was good enough for the Case of the Smart-Ass Punk, and it still satisfies to this day.

I had the duty one weekend and got a call from one of the local hospitals. Could I come down and talk to them about a potential prescription fraud case? Sure. It was a little bit unusual because it wasn't a call from the pharmacy, where these cases usually originate, but from one of the hospital nursing floors. We did get those occasionally, and unfortunately, they usually involved someone on the staff—a nurse or an aide, sometimes a doctor—stealing drugs or scamming some to feed a personal drug habit. Those were never happy visits, and that's what I expected on this morning.

I drove over and went up to the third or fourth floor where all these nurses were standing around, talking to each other. Some looked pissed, some looked worried, and none of them were paying any attention to their patients.

I identified myself and, addressing the crowd generally, said, "What's up?"

The formidable woman who's the head nurse for the floor says they're not really, exactly, certainly, *sure* what's up but they think they're getting scammed. They're not clear on the whom or how parts, but it's been going on for almost a week. She was one of the worried-looking ones.

One of the pissed-looking ones spoke up and said *she* knows what's up and proceeded to fill in the story. Back on Monday, this guy checked himself into the hospital, to have surgery later in the week. The admitting doctor/surgeon had privileges at the hospital but didn't actually work there, so none of the staff was familiar with him. They got a call from the doctor's office confirming the arrangement and ordering up some drugs, including morphine, for the patient, who's now snuggled down into his hospital bed.

Well, the surgery got postponed when the doctor called again and said he had some conflict or something, and the hospital agreed to go along. Then, on Thursday, the doctor came in to check on the patient, who had gone down to the cafeteria or somewhere, so they unfortunately missed each other. The doctor reviewed the chart and all the paperwork and said he had to get back to surgery, ordering some more morphine before he left. The nurses on duty thought it was a little odd because the doctor was wearing full surgical scrubs, including booties, cap, and a gauze mask, but after all, he did say he was on the way to surgery... A little while later, the patient came back, sorry to have missed the doctor.

This same scene repeated itself on Friday, and again earlier that morning, which was when one of the pissed-looking nurses pulled the plug and called me. "I don't think there is a doctor. I think *he's* the doctor," she said. All the other nurses are nodding like little bobbleheads. Yep, they do too.

I started laughing. I said, "So, he's got the scrubs stashed someplace around here and goes and changes like Superman, then strolls in with his mask on and orders himself some more morphine..."

Everybody nods.

"Okay, does this doctor he's impersonating really exist? Did anybody check?"

Everybody nods again. The place is like one of those dashboard hula doll collections. It may have taken them a couple of days to get there, or six, but everybody on this particular nursing floor is definitely on the same page about their patient now. The head nurse says she just got off the phone with the real doctor, who told her he doesn't know this guy and doesn't have anybody in the hospital waiting for surgery. None of the prescriptions issued in his name are any good either, and after six days, multiple orders of morphine every day, there are quite a few of those in the chart. Furthermore, the real doctor says he's about six inches taller than the one who's been "attending," and he's a whole different race. The head nurse looks totally distraught telling me this. I'm still laughing and I tell all of them to lighten up, this is one for the grandkids.

So where is Dr. Patient now? Back in bed, enjoying his morning morphine fix.

I said, "Fine, let me borrow your stethoscope." Head nurse handed it over. I picked the two biggest, toughest-looking nurses, one of whom was also the most pissed off about the whole thing, really steaming, and asked them to come with me. I hung the stethoscope around my neck and walked into the room. (Private, of course, only the best for my new patient.) I didn't say anything right off, just got the chart off the hook at the foot of the bed and started flipping through it. I checked the guy out at the same time.

He's pretty clean cut, mid-twenties, Caucasian. Preppy type. Watching TV. He noticed me, though, and sat up a little, and said, "What's going on? Who are you?"

I said, "I'm the doctor on duty today and I'm here to arrange the pre-surgical procedures."

I could see his mind going about a hundred miles an hour, trying to figure out what to say. Finally, he said, "What kind of procedures?"

I said, "Oh, your enema. Have to have one of those. Maybe two or three; right, nurse?"

They're both smiling grimly now, like they really would like to give this guy an enema. Good and hard.

This news obviously came as quite a shock, especially since he knew neither he nor his "doctor" had ordered anything like that, and he's stuttering, "E-e-e-enema? I'm not supposed to get an enema!"

I said, "No, no, don't worry, I'm going to put it right here on the chart. One enema, extra thorough, coming up." Meanwhile, I'm slipping all of the papers from the clipboard and taking official custody. It's evidence now. After all, he's been writing his fraudulent morphine prescriptions in there for six days.

He got a little composure back and said he wanted to talk to his doctor before we did anything.

I said, "Oh, that won't be necessary. We just got finished talking with the doctor and he gave us a phone diagnosis. He said he thinks you're full of shit, and I have to say in my professional opinion that I concur." The nurses nodded; they thought so too—in their professional opinions. "We've got two ways of treating that condition. You can either stay there in bed and get your enema or come with me." And I pulled out a pair of handcuffs.

He just wilted, but I wasn't done. He wanted to get dressed but I told him, "The hell with that. You've done all the Superman changing you're gonna do for this week."

I transported him in his undies and his hospital gown, those awful ones that tie in back but still don't close and show everything, which is how he got booked into the cellblock. I like to think that made quite an impression on the other inmates.

That was it, my shortest-ever undercover role. In and out in under two minutes. I thought I'd thoroughly put paid to the Smart-Ass Punk, that that would be the end of him, at least until the arraignment and plea on Monday, but no. I still had the duty that weekend, and four hours later, I got a call from the hospital. Could I go back down to the secure floor for a prescription fraud case? Sure.

You probably guessed it. The Punk decided he didn't like it in the cellblock (who does?), complained of chest pains, got transported back to the hospital (same one) for observation, where they put him in a room with a police officer on the door, hooked him up to some machines, and handcuffed him to a bed. Next to a telephone.

Uh oh.

Chapter 13

Punky's Dilemma

Frogville, Oklahoma
February 1978
Five Months Later

Tommy might have made it home but Pat and I had three loose ends back in Frogville. Something had to be done about the Mexicans. We didn't need them as witnesses anymore, had nothing to charge them with except being in the country illegally, and both felt rather strongly they'd suffered more than enough for their little adventure in Frogville, America. We definitely didn't want to leave them to the tender mercies of the Choctaw County sheriff and his 10-5 local train to Nuevo Laredo.

On the other hand, sending three people who, as our informant said, "only know Mexican and how to work in a pot field," back to *Señor* Gene so they could finish processing that year's crop didn't really sound like a great official option for the Oklahoma Bureau of Narcotics. I'm still not sure how my boss would have reacted to that suggestion. Probably not very well. So, I never mentioned it back in OKC, figuring that, like accidental discharges that don't hit anything important, there are some things bosses are better off not knowing. That may not have been the best call, because the road to hell (and Frogville) is paved with good intentions.

We'd gotten Loretta's number in case we needed translation services, and had her call and tell our three motel guests they could do whatever they wanted after they checked out the next morning. We strongly urged, making the point as vigorously as possible, that if they had some other place to go, relatives or friends to stay with, or job opportunities (preferably out of the drug business) elsewhere, they should leave Frogville. The Hatfields, the McCoys, and the sheriff all knew about them and had potential reasons for making life even more difficult than it had been over the last week. We gave them a grace period: two weeks before we'd call the Immigration and Naturalization Service and give up the address of the trailer. Best not to be there if and when INS showed up.

I never saw or heard from them again. I hope they heeded the advice and went home to Mexico. If so, they've all got very interesting stories to tell about their adventures in El Norte.

But not long after, sometime in February of '78, a couple of citizens spotted a body in Muddy Boggy Creek, a sluggish tributary with an alluring name that cuts into the Red River a few miles due west of our search area. (Muddy Boggy Creek has a twin, Clear Boggy Creek. Both real, just like Frogville, I'm not making this up. Obviously, if you're dumping a body—or three—you probably want to use the Muddy Boggy rather than the Clear.)

The citizens told the sheriff's office, which looked in the run-off-swollen winter waters for a day or two before giving up. With Tommy accounted for, the sheriff said he didn't have any missing persons reports or any idea about who it might have been floating downstream. That would have been about five months after Tommy disappeared, and it was a few miles from where Pat and I had been looking, but maybe the Hatfields and the McCoys had gotten back to their old habits, maybe some other Frogville faction was keeping busy, or maybe somebody killed a Mexican that nobody would miss and nobody would report missing. February isn't growing season, and nobody, including OBN, was out raiding marijuana patches that month. But folks down there seemed to have an unlimited supply of grudges and the time and the inclination to act on them. It could be that the two families used their temporary truce from September to bury the hatchet and end the feud, but I doubt it. None of the ones I met seemed like the "forgive and forget" sorts, either bunch of them, and they clearly didn't have any compunction about abusing, shooting, hanging, or killing Mexicans.

Did their involvement in the marijuana business, the secrets they knew about *Señor* Gene and the sheriff get them killed? Did the people who had shot at them and made them dance come back to shut them up for good? They had good reason to. If the sheriff really was in the McCoys' pocket, he could press the Mexicans hard on the lynching and bring kidnapping, assault with a deadly weapon, even attempted murder charges against a whole bunch of Hatfields. That's a loose end, and nobody wants those lying around. Maybe we should have taken the 10-5 option when it came up. I've wondered about that for forty years.

I didn't have to wonder about what happened to the sheriff. I'd described the allegations against him in my case report but didn't think it would amount to much; it seemed like he had Choctaw County on a tight leash. Somebody got off that leash though. In June 1978, two men sued the sheriff, some deputies, and the county, alleging they'd been deprived of their civil rights in one of those 10-5 deals. I left Oklahoma that same month and didn't hear how the case turned out, but was back in OKC on vacation in 1980 and read in the *Daily Oklahoman* that the sheriff had been indicted by a federal grand jury in Muskogee, charged with "conspiring to distribute marijuana, obstructing the investigation of a whiskey shipment and covering up a gambling operation in his county." His co-conspirator on the marijuana charge was a Hugo man whose name came up several times while Pat and I were nosing around Frogville.

In May 1980, the government dismissed the drug counts on former Sheriff James Clifford Buchanan in exchange for his guilty plea on the obstruction charges. Buchanan got a five-year sentence but only served two. I don't imagine those were easy years, a former lawman in federal prison, but it probably wasn't nearly as tough as the thirty days served by the Smart-Ass Punk.

I had noticed something about the Punk when we first got down to the police department and the receiving desk. Maybe he was annoyed with me about the hospital gown thing, maybe he resented being dragged out of his nice, warm hospital bed, getting his regular morphine fix. Maybe he was just one of those guys who wouldn't wise up and listen, but as we went through the booking process, one key point stood out. The Punk just would not shut up. Not in the usual sense. That happened sometimes, people with an urge to confess that you couldn't shut off no matter how little you cared to hear it.

This guy wasn't confessing, which was fine by me, but he wouldn't quit talking either. Or more accurately, muttering. It was more like a cross between grumbling and mumbling, just loud enough to be audible, but not distinct enough to be understood as words with meaning. If you paid close attention, which I mostly wasn't, being occupied with getting all the forms right in the booking process, you could catch a word here and there, generally of the four-letter variety. The tone of the remarks, however, came through clear as a bell. You could tell he was being a smart-ass, no doubt about it, but being one quietly. A sotto voce smart-ass. Naturally, my first reaction on hearing this was to ask to have him speak up and repeat himself, only louder and clearer. This he did not do. He just kept up this low-volume running commentary, the vaguely malevolent, slightly caustic drone, a sarcastic-sounding smart-ass patter.

The receiving desk sergeant at the next desk thought the Punk was talking to me at first, then saw I was busy with some paper as the mocking mutterings continued. The sergeant's eyebrows shot up and he stopped writing in his log book.

"What did you just say?" the sergeant asked.

The Punk answered, but in the same tone, at the same volume, and with the same derisive emphasis flip at the end. Neither one of us understood a word he'd said, but the meaning came through strong enough. The sergeant's eyebrows climbed another inch higher. He leaned over and took in the prison outfit, that hospital gown and a pair of skivvy shorts. He snorted and leaned back. The Punk grumbled some more.

I could see this might turn into a problem. Penal facilities aren't renowned as the safest, most welcoming and inclusive places in society, and definitely not for smart-asses. People who pick up that label make all kinds of enemies, make them at the speed of sound, basically, and enemies are just one more thing you don't need in jail or prison. Plus, this is a white dude, and he's dropping into a penal system in Honolulu where white folks are a) a distinct minority, b) resented heavily by certain occupants of that system, and c) generally much, much smaller and less physically imposing than some of those resentful system occupants. I rated the potential for one-sided mayhem in that situation somewhere between Considerable and Inevitable.

When I got done with the paperwork, the receiving desk officers moved him to a cell, but I stopped at the bars before leaving.

"Buddy, I gotta tell you, you need to lose that attitude or you're gonna have a hard time in here," I said, trying to sound reasonable.

He just muttered some more, and this time, I distinctly caught the F-bomb in amongst the otherwise unintelligible grumblings. I shrugged and went home, figuring I'd see him in court on Monday, but we'd be meeting each other again much sooner than that.

Four hours later, I was back at the hospital, where the Punk was looking up at me very smugly up from a different hospital bed. He was quiet for the moment, smirking silently over his most recent triumph, but the doctor on duty had a lot to say. About an hour after he'd been checked through the emergency room and handcuffed to the bed for observation, the nursing station got a call from "the doctor" requesting that they administer a hefty dose of morphine to the patient, repeating "PRN," which is hospital and pharmacy code for "as needed." They followed the "doctor's" orders to the letter.

Of course, the real physician was shocked and surprised to see his name on the morphine order in the chart and annoyed enough about the whole thing that he marched into his patient's room and jerked the telephone right out of the wall.

The hospital wanted to get rid of him but the police wouldn't take him back as long as he was complaining of chest pains. The Punk knew this and spoke loud and clear about those. No muttering or sarcasm there. HPD, which had been guarding him, wanted nothing further to do with their charge, especially now that he was committing new felonies while in their official custody. Technically, he was a state arrest and the PD held him as a courtesy for us until his initial court appearance, which would be Monday. With no more police presence, we had to put an agent on his door round the clock for the rest of the weekend, which didn't help the overtime budget for the month.

This second escapade blew any chance he'd ever had for getting a low bail set on Monday morning, and I made sure he knew it, knocking a little of the smug off his face.

I spent Sunday going through the paperwork and piling on the counts, and we asked for the max on the bail schedule. He grumbled furiously as I hooked him up to transport him to court and was still muttering when two adult corrections officers shackled him for the ride to the old Oahu Prison, then serving as the pretrial holding facility. They couldn't make out what he was saying, but like me, they heard a few F-bombs detonating quietly amidst the mutterings. From the looks they shot back and forth between each other and the non-gentle treatment employed getting him into restraints and the transport van, I deduced that they'd gotten the general gist of the commentary, and the full measure of the speaker.

I tried again, telling the Smart-Ass Punk right in front of the prison guards that he needed to cut that shit out right now. He didn't acknowledge me, but one of the ACOs told me not to worry, they'd take care of him. This didn't exactly fill me with comfort, but hey, it was no longer my problem and never really had been.

That finally should have been it for the Smart-Ass Punk, a Guy Who Should Have Shut Up and Listened if ever there was one. But I got a call a few days later from his lawyer, who wanted to know if we could recommend a lower bail for his client. Why should we do that, I asked, when we liked him fine right where he was?

Because he wasn't where we thought he was anymore, the lawyer said. He was back in the hospital again. And if it would help, he'd agreed to talk to us.

Hmmm. I said I'd go over and see what the Smart-Ass had to say, and drove back to the hospital where he was in one of the rooms the prison used, an ACO on the door, and cuffed by the ankle to the bed. No phone in sight.

He didn't look like much of a smart-ass now. He had plaster casts on both arms and both hands heavily bandaged. His nose was broken and his eyes were black, both lips smashed, and small silver wires stuck out at all angles of his mouth. He didn't sound much like a smart-ass either, as funnily enough, his diction had improved remarkably. No more mumbling as he told his story.

He'd pulled the smart-ass play for about two days before the act wore out its welcome. A couple of the larger (hulking) inmates caught him and pounded him to a pulp, breaking his jaw and quite a few other bones. Back to the hospital, where the doctors wired the jaw and fixed what other injuries they could (arms and fingers, yes; broken ribs and missing teeth, no), then sent him back to the prison, where he went to the medical unit.

His enemies, of which he now had many, were waiting. They repeated the pounding, broke off his plaster casts, and left them and him on the floor. But first, they got the surgical version of a pair of needle-nosed pliers and pulled out all the wires from the broken jaw. He said the ACOs were in on it, ignoring the impromptu dental surgery and facial rearrangement (with accompanying screams) going on behind the closed medical unit door. "They were supposed to be there but they all disappeared," he said bitterly.

"Well, no wonder," I told him. "The smart-ass act pissed them off too. Congratulations. You managed to irritate everybody you've met since you checked yourself into the hospital the first time. I'd be more supportive if I hadn't told you *twice* already this was going to happen."

Honestly, though, I *was* pretty sympathetic. It's hard not to be, looking at somebody with what looks like a pincushion stuffed into his mouth and visualizing how it got there. Makes me cringe today just writing it. I told his lawyer we'd recommend a lower bail amount since he obviously wasn't safe in jail, and a judge released him on his own recognizance a few days later. The prison people were happy to see him go; I think they visualized the lawsuits coming. He could be charming enough; he'd proved it by getting all that morphine in the first place. And anybody looking at his lawyer's photographs with all those wires would have a hard time saying he didn't have damages.

I sat down with him while he was out-processing and explained how things could go. This time, he actually listened to me, or seemed to. I said he was going to prison for a year or two on the fraudulent prescription charges. He had a prior drug conviction and we had about thirty counts on him, so the prison train was boarding and the boys in General Population were waiting. I said that would give him lots of time and opportunity to work in the law library, helping with the civil suit against the inmate attackers and their ACO enablers. He might even win. But bad stuff had been known to happen at Oahu Prison over twenty-four months. Stuff like getting all your wires pulled out and your jaw re-broken for you. That might even get to be a regular thing since the people you were suing all had lots of (hulking) friends, and undoubtedly many, many more than you did.

On the other hand, I might be able to talk the prosecuting attorney into filing a single count on one fraudulent prescription. Take the thirty or ninety days, suspend the rest, get his probation transferred to California or Nevada, someplace where they appreciated smart-ass punks with innovative prescription schemes. That implicitly meant giving up the lawsuit, however well-founded the claims might be. A win for the state, but one for the Punk too, who got to survive to enjoy his winnings.

In his smartest move yet, the smart-ass chose Option B, getting the case kicked down to one manageable count. He got thirty days on that, with credit for the (very hard) time he'd already served, telling the judge with hardly any snark that he was sorry for scamming the hospital and wouldn't do it again (in Hawaii). As a goodwill gesture, he suspended his lawsuit against the prison, subject to reopening if more bad stuff came down, which gave the ACOs a powerful incentive to protect him. A month later, he left Hawaii behind forever, his lawyer begging to work with me on more of "these great deals."

"I can't wait," I told him.

He'd worked a terrific scheme. Original, daring, requiring nerve and enough intelligence to fool, not just the usual idiots on the street, but trained professionals on their home turf. And it hadn't been just a quick in and out. He'd run the con for almost a week. Even some of the nurses admired him in a grudging way and used his scam to plug some of the holes he'd shown them in their system.

Never saw or heard from him again. I like to think he's refined his technique, got the bugs worked out, and is right now lazing in a bed on a nursing floor somewhere, enjoying the warm flow of the morphine buzz as it kicks in every morning and afternoon, and evening if his "doctor" feels like a nightcap. He won't hang around as long, bilking for three days or four, lightening the touch before going out to the supply cupboard, suiting up, and walking out the front door into the sunshine, nodding to witnesses anonymously from behind the mask. There are a lot of hospitals in America, and somewhere, somebody will probably fall for that.

Like I said, I thought I did pretty well in my undercover role as a doctor. But really, the Punk put me all to shame. I only had to pull it off for a minute. He'd played the same role, convinced a bunch of alert experts, and kept it up for six whole days.

A FAILURE TO TAKE OFF

Things don't always go from bad to worse, of course. Sometimes people get lucky and the ball rebounds in their direction. The luckiest bounce I ever saw happened at the Clarence E. Page Municipal Airport in Canadian County, Oklahoma, early one Sunday morning. I got called by the Canadian County Sheriff's Office to assist with the identification of some drugs they'd found in a motor vehicle accident at the airport. I pulled up to see some deputies standing at the side of an airplane hangar.

There's a perfectly rectangular hole in the wall, precisely, as it turns out, the size of a Chevrolet Impala. The hole looked like it had been laser cut. No car in sight, so I'm assuming it's inside someplace. Yep, go in the hangar, and there's a couple of airplanes and a very short Chevy with a Maryland license plate, halfway out through the wall on the far side. The corrugated metal sides of the hangar might have been thin and flimsy but he'd gone under a big steel support beam that took everything above the dashboard off just as neatly as you could do with a blade. Ooh, that's not good. I figured I'm going to find almost exactly half a driver in the car, but it's empty except for a thick layer of shattered safety glass, some books about motivational selling, and some white pills that the deputies wanted me to identify.

Easy, meth tabs, very popular with long-haul truckers and others wanting to drive for extended periods of time. (See *Vanishing Point*, 1971; great film.) But where's the driver? Oh, he's sleeping in one of the sheriffs' cars. Not a scratch on him, the deputies say. What the hell?

Apparently, he'd been driving west with MethAssist for a couple of days, heading for greener pastures out west. The north end of the airport runway was about one hundred yards across an open field from the eastbound interstate lanes. As best the deputies could tell, he'd fallen asleep, drifted off his lane, across the median, across two lanes of oncoming traffic, down a ditch, up through a barbed wire fence, across the field, and onto the runway. A witness in the tower said he'd driven at highway speed (seventy miles an hour) to the end of the runway, out into the field (failed to take off), turned around, driven back even faster to the other end of the runway, turned off onto a taxiway and then the apron, through a dozen parked planes, and straight through the side of the hangar. He must have finally lost consciousness at exactly the moment before he hit the wall, and since he was not wearing his seat or shoulder belt, he slumped sideways on the front seat about a tenth of a second before the steel beam sheared off the top of his car. Then he missed both of the planes in the hangar, going under one of them, which wouldn't have been possible if he'd still had an undamaged Impala, and hit the far wall, finally stopping. He hadn't put so much as a nick on a single airplane, and there were millions of dollars in planes out there. One of them in the hangar was an executive jet.

I'm shaking my head in amazement as they tell the story, and then the deputies wanted to know, did I want to bust him for possession? Nah, but I did want to say hi to the luckiest man in Oklahoma. Went over and woke him up, asking him if he knew where he was. He says he's a "little lost but coming up to Memphis." He's got a job waiting in New Orleans and can I give him some directions. The deputies and I are laughing. I told him, "Yeah, make a U-turn and go back that way for two states and the Mississippi River, then turn right."

How did he manage to make it all the way from Memphis to Canadian County without killing himself or ten other people? He'd driven 487 miles past the New Orleans exit, clearly asleep most of the way. To this day, I have no idea, but this, kids, is why you don't use drugs and drive. On account of a guy from Maryland used up all the luck and there's none left for anybody else.

CHAPTER 14

LAST NIGHT I HAD THE STRANGEST DREAM

OKLAHOMA STATE PENITENTIARY
MCALESTER, OKLAHOMA
APRIL 23, 1978
34 DAYS BEFORE BLACK FRIDAY

I'd passed through the forbidding white walls of McAlester's Oklahoma State Penitentiary a few times, doing inmate interviews, following up on information in my cases. In 1978, OSP was seventy years old and showed its age. Built in another era when times were hard on the outside of the thirty-foot walls and time inside was still brutally harsh. One of the worst prison riots in American history wracked the place in 1973, killing three and injuring twenty-one. Rioters burned twelve buildings and caused more than thirty million dollars in damages. In the three years preceding the riot, the prison recorded nineteen homicides, forty stabbings, and forty-four serious assaults. Five years later, a federal judge in Oklahoma City found the prison conditions unconstitutional and took control away from the state's Department of Corrections. On April 23, two inmates cast their own votes on conditions at Big Mac.

Claude Eugene Dennis and Michael Lancaster were bad boys, locked up at Mac for manslaughter and armed robbery, career criminals who would not shy from more killing. Both had broken jail before, fleeing previous sentences. Prison officials originally thought the pair climbed the wall, the same route taken by three other escapees in January, but soon discovered a hole chopped through a concrete barrier in a utility tunnel. The tunnel got them under the wall and left only a chain-link and razor-wire fence between them and freedom.

After scaling the fence, they ran to the home of a McAlester guard, breaking in and taking his wife and ten-year-old daughter hostage at knifepoint. Although Lillian Key fought herself free and went for help, Dennis and Lancaster didn't leave empty-handed, driving off in the family car with a shotgun, a high-powered rifle, and a .357-magnum revolver. Now armed and as dangerous as they come, the two inmates vanished into the southeast Oklahoma countryside. There would be no sign of either of them for seventeen days, but you didn't need to be a fortune teller to know what was going to happen next. Or that there would be blood; that was certain. No one, even a psychic in her worst dreams, would have guessed the body count would reach eleven before the sun went down on Black Friday.

***

Her name was Lin Chan. She had a great reputation around Honolulu for her unusual talents, though not everybody, including me, believed in them. Those who did believe said she had psychic abilities, and she said I had them too. I didn't buy that either, but I have to admit, she did say a couple of other things that made me think, hmmm.

Lin kept a small office, something like you'd see in a solo dental practice, with a waiting room out front and a couple of consultation rooms in the back. People packed the waiting room every day she worked, and a line out the door usually, each of them with burning twenty dollars, questions, and their belief in the psychic world as they waited for their turn with Lin.

I knew of her because Connie, our receptionist at State Narcotics, saw Lin regularly, and believed with great fervor. Like many others in town, Connie didn't do anything big in her life without checking with Lin first. Such as buying a car. She went to see Lin, who told her that she was thinking about buying a new car (apparently true), and that she'd be getting a white Toyota.

"And it was exactly like she said," Connie told me solemnly. "I *was* thinking about it and I did get a new car. Only it was a Honda. And it was gray."

I think I stared at her a little. "Well, they are both made in Japan..." I said finally. "Eerie..."

"Yes," she said earnestly. "And how did she know I was going to buy a car?" Hmmm.

Based on stories like that, I was more than a little skeptical about Lin and her psychic abilities, but two things happened to make me take her more seriously. One of them involved an undercover agent. The other involved my wife.

While a lot of people like Connie really did want Lin's predictions, sought them out to plan their futures, others saw her strictly for the entertainment value. For twenty bucks, you could spend ten or fifteen minutes listening to Lin tell you about yourself and your future, marvel at how much (or little) she got right, and try to figure out how she did it. My wife and her sister went to a session for exactly that reason.

"Have a good time," I told them as they headed out. "Just don't come home saying, 'Lin says we're getting a new Toyota,' because we're not. Or a Honda either." I'd told her Connie's story.

You didn't tell Lin anything other than your first name when you got there, so she started off with near-zero information, at least on her new clients. This was especially true of someone like my sister-in-law, who had just come to town from Oklahoma for a two-week visit. Lin could not possibly know anything about either one of these two ladies before they sat down, so how did she do? I got the full account from my wife when she got back.

Lin knew they were both married and correctly got my name and my brother-in-law's initials. She said that my sister-in-law had just come from the mainland and was pregnant, something she'd only found out a couple of weeks earlier. Lin said it would be a boy and didn't know the name, but did know his initials: G.H.G. Both of these predictions came true a few months later, so Lin didn't do too badly on the Oklahoma branch of the family.

On our side, my wife said, "She got your name right and she said you were in law enforcement, a detective. But she said somebody shot at you last week, so that part was wrong."

Lin also asked whether I had any psychic abilities. "I told her I didn't know, but she said she saw it and you did," my wife said. "And she said we've got one son but we're going to have two."

Hmmm again. Interesting, except that we weren't planning at that point for any more kids, so I thought that prediction was way off. As to my psychic gifts that she'd "seen," I didn't have a psychic bone in my body and I didn't believe Lin did either. I thought the whole act was basically a carnival fortune-telling stunt. I don't know how she did it, getting my job and our one son right and my sister-in-law's pregnancy, but I'd pegged her accuracy rate at fifty percent, about what you could get by guessing. Still, she got enough right that it did give me pause. Hmmm.

By an odd coincidence (one which I don't know if the storefront psychic or anyone else "saw" coming...), Lin's name popped up shortly thereafter on official business. We were working on a major cocaine and heroin trafficker and a long-time local organized crime figure, a career criminal with connections to the Japanese Yakuza crime groups and who went by the street name "Japan."

Our informant had known Japan for a long time, and although he was much younger, they were fairly close, personally and professionally. But the CI was facing a really long prison term for dope and decided he didn't like the guy *that* much, so he introduced an undercover agent who had a scheme to launder dirty money for Japan and maybe his Yakuza buddies. This was a hot prospect because at the time the Yakuza crime groups were investing heavily in Hawaii real estate, buying expensive houses, condos, even golf courses. Tapping into that cash flow could turn into a multi-million-dollar money laundering case. Japan and the undercover hit it off and they started talking about the laundering and a multi-kilo cocaine deal. Everything was looking good.

Then Japan threw in a wrinkle. Something had spooked him and he got suddenly leery of the undercover. He told the informant he wanted him to take the UC to a psychic, and if she said he's okay, Japan will go ahead and do the deal. The psychic was Lin.

This was a problem for us because if we go and Lin says he's a cop, for whatever reason, because of a "psychic vision" or a hunch or just because, then the deal's sunk, and maybe the CI's in big trouble. It could put the undercover at risk; Japan had some very violent friends. If she tells the informant the UC's a cop and we go to Japan and "Lin says no problem, everything's cool," he could still check directly with her and find out we're lying, which also burns the informant and the undercover. But what good excuse do we have for not going to visit Lin? I mean, we don't really believe in this stuff, do we? We don't, but Japan apparently does. Hmmm.

We finally just resolved it by hurrying the deal up so that there was no time to visit the psychic. The informant made an appointment with Lin, but then had the "out of town connections" with the money arrive sooner and the whole thing went down fast, Japan's greed taking over ahead of caution. I always wondered what Lin would have said if the informant and the UC had turned up in her office with twenty bucks each. And I wonder if she hadn't already cautioned Japan in a previous session because he'd been to see her; he told the CI she knew things about people she couldn't have known and her predictions about his future had come true. Maybe she'd spooked him in one of those readings, told him she saw a thirty-year prison sentence coming his way. Maybe she looked into his future and saw him dying in a federal prison hospital a long way from Hawaii. That's what fate actually did have in store for Japan, but I don't believe I've got a psychic bone in my body, and I didn't believe Lin did either. So I doubt Lin told Japan those things were waiting down the road.

But maybe she had. Could be that was why he suddenly got nervous about the undercover. She did know a lot of stuff about me that she had no plausible way of knowing. Not about me having psychic abilities. I'd never seen any sign of that. We did have that one son, so she hit that on the nose, and not long after, we decided we wanted more and had that second boy, just like she said we would. And I was a detective, sort of; she definitely got that right, which I'll admit put her pretty close to one hundred percent. But what about the other part, me getting shot at the week before that my wife said she'd obviously gotten wrong?

Well, the thing is, I *had* almost gotten shot almost exactly a week before, narrowly missed by a bullet fired in an accidental discharge by another agent while we were making an arrest. Nobody was hurt and we never publicized the incident. In fact, figuring there was no point getting her worried or upset about something that could've been much worse but wasn't, I hadn't said a word about it to my wife before she saw Lin. I never said anything about it afterward either, so she's hearing about it for the first time if she reads this. Which explains why she didn't know it had happened when Lin mentioned it.

So my wife didn't know about that near miss, but it left me with a nagging question. How in the hell did Lin know? Hmmm.

THE LIGHTNING-STRUCK TOWER

Even after Lin, I thought the whole psychic business was total baloney. She'd gotten almost everything right, couldn't argue with the facts, but it still seemed to me that there should be a logical explanation. Remember that she said I had some kind of special supernatural abilities? That was really the sole thing she said about me that turned out to be wrong. But my other extrasensory experience made me wonder if there wasn't something to it after all.

We'd made a couple of buys from Eddie, Callie's husband, and wrapped the case up with a search warrant at their house. Callie lived in Wahiawa, not far from the army's big base at Schofield Barracks and a couple other military installations, and she was home when we served the warrant, though Eddie, a service member, was off getting arrested separately by the military cops.

My job for the warrant was to interview anybody present while the other agents searched the place. Callie had been home alone, so we put her on the couch in the living room while I took her personal information. When that was done, I started looking for a rapport builder, one of the key elements in an interview or interrogation. You want the subject to relate and identify with you, to see you as a like-minded person. Someone they can "like" and trust. You build that rapport by finding out the subject's background and interests, then share points of contact or mutual interests. If the guy has a classic car, you show some interest and talk about a similar one you used to have. I used that one a few times, my '67 Camaro coming up for discussion and comparison. There's no pressure here, just gently nudging the witness toward the state where she doesn't look at you like an armed alien invader.

You wouldn't think I'd have much in common with Callie, but she had children and so did I, and she was from the Midwest, which is where my family is from, so we hashed that over while I fished for something a little stronger. That's when I spotted a stack of tarot cards on the coffee table.

"Are you into this tarot thing?" I asked, pointing at the pack.

"I do readings. I use the cards to help me See," she said, rather sullenly, but saying "see" like it was supposed to be capitalized. A word with import.

"I See," I said, but if she got it, she didn't let on.

I riffled through the cards, checking out the pictures, thinking the only other deck I'd ever seen was in a movie— the James Bond film, *Live and Let Die*—and that the tarot reader, Jane Seymour's Solitaire, was considerably hotter than Callie. But Looks probably aren't as important as Seeing in this field, if you know what I mean. In the movie, the master criminal, a big-time heroin dealer, had used the hot Seer to burn undercover agents. Maybe our drug dealer Japan had seen the movie and thought Lin could be useful the same way, although my wife said Lin hadn't used tarot cards or any other props to See whatever she Saw. I didn't think the cards were going to be much good to Callie at the moment, who, if the searchers at work in the house found anything illegal, would be Seeing the inside of the police cellblock and a courtroom before she did any more readings.

"I had a psychic tell my wife recently that I had psychic ability. Do you know Lin? A lot of people in town go to her," I said.

Callie perked up, looking impressed. "I do know her. I've been to see her too. She has the Gift." Saying "gift" like it was capitalized.

"Well, let's check it out." I held up the cards. "What do I do first, shuffle them?" But I didn't wait for instructions, shuffling the deck a couple of times, spreading them out, faces down. She showed me how to lay them out in the form of a triangle, with one card higher than the other two. Past, present, and future.

"Is this your reading or mine?" she asked. Good, maybe we were developing a little of that rapport I was supposed to be building.

"We'll make this about you. You need it more than I do. What's going to happen to Callie? You probably want to know about that, right?"

She didn't answer for a couple of moments, both of us listening to the other agents ransacking her place. "Okay," she said, sounding skeptical, like she didn't have much confidence in my ability to read her or get anything right. She clearly didn't think I could See beyond the end of my nose.

That was okay, since this whole thing was basically a joke, and she was definitely right about me knowing what significance the cards held. "I guess you'll have to tell me what the cards mean unless I can figure it out on my own somehow. Maybe it'll be obvious," I said and turned over the card at the top of the triangle, the point nearest to her.

Hmmm. "Justice." The robed Lady Justice, holding her sword in one hand and scales in the other, not blindfolded like you see on some of the statues, but familiar enough that this seemed like one card I didn't need a pro to explain.

"I think I got this one," I told Callie. "Seems pretty clear, really. Law, justice. Got the scales and the whole sword thing going. That's always punishment, right?"

She didn't say anything, just looked thoughtful. Maybe we were relating, coming around on the whole rapport goal. I flipped over the second card, the one for the present.

"The Tower." A stone medieval castle tower, getting hit with a vivid-looking lightning bolt, knocking the top off and sending two people, a man and a woman, plummeting off the building. The woman was even blonde, just like Callie. Hmmm. Well. That was kind of an eye-opener. I suppose Justice had just arrived at her home with at least the force and fury of a lightning bolt, and we'd definitely broken her place—and her life—apart. And unless I missed my guess, a man and a woman were going to go tumbling out of this tower too.

"I got this one too," I said. "Justice, which would be me, came and cracked open your castle. Now you and Eddie are taking a fall. Things aren't looking too good in CallieWorld. How am I doing so far?"

She didn't answer, her eyes flicking back and forth between the cards and my face. She seemed a little shook, doubtful about me or the cards. That fit in with my own skepticism but wasn't really good on the rapport-building front.

"That just leaves us with this one," I said, reaching for the third, future card.

"No. Don't. I don't want to see it," she said, saying "see" this time in a normal, and, I thought, sharp and slightly panicky way. Now her eyes were wide and fear-filled, and she stared at the card like it was a snake as I sat back away from the card table. Maybe she really believed in this tarot stuff and it wasn't all just a scam for the neighborhood rubes. Maybe she could See the other side of the card already. It didn't matter. I wasn't there to read her fortune or play tarot games. Rapport-building meant I was supposed to work with her, get her in a mood to cooperate with me and the investigation, not piss her off.

"Sure. No problem." I gathered up the cards and stacked them on the table. "Let's talk about your situation and what you can do about it…"

We had a nice chat and got a few things accomplished before everybody left to go back to the office, Callie coming along since we'd found some coke in her bedroom. Before we left, I sneaked a peek at that last card, the one she hadn't wanted to See. I'd made sure it was on top of the deck when I dropped it back on the coffee table. It was "Death," which, as far as I was concerned, just went to show that those first two cards were a coincidence, nothing more and this tarot stuff, and all of the other "psychic phenomena" was a complete crock.

However, we never took the case on either of them to court. We didn't have much on Callie, just the small amount of cocaine the searchers found in the house, and Eddie took responsibility for that.

And a week later, Eddie killed himself.

Hmmm.

I Got a Funny Feeling...

Despite my wife's experience with Lin and my own brief, ambiguous turn as a tarot fortune teller, I'm still not buying the whole ESP paranormal thing. Sure, clairvoyance could come in handy and I can't explain how Lin knew the stuff she did. Telepathy, reading people's minds, might be fun, although I think you'd learn a lot more about somebody than you really wanted to know. But if Lin really had precognition, could foretell the future, how come she didn't just take the gift to Las Vegas and spend twenty minutes at the roulette wheel? If you can See the next number ten times in a row, you walk away owning the place before Caesar's Palace can throw you out on your ear. Connie, a Honda-owning Lin fan, said her fortune teller went to Las Vegas a lot and never came home owning a casino. Chalk the tarot card thing up to coincidence. I've seen how the "bending spoons with your mind power" hoax got debunked and some other psychic scams too. It's pseudoscience, magic tricks, and as somebody conditioned to operate on actual evidence,

I think they're all fantasies. Except... I can't really explain Liberal, Kansas, either.

For a story this weird, you need some background. I'd never been to Liberal. In fact, I'd never even heard of the place until shortly before that very chilly December night. By the time I got there, I'd been working undercover for a couple of years, had plenty of practice, and had developed the skills I needed to survive in that harsh and very demanding environment. Undercover is a talent, and some agents had the gift. Others didn't. We had one agent at OBN who could go under anywhere, anytime, and with any subject, fitting in almost effortlessly. My later partner in Hawaii, likewise. She could buy dope from anybody, had absolute confidence, was always in control. I didn't possess the undercover Gift, had far fewer of their natural talents, and had to learn from agents like those two, and Jimmy, who did.

One critical ability was "reading people," a skill that did get to be almost intuitive, but is based on observation—listening and watching, picking up verbal and nonverbal cues. That occupied ninety percent of my time in an undercover encounter. "Listen to everything" became one of the Iron Laws, and that meant tuning into everyone present, to people coming and going, and sometimes, to a roomful of total strangers, most of who didn't know I existed. I got good at it, could monitor several conversations at once and still hit my cues in the one I was most interested in.

I *think* that's how it worked that night in Kansas. Liberal isn't a big town, maybe 15,000 back then. That's the most people in one place for about fifty miles in any direction, and I didn't know any of them. I was working with another agent in the Oklahoma Panhandle and our informant thought he could find some of the local connections at a cowboy bar across the state line in Liberal. I'd been up there in that part of the state off and on for a few months, but this was my first time in Kansas.

The CI was right. That saloon, about two miles north of the border, was the only thing happening for a hundred miles around, jammed full of people, country music blasting, every table full, dancers going, folks having a great time. We took up a spot at the bar while the CI went off into the crowd, trying to find somebody he knew. As I've mentioned, I ordinarily stayed away from bars, even for negotiations, preferring quieter settings with fewer people around. You never knew who you were going to run into, but that night I thought I'd be okay, since I didn't know a soul in Liberal, Kansas, and none of them knew me.

We ordered a couple of beers from a harried waitress and settled back to watch the crowd and wait on the CI, which is when the Alarm kicked in.

I've never talked about the Alarm before, mostly because it makes me sound like a complete nutter, even when I'm working on it in my own head. But I believed in it and had good reason. Earlier in my UC career, I'd been startled to notice a strange sensation, a kind of awareness that someone I knew was present. It was beyond a feeling, more like a sense, a flash of recognition, going off before I actually saw or even heard the person I recognized. I suppose it was technically an extra-sensory perception since none of the regular senses explain it. As a superpower, it's definitely from the third or fourth order, like being able to sneeze with your eyes open or counting backwards from a thousand in Klingon. Still, the Alarm came in handy.

The Alarm didn't tell me who this familiar person was, only that somebody known or acquainted was there. Strange, but real. I got the Alarm once on a UC deal in a remote farmhouse, hearing some people come into the other room, certain that I knew one of them before they spoke or entered the kitchen, where I was sitting with the drug dealer. It turned out to be an informant from another case, who knew better than to say anything when he saw me, but the experience made me more of a believer, especially when the same thing happened on several other occasions.

The Alarm didn't always go off for these close encounters of the personal kind. Lots of times, I'd walk into a room and somebody I knew or who knew me would come over and say hello before I was aware that they were there. But here's the thing. The Alarm was *never* wrong when it did go off. If I got the sensation, I'd start looking, and sure enough, I'd find somebody I knew. Sometimes it was a co-worker, sometimes a friend. Occasionally, I'd turn around, and the person would be walking in the door from outside a restaurant or an office. I chalked it up to the hyper-vigilance I deliberately cultivated to work undercover, trying to be extra-aware of everyone and everything around me. And when I eventually stopped working undercover, I lost the Alarm and haven't seen or felt it since. I've never found out if other people have the same experience; maybe it's something common, I don't know. But one thing was for sure, the Alarm was sounding loudly that night, where I didn't know a single soul in that cowboy bar, in Liberal, or in the whole state of Kansas.

I started checking out the crowd, looking for any accustomed faces, watching for anyone interested in us, getting a stronger sense that something was seriously wrong.

"We're going," I told my partner. "Where's the CI? Let's get him and get out of here."

"We just got here," she said.

"Get your coat on," I said.

At this moment, the informant wandered back out of the crowd.

"Here's your coat. We're leaving," I told him.

"Oh, you saw him, huh?" he yelled over the crowd and the music.

"What? Saw who?"

"Some rounder named Jake from Guymon," he shouted in my ear. "I don't know him, but I know the people he's with."

"No, I don't know anybody from Guymon except you and the sheriff," I yelled back, shrugging into my parka. "Why?"

"Well, he knows you. He said you're the state narc that busted him for selling. He said he was going out to the truck for his shotgun. I dunno. Maybe he's from Buffalo."

The Alarm switched off as I abruptly remembered two very important facts. First, I *had* recently met a Buffalo Jake, paying in gold for some methamphetamine, busting him down in Harper County, a full eighty-five road miles away. We had a date in court in a month or two. Second, we were having this suddenly unpleasant little chat in a bar in Liberal, *Kansas*, at least two miles outside the jurisdiction of the *Oklahoma* Bureau of Narcotics. This would make shooting Buffalo Jake a problem, even if he and his shotgun didn't get me first.

"Is there a back door to this place?" I asked the informant, looking for a way out.

There was, and we left the bar and Liberal before Jake could shoot us or burn us with everybody else in the place. I crossed Kansas off my destination list for a while and made another note to myself to avoid bars. I'd been burned in them before, and this was a vivid reminder of how quickly a burn job could happen and how fatal the potential consequences could be.

And I made another mental note: listen for the Alarm, and pay attention when it goes off, even if you've got no earthly explanation for how it works or why you're hearing it. Maybe I did have a psychic bone in my body after all.

Chapter 15

Patterns

Rogers Superette
Denison, Texas
May 10, 1978
14 Days Before Black Friday

They were Oklahoma boys, born and raised, and that's where the manhunters started looking for Claude Dennis and Michael Lancaster, in the state's southern counties along the Red River. OHP had roadblocks up and extra troopers out searching; I'm sure Lewis wasn't getting much sleep again. He worked the roads of Bryan and Choctaw Counties, both hard by the Red River and Texas, which is where most people figured they'd be headed. We had the escapees' pictures up in the office but nobody thought they'd be coming to Oklahoma City, and Dennis had kin in Bryan County. They had a car, guns, and a partiality for crime and killing, so everyone guessed they'd turn up soon enough.

Oklahoma had a history of that sort of thing. The two escaped Wagoner County inmates who killed Undersheriff Kenny Miller and his friend in Beaver only a few months earlier served as one recent example. Three other McAlester convicts busted out of Mac on January 7, climbing over the wall at night and disappearing into the darkness. That breakout set off an orgy of kidnapping and car theft that terrified people from New Mexico to Illinois. Based on past experiences like that one the latest escape already had people on edge. The January escapees hadn't killed anyone before they were recaptured, but we wouldn't be so lucky with Claude Dennis and Michael Lancaster.

In another Clint Eastwood film, *The Outlaw Josie Wales*, one of the pursuers says, "Not a hard man to track. Leaves dead men wherever he goes." On May 2, Dennis and Lancaster started leaving tracks. 160 miles south of McAlester, the convicts robbed a gas station attendant, thirty-one-year-old Mithal Mathew, taking one hundred dollars before shooting him to death. Witnesses positively identified Lancaster as the shooter, but the "thrill killers," as the papers started calling them, weren't done in Texas yet.

When twenty-six-year-old Garland minister David Bobo failed to return from a fishing trip, Texas authorities went looking for him, finding his body on May 16. He'd been shot to death a couple of weeks earlier, so the trail had gotten a little colder and another man, John Dowdy, 57, had been missing from Hemphill, Texas, since May 5. His body was found several weeks later in a garbage dump, shot in the head with a shotgun.

On the evening of May 10, sheriff's deputies in Denison, Texas, ninety-five miles from McAlester, responded to a call about gunshots and screams at the Rogers Superette. Bobby Lee Spencer, twenty-nine, who operated the store and bait shop with his wife, had been shot multiple times. The killers were gone and so was Spencer's wife.

Police found her the next day after she fled from her captors at their Lake Texoma campsite. She said she'd been chained to a tree, tortured, and raped, but managed to free herself and ran blindly through the woods toward the sound of traffic. By the time an army of troopers descended on the campsite, Lancaster and Dennis were gone, and they evaded the roadblocks thrown up on every road in the area on both sides of the state line. Her panicked flight had saved her life, but she never fully recovered from her ordeal.

By now, the residents of Oklahoma and North Texas were scared to death they might be next. "The fear was so thick, you could cut it with a knife," one lawman said. These weren't your normal prison escapees who seek to get out and disappear. These two wanted to kill as many people as they could before getting caught and to take as many law officers as possible with them. They were going to get their wish on Black Friday.

***

Blame Hollywood. People always wonder how many people you've shot, how many gunfights you've been in, how many times cops have needed to use their guns or had one used against them. Blame Hollywood. Cops get shot at a lot on film and shoot people regularly in the movies or on TV, so people are always surprised to hear that most law enforcement officers in real life go their whole careers without firing a shot or hearing one fired at them. Some cops will tell you they never drew their gun except at the range. I'm not one of them. I drew mine all the time. And I was surprised to find at the end of thirty-five years, that shootings had happened often enough to me that I'd actually lost count. When I finally added it up, it came to seven. Maybe eight.

You'd think these would be life-changing events. A "deadly force" incident, or the much more euphemistic "officer-involved shooting" is by definition a close enough brush with somebody's death. Even if nobody's hurt, these incidents suck in huge amounts of energy and attention, nowadays requiring mounds of paperwork, weeks of reviews, and sometimes scrutiny by national and international news media, depending on the circumstances. Even the accidental or non-fatal use of firearms these days can be the cause for much analysis and evaluation, plus second guessing by everybody who wasn't there and has a conjecture or an opinion. Yeah. Almost half of mine weren't even reported and the first time anybody's hearing about them is right here.

So to the questions people ask or want to ask, and have asked over the years, and the honest answers for the first time.

One: "Have you ever been shot at?" Yes. Twice. Once on purpose and once by accident, but when you cut right down to it, the bullet doesn't know whether it's been fired by negligence or with malicious intent, and you're just as dead if it hits you in the right spot, so... And that's not counting Jimmy's blank.

Two: "Have you ever killed anybody?" No. But not for lack of trying. Only fired my weapon three times in thirty-five years. Didn't hit the man fatally, and I'm still thankful every time I think about him. I passed on two other guys who probably had it coming and barely missed on a third that would have been tragic.

So, as Hollywood would say, let's cut to some of those seven (or eight) shooting situations and see what really happened.

POT'S NOT SO MELLOW AFTER ALL

In the book on his adventures in the Boer War, *The Story of the Malakand Field Force*, Winston Churchill said, "Nothing in life is so exhilarating as to be shot at without result." Getting shot at is not a good feeling, and sorry, Mr. Churchill, I didn't find it especially exhilarating. Just scary. Three of us were doing marijuana eradication one morning, not too far off the beaten path. Civilization—people, cars, houses, and businesses—was no more than a half mile away, but nobody was obviously visible when somebody with a high-powered rifle took a shot at us. He was pretty far away because the sound of the report wasn't that loud. The round going past about a foot or so from your ear at three thousand feet per second: now *that* makes an impression. It's a miniature sonic boom that tells you, "Hey! You're still alive but not by much."

We all stared at each other, wondering if that was what we thought it was. Not an especially helpful reaction, considering that a serious shooter would be adjusting his aim right about then. But nobody really expects to get shot, so a little skepticism is normal. There's no time for any of Mr. Churchill's exhilaration or even relief, just an overwhelming desire to not be on the receiving end of the next little supersonic missile.

And in Hawaii, that's attempted murder of an LEO, which is a mandatory-life-without-parole offense. Possession of a couple marijuana plants is likely to be a misdemeanor or, at most, a Class C felony, five years, almost always suspended by the judge. Nobody's going to jail over a few stupid plants. Jeez, really?

We found somebody who probably took the shot, but he denied even owning a gun and didn't have one that we could find. There weren't any plants in the little clearing where he'd parked his car, and even if we'd found some in the vicinity, there'd be no way to connect those to the shooter. We left the area with nothing more than the sharp memory of that little piece of copper and lead zipping past a couple feet away from accomplishing its only purpose in life.

ACCIDENTAL DISCHARGE

Whether you call them "accidental discharges" or "negligent discharges," they're no good and no fun. I literally dodged these accidental bullets not once but twice, getting off much luckier than a friend and was reminded just how sudden and close a near miss with a gun can be.

The National Rifle Association is fond of saying "Guns don't kill people. People kill people." True, but chainsaws send tens of thousands to the hospital every year, and kill a few too, and I don't like them any more than guns. They're both power tools, designed for industrial purposes, and sorry, NRA, I always treated them both as if they'd kill me if they got the chance.

Consequently, they never got that chance. I've never held a running chainsaw in my life, and left guns aside as much as possible. I didn't collect guns, hunt, or target shoot. I've got no problem with people who want to do those things and enjoy them, so long as they don't endanger me with their hobbies. Still, being required to carry a weapon on and off duty for thirty-five years means hanging out with guns and other people with guns. Twice that bit me.

OBN issued us a handgun, a 12-gauge pump shotgun, and a 30.06 rifle, plenty of firepower to get the job done whether you're in the city or out in the country. I carried a stainless steel .357 revolver, but it was bulky and only had the traditional six shots, so, like most of the agents, my partner, Mark, and I bought backup guns. We went together to pick them up at the police supply place, ordering ahead and getting the discount. I picked a stainless steel .38 revolver, the famous snub nose, a little gun with only five shots that with any luck, I'd never need. It was a good undercover gun: easily hidden, safe, and, above all, reliable. Pull the trigger and it fires; otherwise, it just sits there, a chunk of stainless steel and rubber.

Mark was an automatic kind of guy, carrying OBN's big Model 59 Smith and Wesson. He had fifteen rounds of 9mm ammunition in the pistol, and really didn't need a backup, so for his undercover piece, he picked the Walther PPK in .380, James Bond's gun. It's little, it's flat, and hides easily, and while it can't make you look like James Bond, it doesn't make you look like a cop either if somebody sees it when you're pretending to be a drug dealer. We drove away from the gun store, pleased with the purchases.

Before we headed out down NW 23rd Street toward the office, I loaded my Smith and Wesson up and stuck it in its new holster on my ankle. Mark's gun posed a more difficult problem. He loaded the magazine, chambered a round, and then puzzled over the action. Neither of us had any experience with Walthers except what we saw in the Bond movies. Which counts as fantasy and was no help.

"So which one is the release?" he asked, examining the buttons on the pistol.

"The one on the bottom," I said, looking over from the driver's seat as he pressed the magazine release and the full magazine dropped into his lap.

"Same as the 59. That's good. Now does this have the other safety?" he asked, talking to me this time. He meant the one on his Model 59 that prevents the pistol from being fired unless the magazine is seated.

I could see the red dot on the left side of the pistol, Walther's little aide-mémoire that this power tool was plugged in and ready to go. "I don't know," I said. "But I can see your safety is showing re—"

Pow! The sound of a shot firing in a closed car is terrific. Even a .380, not a high-powered round, is literally deafening, especially when it goes off two feet from your head. Bits of metal and plastic pelted my face and arms, and something more substantial hit my right ankle. The smell of burnt powder filled the car, and I jerked it to the side of the road and parked haphazardly.

We stared at each other as the shock cleared, eyes wide, mouths open, nothing to add to the recent explosion. Then it was inventory time. Nobody was bleeding. I had a few pieces of plastic on my shirt and in my lap. Whatever had hit me on the ankle never even left a mark, so that was good. Nothing had gone in Mark's direction; he was holding the pistol, the slide locked back and definitely empty now, looking at it like it had just bitten him. Which it had.

I started checking out the state car we had just shot, already thinking that the bullet hole was going to be difficult to explain, especially if it had taken out one of the dials or drilled through the dashboard. Or worse, the windshield. Or worst, the windshield and the car in front of us. Except there was no bullet hole. I found the spent bullet on the carpet down by my foot, handing it to Mark. But how in the hell had it gotten there?

It took a minute, but we eventually found that, incredibly, it had gone directly through one of the air-conditioning vents, breaking off only one of the little vanes, barely visible damage from anywhere inside the car. Further on, it bored through the back of the vent, then hit the more substantial firewall between us and the engine, finally bouncing off my leg and onto the floor. You couldn't see any of this damage either, although it had taken out a substantial piece of plastic, the shards of which I was brushing off my clothes. Couldn't have aimed it any more perfectly or come out with a better result.

Why? Because the accidental/negligent discharge didn't have to be reported. No harm, no foul. What the boss didn't know wouldn't hurt him, and it seemed to both of us that there was no urgent need for all that paperwork, difficult questions, and embarrassing answers. I couldn't do much to permanently fix the hole in the back of the AC vent, but a few layers of duct tape sealed it off nicely and the AC worked fine. Better than before, maybe. I could get a replacement for the broken vent easily enough from the dealer but nobody ever noticed the missing vane and I forgot all about it. The agent who drove the car after me never mentioned it either, so the whole incident really was non-reportable under the "no harm, no foul" rule.

It was a totally understandable mistake. Mark assumed his new, little semi-auto pistol would function exactly as his old, big semi-auto pistol. I could make the exact same assumption about my new revolver and be one hundred percent correct. But Mr. Walther didn't put the extra safety into his PPK. When you pulled one of his triggers with the safety off, James Bond's gun performed exactly as advertised by the red dot. Having it go off unexpectedly inside a car, however, is way more exciting than most Bond films I've been to, but all in all, I'll stick with the movies.

Accidental discharges happen all the time to cops. Whether you hear about it or not depends on the presence of witnesses and their willingness or reluctance to say anything about the sudden and surprising explosion in their midst. And because these are people with guns and guns are everywhere, these things happen everywhere guns are. It was common knowledge at OBN that one of the agents had accidentally killed two television sets and a Princess Phone at his house, all on different occasions, which seemed to indicate he was accident-prone and not learning much from experience. Another agent I worked with shot himself in the leg and barely made it to the hospital before bleeding out, and a third from another state agency shot himself in the... very high upper back leg... at the pistol range, making it hard to sit down for a while.

I didn't personally witness what I considered the most frightening of accidental discharges (other than Mark's) but saw the aftereffects frequently. To get to the Oklahoma City Jail, you had to ride an elevator to the upper floors at police headquarters downtown. The elevator was an austere stainless-steel box, designed for the security of the prisoners going upstairs. Officers checked their weapons into gun lockers when they got off the elevator, so there were plenty of guns going up to the City Jail.

The first time I noticed the dent in the door, I pushed my finger into it, idly wondering how it had gotten there and what had made it. It was a deep gouge in the metal, but it hadn't penetrated, just gone in hard, then trailed off toward the ceiling. Probing the mark, it came to me: this was a bullet hole.

I knew right away what had happened. Someone, getting ready to check his weapon, got it out to unload it, then became just distracted enough to pull the trigger. Huh. That was a sobering thought. Imagine being stuck in a little six-foot-by-six-foot steel box when suddenly, you're sharing it with a lead projectile furiously rocketing off the walls at a thousand feet per second. Imagine the noise and the smell of the powder. Imagine your terrified partner or prisoner, sharing this bowel-moving moment with you. Imagine the paperwork when the bullet stopped flying in one of the occupants.

I rubbed the mark, thinking about where the bullet might have gone, letting my gaze drift up toward the ceiling. There I discovered that the first dent wasn't a one-off. In fact, the jail elevator was fairly pockmarked with places where bullets had left deep physical—and no doubt, emotional—impressions. I'm sure I got off on the jail floor with my mouth hanging open and a firm resolve to be extra careful clearing my weapon.

I'll guarn-damn-tee you one thing though. Not one of those big dents or gouges ever got reported by the one who made it. No accidental discharges in that elevator, no, sir. Whoever made them can still hear them though. I'd guarantee that too.

GETTING THE LATE NITE SPECIAL AT DENNY'S

Somebody asked me one time, "What's the dumbest thing you ever did as a cop?" Unfortunately, with thirty-five years of experience, most of it gained right after I urgently needed it, I had an abundant supply of possible answers. Still, I didn't have any trouble picking the single most stupid moment in all those years. It was the night I made an arrest in a double homicide.

I wasn't looking for trouble that evening, just a Coke and a little conversation. But sometimes, even when you're not looking for gun trouble, it finds you anyway. And that trouble always has a much easier time latching onto stupid people, which is exactly what I was late that summer night at Denny's.

At the boss's request, I was taking Freddie, a new agent, around to make some introductions. He was so new that he didn't even have a gun or badge issued yet, a situation that would be really important a few minutes after we pulled into Denny's off I-35 in southeast Oklahoma City.

Denny's was normally a great spot for introductions because cops hung out there in the evenings—Oklahoma City Vice and Narcotics officers, detectives from nearby Midwest City, Del City, and Moore, state troopers, and sometimes other people from OBN or OSBI. It was where the hunters paused from their night stalk to get a coffee or something to eat, and you could usually find somebody to talk to at Denny's, but not tonight. For whatever reason, we seemed to be the only law enforcement people in sight, though the restaurant was doing good business.

We had a booth by the big plate glass windows that overlooked the parking lot, although it's well-lit in Denny's and you can't see much outside where it's darker, just the shapes of cars and outlines of people. But I could see the bright flashes of gunfire, about five feet away from me on the other side of the glass, and heard the shots, POW! POW! POW! POW! Four of them, muffled only slightly by the window.

It got really quiet in the restaurant for a few seconds while everybody processed the new information on the Late-Night Special, then a lady came running in from outside, screaming. By that time, Freddie and I were already squeezing out of the booth as other people started yelling and pointing.

Looking back, I should have stopped there and got my gun out, I but didn't want to pull it until I got outside. That's because candidly, I looked like what we used to fondly call a "maggot," with long hair, a beard, jeans, and a crummy t-shirt. Running through a crowded Denny's after shots had been fired, waving a gun and looking like a scrawny reject from a biker gang was probably asking for that trouble I hadn't wanted, so I thought I'd wait. That plan went south when the lady at the door started yelling about people getting shot outside, so now, I went for the gun.

Unfortunately, like most undercovers, I hid mine, and that night it was in the new ankle holster I'd bought when Mark and I picked up those backup pieces, and it was a long, long way from where I needed it in my hand. I started grabbing for it, trying to unsnap the holster while lifting the pant leg, all while still trying to run, which resulted in a sort of jerky, skipping movement that Freddie unkindly described later as "the crow hop."

Really, I've seen crows hop, and while I'll admit there might have been a passing resemblance, it hardly bore mentioning. To everybody and anybody who would listen. Much less repeating about five hundred times over the next year or so.

Hopping, er, running up to the cash register, I asked the lady what she'd seen outside as I finally got the gun free. She said, "There's two people shot dead out there."

Freddie looked at me and said, "I don't have a gun. Have you got another one?"

I had a shotgun in the car, but there was no time for that. "Just call the police and get somebody down here," I told him.

"Well, give me yours, then," he said as I headed for the door.

I'm sure I looked back at him like he'd just sprouted another nose. Give him the only gun? That was pretty presumptuous, not to mention totally unrealistic, but there was only one response to that sort of lunacy. "Screw you, buddy," I said and took off through the door.

A little knot of people stood in a small circle on the sidewalk in front of some parked cars. Our empty booth in the restaurant was just on the other side of the low wall and the window. Everybody in the circle was looking down at something on the ground, and as I ran up, I could see it was two bodies: a man, laying partly on top of a woman, both facedown. They weren't moving and both were bleeding.

I pushed into the group and said, "Police. Did anybody see what happened?"

Nobody answered right away, and you probably see the problem already. With nobody talking, I tried again, although the bells should have been going off.

At this, a hillbilly-looking guy, dressed like a farmer in overalls, scraggly hair, and beard, spoke up. "I seen him. He run off over there, between those buildings."

He turned and pointed to end of the parking lot, toward two long, two-story structures back to back, with a passage or alleyway running between them. At least one of them was a motel, and aside from the occasional light from a partially curtained window, there was absolute darkness down that alley. Whoa.

I contemplated that grim scene for a few seconds, then checked back with the farmer to make sure that's really where he was pointing. Yep, straight down that silent black passageway. I remember thinking that that's right where I'd go if I'd just shot somebody outside a busy restaurant next to an interstate highway. It looked like the kind of black hole you could disappear into and come out on the other side of the universe.

I was suddenly not real anxious to go racing down into that spooky blackness, especially chasing after somebody with a gun who'd just killed two people in front of God and everybody in a Denny's parking lot. The, um, *sensible* course seemed to be to stall a little until some help finally got there with uniforms and dogs and lights and helicopters and lots more people. Which showed some of the stupid was beginning to wear off. But not enough.

After telling Freddie to check on the two victims, I started quizzing this 'billy on a description, going to make it as detailed as I could for the arriving OCPD. Oddly, the witness immediately got very vague, sounding like he hadn't really seen much at all. Those clamoring alarm bells were finally, faintly tinkling, starting to penetrate the dumb.

I was just going to call him on it when this other guy standing there spoke up and said, "That's not how it happened. She did it." and he pointed straight at me. I turn around and right there, no more than eighteen inches away, was this mousy little lady, probably forty years old, five feet nothing, and about ninety-five pounds, looking up at me.

We'll call her Gladys because she had short brown hair, parted down the middle, and worn just like Gladys Ormphby, comic Ruth Buzzi's drab and frumpy character from the old TV comedy, *Laugh In*. She even had a little brown purse like Gladys Ormphby, and I immediately noticed she had her right hand in that purse, but what struck me most was her expression, which said everything that needed saying. She had the look on her face you see on a golden retriever when you come home and the contents of the garbage can are all over the kitchen while he's been locked in alone while you were gone. It's obvious what happened, it's abundantly clear who did it, and although he's not even slightly sorry about all the mess, he's distressed that you're going to be mad at him about it. There's no mistaking it. It's the original hangdog guilty look. Gladys had it, big time.

I said, "Yeah? Is that right?"

She nodded and started pulling her hand out of the bag. I shoved her backward and got her off balance, getting her gun hand by the wrist, pulling it out of the purse. Sure enough, she's got a little silver pistol in her fist. I twisted it away and marched her over to the state car, where I kept two sets of handcuffs down on the parking brake pedal. Once she was safely hooked up and belted into the back seat and the car locked, I headed back over to the crime scene with the other set of cuffs.

The hillbilly had disappeared while I was busy—maybe down that dark alley—which was very fortunate for him since I intended to impart a forceful lesson about making false reports to LEOs. But he was apparently smarter than he looked, and definitely a lot smarter than I'd been, saving himself some handcuff time and a ride to the city jail.

It turned out the man on the ground was Gladys' husband and the woman was his mistress. She'd followed the lovebirds, confronting them as they parked for the motel and a snack at Denny's next door, then shot them both in the back as they tried to flee. That should have been what happened to me, standing there with her a foot away and me with my thumb up my... well, definitely not using my head. She still had a few bullets in her gun. That mousy little lady could have put two or three in me, no problem, and she could have easily gotten the home run and Freddie too, since he was kneeling there at her feet, unarmed.

What I *should* have done was to approach the scene as if an armed and dangerous assailant was standing right there over the victims, deciding whether or not she needed to shoot them some more to finish them off. Because that's exactly what she was doing. Instead, I made the daft assumption that the perpetrator had fled, listening credulously to some total stranger (who also might have been the shooter) confirm my false hypothesis. Pure dumb luck, that's what got me out of there unventilated; that and the fact that Gladys decided she'd already plugged all the people she'd come to shoot that night. Saved from sheer stupidity by an extra helping of luck that evening at Denny's.

Of course, it wasn't over when Freddie and I drove away from the restaurant. I spent the next several weeks at the office enduring the nickname "Crow Hop." That was thanks to Freddie, who, happily telling the whole story to anyone who hadn't heard it—and repeating it often to everyone who had heard it already—highlighted my unreasonable selfishness about not sharing my gun. He evidently held a grudge about it, I guess, because he called me Crow Hop for as long as I knew him.

But secretly and silently, I was awfully glad that was the worst price I had to pay for all that foolishness, and never complained.

GRIEF AND ANGER—THE ONLY WARNING SHOT

Warning shots are a bad idea, and almost every law enforcement agency forbids them. Virtually no good can come from that loosed round: where it will come down, what it will hit, what mischief it will do, no one can know for certain when the trigger is pulled. Nowadays, the paperwork for a warning shot would be monumental, and all of it would be ammunition for the inevitable administrative action to take your job. All things considered, warning shots are to be avoided like a trailer park in a tornado. Except, once in a very great while, maybe only once in a career, I suppose you just have to let one go.

That one time for me was the very wee hours of December 10, 1977, a little after 3 a.m., when all on America's Great Plains lay sleeping or would have been, if not for murder. OBN had sent two of us to work for a few days with the Texas County sheriff, trying to make some drug buys in far northwest Oklahoma. Texas County is the middle of three in Oklahoma's famous Panhandle, and it was a long, long way from my usual haunts in the city. Heck, Texas County is a long, long way from just about anywhere.

We hadn't had much luck; Guymon, the county seat, was quiet that Friday evening, and so was Beaver, seventy road miles east. Even Liberal, Kansas, the biggest town in the neighborhood, which isn't saying much, and had bars open late and people in them, hadn't panned out. By 1 a.m., we ditched the informant and were back in Guymon at the sheriff's office, planning out our move for the morning and thinking about the motel.

By geography, these counties are big and rangy, but there are few people in them and their police departments are small too. We'd worked the whole night with the sheriff, never saw a deputy, and I don't think any—if he even had more than one or two—were on duty. The same went double for Cimarron County (west) and Beaver County (east) which had even fewer people to protect and serve. I think Beaver County had a sheriff, an undersheriff, and maybe a jail deputy at the time. But shortly after 1 a.m., somebody cut into those numbers pretty drastically.

Back in Guymon, the sheriff took a call and got off the phone looking shook up. In a voice tight with anger, he said that Kenny Miller, the Beaver County undersheriff, had just been found murdered, shot in the back of the head by somebody who stole his gun and patrol car. Whoever killed Miller also gunned down a civilian with him. They had ridden out together to check on a report of a motorist possibly in trouble and trying to stop traffic. Now Miller and his friend were dead, the distressed motorist had vanished, and the Highway Patrol wanted every road leading out of Beaver County blocked. Two of those roads, US 64 and US 412 drove west into Texas County. The sheriff asked if we could back him up, as the only OHP trooper in town went north to set up on US 64. We took 412, to the south.

It was cold that night, arctic cold, with a cruel wind from a thousand miles away in Canada dropping the wind chill to well below zero. We cut through the icy darkness on a forsaken highway, headlights lancing out over the asphalt ahead, nothing but emptiness on either side. It was a bad night to die, and a lonely one, and Kenny Miller, who'd been doing the exact same thing only an hour earlier, now rode with us.

I edged our car to the side of the road, partly blocking the westbound lane and a shoulder that ended in a shallow ditch and a barbed-wire fence. The sheriff slewed his cruiser across the rest of the road, keeping the roof lights going for a minute, then turning everything off. I got the shotgun and checked it, standing outside in the frigid night, looking up at the stars in the moonless sky. The Milky Way wheeled, vast and silent overhead, a billion tiny sparks shining down, combining to share enough light that I could see the chamber of the shotgun, the safety on.

I stood outside for another minute of awed silence, amazed by the immensity of the blackness all around me. No city lights, headlights, or the yard lights of farms or distant ranches anywhere. The emptiness of the Great Plains stretched away under the great starry vault, vanishing into yawning darkness on all sides. Except for the parked cars, we could easily have gone back in time, traveled through history to the Old West. In those bygone days, the Panhandle, unfenced and wide open, had been part of Texas, which gave it up for some reason. Maybe it was too rough and remote even for the Lone Star State. Nobody else wanted it either, so the unclaimed land became a forsaken place, run before Oklahoma's statehood without law, wild and rugged, where the gun ruled and desperadoes—men on the scout, lived without fear of justice. Sixty years earlier, a gunman shot down my own great grandfather here on these plains, and he was far from the only murder victim in a Panhandle cemetery.

Enough of history. This night, it was beyond cold out there under the stars, the wind chill deadly, and me unprepared. I had a jacket but no other winter clothes, having planned, as usual, to do most of my undercover work indoors. Staying outside in this weather for more than a few minutes would be dangerous enough, even without trying to stop a cop killer. I took a box of road flares out of the trunk and walked a couple hundred yards east on 412, dropping the box on the side of the road, lighting one flare and setting it on the centerline, the spiteful hiss of the flame now the only sound.

No cop killers were coming our way. In fact, nobody seemed to be headed west on US 412 that morning. When the first car did appear, we could see it coming from miles away, spotting the pale thinning of the darkness, then the loom of the headlamps and a halo of soft, bright white light against the urgent center as the car pushed closer to the flare. This stretch of highway is notable as it is the straightest piece of road in the entire United States, 65.5 miles of unswerving blacktop not requiring so much as a twitch of the steering wheel through two Oklahoma counties. And it's flat, only a few low rippling hills and an occasional tree darkening an already black landscape, so we got plenty of warning when we needed to light up the cars and get ready to go out into the cold.

We agreed on a routine and settled into it, waiting until the oncoming vehicle got close—a few hundred yards away—and then lighting up the emergency signals, our cars blocking the road. While the sheriff spotlighted the drivers and talked to them from behind his own patrol car, one of us flanked out to one side of the road in the ditch with the shotgun and a flashlight as the other covered from the state car. When it came time to search the vehicle, we'd get the occupants out and stand them at the edge of the road, under the guns and shivering, while we took a quick look in the back seat and the trunk.

In the beginning, we got only the vaguest information from the OHP radio under the seat of the car, just a lookout for a "white male," and this didn't improve even after the Patrol dispatcher identified two possible suspects, escapees from the Wagoner County Jail east of Tulsa. Honestly, none of us was worried that we didn't have a clear description because we all figured the real killer would identify himself quick enough by opening up on us or trying to run the block. He'd already killed one cop. Oklahoma had the death penalty for that sort of thing and wasn't shy about using it. Whoever the murderer was, he had to know what he had coming to him, whether he got it in the electric chair down at McAlester or from a 12 gauge on a lonely road in Texas County.

Searching those cars was no fun, but the worst were the semis, with their sleeping compartments behind the cab. Easing up and sticking my head into one of those, wondering if I was going to be looking into the barrel of Kenneth Miller's stolen service revolver was a heart-hammering, breath-holding climb that took a couple months off my life, at least, each time. But it was always nice and warm in the cabs, so there was that.

Fortunately, the traffic was light, a car or truck every ten minutes or so. We never had two at a time in sight. The time dragged, and every stop got a little harder, the effort it took to climb out of the warmth of the car into the cold a little greater each time. I couldn't wear gloves to work the shotgun, didn't have any anyway, so I had to hold it and my frozen hands over the heating vents after each car departed. My partner and I had started alternating our turns in the ditch but I eventually just took them all, crunching sleepily to my spot in the brittle prairie grass, cradling the shotgun, keeping one hand in a pocket for as long as possible while the lights in the distance got nearer.

Headlights, a semi. He slowed down as our flashers went on, then ground to a stop, the air brakes whining, shutting down with a sharp hiss. The driver leaned out of the window and the sheriff told him to climb down so I could check his compartment.

The guy said no, he's not getting out. He'd already been checked twice.

Hmm. I'd been listening to the highway patrol radio in the car but that's the first we've heard that somebody is working on 412 closer to Beaver. *If it's true.* The sheriff argued back and forth with him for a few seconds, getting more insistent while I'm shivering in the ditch and the trucker bitched and moaned. Maybe the trucker missed it, but I could clearly hear the sheriff losing his patience.

Then... BOOM. Big flash, reached out toward the truck, right over the top of the cab. What the hell? Ears ringing, I dropped down to a knee to make a smaller target, aiming in on the guy in the window.

The sheriff yelled at the driver again to get out of the goddamn truck, but there's no need, he's already scrambling, hauling ass down to the pavement in shorts and a t-shirt and a pair of socks. I covered him with the shotgun, though he's clearly got no weapons, moving closer while still trying to keep an eye on the open driver's door, and telling him to stand next to the semi's drive wheels where it was a few degrees warmer (I'd learned that trick pretty quick).

Man, I did *not* want to stick my head into that sleeping compartment. I asked the driver a couple times, maybe three or four, increasingly emphatically, if he had a rider and he denied it every time. He said the cabin was empty, so I made up my mind to shoot anything that moved, breathing hard, my ears still ringing, trying to listen, trying to feel any movement over the rumble of the idling diesel. But nobody was waiting, and we let the guy get back into the cab and be on his way.

That was the only warning shot I ever heard in thirty-five years. There was absolutely no chance of that .357 round coming down on any inhabited area, nobody but the four of us, some cows, and maybe an antelope for ten miles around. But it scared the living hell out of me. My partner, who was covering from our car, was equally surprised because she had no idea what was going on, who was shooting, or if anybody had been hit. And numbed by the cold and lulled by the routine, it took me a second to work it all out too, that big boom coming out of nowhere behind me, the flash literally splitting the night.

Warning shots are a bad idea, and there are good reasons for prohibiting them. But this one sure got that trucker out of his comfort zone in a red-hot hurry. He knew the next one wasn't going to be a warning; it was coming right through the windshield and into his face. No apologies from here. We were looking for a couple of cop killers (who had also killed that civilian in the same incident and had done both "execution style," so those boys weren't shy about pulling a trigger).

On this night, that trucker drove his semi clear out of 1977 onto the High Plains of the Old West to the rough cut and untamed Oklahoma Panhandle of eighty years before. Out there, on the solitary, ruler-straight road that traverses the entire length of No Man's Land, he met three people all alone in the world except for a passing stranger and, somewhere unseen in the cold and the darkness, killers with the blood of two still warm on their hands. Out there, with only a billion tiny stars watching, there were no policies or procedures, review panels, or four-inch-thick operations manuals. Enough talk. Let's get to shootin'.

I got it, and you'll understand too. That sheriff knew Kenneth Miller personally, knew his wife and four daughters, had been to barbeques or church functions with them, shared time with the loving family of another Oklahoma lawman. None of us had to use much imagination to picture the scene in Beaver, seventy miles away, where that family, now shattered forever, was waking to a knock at the door, a pastor or a trooper on the doorstep, and their worst nightmare beginning.

And Undersheriff Miller wore the badge, was killed for wearing it, gunned down for doing his duty, for leaving his home and family to go out into a hellish, frigid night to offer help to someone he'd never met. His cold-blooded murder was an attack on law, order, and the rightness of things that no other peace officer could abide.

So, yes. Yes, warning shots are bad policy, but on that forsaken night, a grieving and angry Oklahoma lawman had had all he was going to take from some truck driver passing through his county. Boom.

We never reported the shooting, obviously. Never said a word, and I'm sure the sheriff forgot all about it five minutes after he reloaded his .357. No piles of paperwork or weeks of administrative leave, no waiting for some management types to decide whether that trigger pull had been "in policy" or not. Today, the thing would probably be on the trucker's YouTube channel by the time we got back to Guymon, the "warning shot heard 'round the world." Today, that "use of deadly force," or "officer-involved shooting" is just the beginning of a long process of second-guessing with an uncertain outcome at the far end. Back in the day, the "no harm, no foul" rule (closely related to the "what the boss doesn't know won't hurt him" regulation) might still have applied. I stretched it a little to invoke it myself at least once.

But grief and anger are powerful motivators and that warning shot prevented an escalation into something much worse. It doesn't get much worse than murdering police officers, or gas station attendants, preachers, or store managers either. Kidnapping and rape weren't far behind, and the line has to be drawn someplace.

Chapter 16

Save the Life of My Child

Cuba, Alabama
May 23, 1978
Three Days Before Black Friday

Maybe the heat was too high in Texas and Oklahoma. Maybe they were carrying a grudge and with time running out, couldn't let it be. Maybe they just wanted to go somewhere new. There were victims in Mississippi and Alabama too, so the evil pushed eastward in another stolen car, toward more crime and killing.

Before they left, Lancaster and Dennis kidnapped a young boy from Denison, letting him go before hitting a couple of places in southern Oklahoma again, stealing cars and failing to carry off a home invasion. Each new sighting drew an increasingly massive law enforcement response. The Oklahoma Highway Patrol alone had more than two hundred troopers on the hunt, which now included hundreds of local and county police, OSBI, the Texas Department of Public Safety, Texas Rangers, and the FBI. Police blocked roads and bridges for fifty miles around each incident, but Lancaster and Dennis got away clean.

They turned up with a bang in Butler, Alabama, on May 16, attacking a Butler police officer, Dean Roberts, with a shotgun. Though wounded, Roberts, who would be crippled for life, survived, as did Alabama State Trooper John Christenberry, whose patrol car was riddled with bullets before the two killers disappeared again. They stayed busy though, burglarizing houses, stealing guns, food, and the camping gear they'd need for living rough near the border between Mississippi and Alabama.

Stacie Virginia Beavers returned from a church social on the evening of May 22, finding hell had descended on her little home in Cuba, Alabama. Lancaster and Dennis beat the seventy-year-old retired school teacher, then cut her throat. Police found her the next day as the people in the rural areas on both sides of the Mississippi-Alabama line went into panic mode. Back in Oklahoma, OHP had information the killers planned to come back. Troopers from all over the state, many who had been sent home when it looked like Lancaster and Dennis had left for greener pastures, now flooded back into southeastern Oklahoma. They were concentrating on Bryan County, one west of Choctaw, where Dennis' ex-wife lived. Word was, Claude Dennis planned to pay her a visit. With a car full of guns.

*** *** ***

You often hear people say they want to go into law enforcement to help others, and police officers, especially those on patrol, do get that opportunity. Officers working traffic accidents and responding to calls for assistance frequently arrive at a scene before the ambulance and provide vital, even life-saving aid to people who badly need it. I'm sure Pat Grimes got plenty of opportunities, being a Highway Patrol Trooper and first responder. Maybe he'd gotten the chance, as some officers do, to deliver a baby or pull people out of a burning building; that sort of thing does happen, and it's one of the reasons society funds police departments. Saving lives happens, and it's a tremendously rewarding opportunity in a profession that has few enough rewards. I'd started my career saying the same thing, picturing myself riding to the rescue, but I only got two real chances in thirty-five years. By an odd coincidence, my opportunities both involved people lost in the high grass. One, of course, was Tommy Hatfield, somebody I'd been assigned to help. The second was a total accident.

There isn't a lot of high grass at FLETC, the Federal Law Enforcement Training Center, in Glynco, Georgia, where I was attending a two-week advanced training course. Dozens of federal agencies do their training at FLETC, and the place is always busy. While the criminal investigator and basic police training classes generally stay in housing in the center, the advanced trainees often stay in motels in the area. I was in a motel about five miles south of FLETC off I-95, driving a rental car to and from the center each day. FLETC had a rule prohibiting students from bringing their guns to the Center, which was about to become real important that day.

On this afternoon, I was headed back from class and took the Cloverleaf Exit off the interstate toward the motel. Coming through the curve, I saw a car—an older model Ford Escort—stopped on the dirt on the inside of the cloverleaf, a cloud of dust thrown up in the air around it as if the car had just spun, coming to rest with the nose of the car facing toward the off-ramp. Thinking there may have been an accident, I slowed down, seeing two people, a man and a woman, in the front seat.

As I went by, the man jumped out of the driver's seat and runs around the front of the Escort to the passenger door, where he unloads on the woman, punching her repeatedly through the open window. He's really connecting; she's trapped by the seat belt, and he's got a hold on her with one hand, nailing her with the other. Whoa. Wasn't expecting that.

I eased down the ramp about fifty yards, pulling off to the inside and stopping while I fumbled for my phone and started dialing 911. I was hoping to get the Glynn County Police to answer, or at least the Georgia Patrol, but wasn't sure who would pick up and was trying to remember the number of the exit we were on when I checked back on the Escort.

The man had quit pounding on his passenger and was climbing back into the driver's seat. From my position, stopped on the off-ramp, I couldn't see the license plate, just the passenger side of the car, but now it looked like they'd be moving, and I thought I'd see the tag when they drove down past me.

But as soon as he got all the way in, she jumped out, flinging the door open and tearing off through knee-high grass and weeds down the slope directly toward me. Even from as far off as I was sitting, I could see the terror through the blood on her face; this was somebody running for her life.

Behind her, the guy put the Escort in gear, floored it, jerked the car around, and accelerated right through the woman, just flat running her down. The bumper took her at the knees and she folded up backward, slamming down on the hood, legs up, both shoes flying off, bouncing off the windshield, then sliding down the far side of the car where I couldn't see her.

I'm thinking, *Holy shit!* and completely forgot the phone for a minute as he put the car into a skid, turning like he's going to take another run at her, throwing up a cloud of dust that drifted down through the weeds, wafting past my car. He looked exactly like a bull, taking a second shot at the matador he just missed.

What with the tall weeds, the dust, and the Escort in the way, I couldn't see anything of the woman anymore, but I knew for sure that she's completely helpless if he decides to run her over. And this looked like the guy's plan as he made his skidding U-turn in a cloud of dirt. Couldn't let that go, so I put my car in reverse, hoping to hit the Escort before he gets back to wherever it is she was lying. Or maybe I could put myself between him and her. He's going in forward and I was in reverse, but I'm on the pavement and he's still off in the grass, so I'm gaining. I guess he saw me coming because he changed the plan and swerved away, bouncing across the ramp and down onto the access road and onto the on-ramp to I-95 South, taking off at high speed toward Jacksonville.

By the time I get to the woman, she's pulling herself up out of the weeds, starting to hobble over to where I've stopped. She didn't look too good and she's limping hard, but she could still stand, which is a surprise, considering. Thinking we should get out of there in case the guy changed his mind and came back, I popped the passenger door and told her to get in, then headed for the county safety complex—police, fire, and paramedics—at the next exit north.

"He tried to kill me," she said, disbelief in her voice. No kidding.

"Who was that guy? Do you know him?"

"He's my husband. He tried to kill me." She gave me his name, address, and even the license number on the Escort, and said he was heading down to Camden County, the next one south.

I gave all that information to the county police while the ambulance people took her, promised I'd make a written report, and headed for Walgreens to get some hydrogen peroxide to get all the blood off the rental (helpful household hint).

I saw her again at the trial, called back to testify for the prosecution. Georgia charged her husband with kidnapping and attempted murder, and he got thirty years for it. Seeing somebody almost get killed right in front of you is shocking enough, but the biggest jolt came when the defense attorney got me on cross-examination. He didn't have any questions about the actual attempted murder I'd witnessed; I guess he didn't want the jurors dwelling on that. What he wanted to know, was very interested in hearing, was whether I'd seen the sawed-off shotgun the prosecution alleged he threatened her with to get her in the car in the first place.

There was a long pause in the quiet courtroom, the jurors turning to me to wait for the answer. Um, no... No... No, now you mention it, I hadn't seen any shotguns, sawed-off or otherwise. This is the first I've heard...

Apparently, I had brought an Avis to a gunfight in the high grass.

Chapter 17

7 o'clock News/Silent Night

Kenefic, Oklahoma
May 26, 1978
The Morning of Black Friday

Claude Eugene Dennis was finally going home. The thrill killer had terrorized people in five states, literally leaving a trail of death and destruction on his month-long rampage. He and Michael Lancaster had dodged a thousand roadblocks, outrun, outshot, and outwitted law enforcement officers from hundreds of agencies in tiny hamlets, small towns, and big cities, their run fueled by rage, hatred, and a burning, all-consuming desire to die free. Now, he was heading back to Caddo.

OHP knew that the Lancaster/Dennis tornado had circled back around to Oklahoma, heard that Dennis wanted a chance to see his ex-wife Katherine and their three children before the law caught up to him. He and Lancaster had been through Caddo, a little place with an Old West main street and fewer than a thousand residents before, only stopping long enough to steal a new car. This time, they wouldn't be leaving, and they knew it.

Everybody found out the killers had returned when they broke into Russell Washington's farmhouse, just south of the even tinier hamlet of Kenefic. Dennis confronted Washington and his hired man, G.D. Busby, who both knew what was up and were prepared to die, but Dennis asked if Washington remembered that he had let Dennis hunt on his property a few years before. Washington said he did remember.

"You're a hard-working ol' boy, and a family man, and I'm not gonna kill you," Dennis said. He tied the two men up and told Washington that he was taking his blue pickup truck, promising, "I won't hurt it, won't tear it up, but I'm not going back alive. And I'm taking every cop I can with me."

The extremely relieved Washington and Busby freed themselves and called police, who finally had a recent sighting in a narrow area, and OHP units converged on Kenefic from every direction, putting the description of the truck onto the air. Minutes later, just a few miles from Washington's farm, two troopers rolling down a gravel back road came onto a blue truck, blocking the way toward Caddo.

HONOLULU, HAWAII
1986
NINE YEARS LATER

Very few cases make the big time, get the media attention and notoriety that some criminals—and some cops—crave. Hitting the big time is a lot easier when you start out with a big name. The murder of Nicole Brown, O.J. Simpson's ex-wife, and her friend, Ron Goldman, would have been a page 15 story if she was Mrs. Joe Blow. Having a much bigger celebrity as the suspect made it the Case of the Century. I dealt with far more people who may be remembered only by their families and friends, but ran across a fair number of luminaries too over the years. I knew a couple of cops who liked going after celebrities. Big ones or little ones, they knew the notoriety and the scandal would get publicity, hitting the newspapers and maybe the TV and cable news. They're hoping a little corner of that spotlight will catch them as it paints their star target. Maybe they see a book deal in it or something, an "I Busted O.J." tell-all. I don't really understand the thinking because the last thing I wanted was any of that limelight washing over me.

I had my chances. Hawaii gets its share of stars and superstars; movie icons vacationing, TV actors filming shows on location in the islands, recording artists and others coming to paradise for a little sun, fun, and maybe some chemical entertainment just like back home in Hollywood or New York. The opportunity to play Celebrity in Jeopardy came up more often than you might think, because lots of people (not just celebrities) come to the islands for vacation thinking normal rules like the laws of physics, calories, and marriage vows don't apply; like Vegas, you can do whatever you want and get away with it because, hey, you're in Hawaii, and some of these people aren't thinking all that clearly to start off with.

I had a rule that covered this situation, Number 5 on my list: *Never spend more time on the case than the crook will spend in jail.*

Since almost nobody goes to jail for misdemeanors or marijuana, that let everybody off those offenses straight away. No juveniles go to jail for practically anything, certainly not narcotics, so they were all strictly off limits. And this led early on to an amendment to Rule 5, a corollary I called "The Luminary Law."

I didn't like this particular luminary. Not as a person, since I never met the guy, but as an actor. I didn't think he was funny, found his shtick annoying, hammy, and him way overrated as he consistently played the kind of people I wouldn't want to hang around with in real life or even for two hours at the movies. So when I got the chance to bust him… I passed. Rule 5—and its corollary, the Luminary Law—said if you wouldn't bust an ordinary person for something, you shouldn't go after a celebrity—even if he's an Academy Award winner—for the same thing.

The informant came in and told me that these Hollywood people were partying big out on Oahu's North Shore one winter, escaping Los Angeles' fierce January chills, I guess. Lots of booze, lots of coke, which they were buying from the locals. That's when the luminary's name came up.

"There's a couple of them are stars, one big Hollywood guy. He'd be a good bust," the informant said helpfully.

"Oh yeah? Like who? What's his name?" I asked.

"I don't know. He was in that thing with the two old guys." He described the film.

"The movie or the TV show?"

The CI shrugged. "I dunno. They all look alike."

I knew the film, undoubtedly, in my opinion, the Luminary's most annoying role.

I was a little surprised. "Isn't he kind of old for that shit?" I asked the CI, who just shrugged and said nobody was too old to get high. I'd heard the actor had a drinking problem at some point, which, unlike some in Hollywood, he didn't make a big deal about, just rehabbed and got on with his life, but maybe he'd fallen off the wagon or hitched it to another set of horses. I don't know and to borrow a line from another Hollywood alky, frankly, my dear, I didn't give a damn. Even if the informant's information were true, busting the actor and his coker pals would accomplish absolutely nothing of value to the taxpayer, have zero impact on the drug traffic, and waste everyone's valuable time. This was before we had drug courts, so even the polite pretense that we were "doing it for his own good" to get him into rehab (when what we really wanted was to watch a celebrity squirm in the scandal spotlight) smelled exactly like the bullshit it was.

I told the informant to go find a real dope dealer (not the ones providing small quantities to rich visiting Californians on the North Shore) and left the Oscar winner to drink or snort or whatever and go do another crappy movie.

A similar opportunity came up to nail a standup comedian and TV star whom I also never met but did like and thought was very funny. Like the actor, the comic was partying with friends in the islands and unlike the actor, the comedian's reputation for heavy cocaine use went far beyond rumor or a possibly unreliable informant's tip. Making a case on him for coke possession would hardly have posed some great challenge; he practically wallowed in the stuff. Unlike the actor's crew, the comedian's harder partying entourage was being supplied with more serious quantities of coke.

Pass. Again, what's the point? No Hawaiian judge was going to put this guy in prison for snorting some cocaine nor should they. All it would have accomplished would have been to get some cheap headlines and bad PR for a guy who probably didn't care that much anyway. After all, this was somebody who owed the IRS something like three million bucks and clearly wasn't eating himself up with remorse over that. We looked into the people supplying the coke but eventually decided it wasn't our concern, leaving it for the Honolulu cops.

Still, I wonder. Cocaine and heroin literally killed a lot of talent in the 70s and 80s and it probably contributed to the comic's too-soon death at age sixty-eight. Maybe if somebody had jerked him up and forced him into some court-mandated treatment program, made him go to the Betty Ford Clinic or someplace like it, he'd have been around making people laugh for another fifteen or twenty years. Maybe there should have been an exception to the Luminary Law called the Funny Man Follow-On. The point has merit, but not enough for me to break Rule 5.

I didn't make any exceptions for the actor on one of the popular TV crime shows that filmed in the islands for a few years. He wasn't the lead, in case you're wondering, but he is still acting, so I'm not giving him or his show up, but he fit the Rule 5/Luminary Law limits perfectly. Again, there was an informant, this time a sex worker, who said she'd been providing some pretty exotic sexual services and knew about the supplier of the cocaine that allowed the all-night parties and all-day filming to carry on uninterrupted. This was apparently a fairly normal lifestyle in the Los Angeles entertainment world at the time, and may still be, and she'd gotten used to it, and a couple of her sex worker friends too.

They sure liked the coke, the money, and the glitter of associating with the Hollywood types, but none of it was enough to convince me that we ought to go after her kinky client. The Luminary Law basically said that if we wouldn't bust the anonymous guy down the block for the same crime, we should pass on the celebrity. Based on what she told me, I figured AIDS or hepatitis or something else nasty would be catching up to him fairly soon anyway, so he probably didn't need any help from me getting to some new low point in his life. (He seems to be doing fine. Maybe all those cautions about the benefits of clean living were horse manure after all.)

And there were the home-grown celebrities, minor stars in the brighter galaxy, though of course they don't see themselves that way. A TV newsman, a radio personality, couple of local entertainers. Drugs reach into every corner of our modern society; we all know this and see it all the time. Busting them would have made a big splash in a smaller pond, the scandal lights burning just as brightly but invisible to people separated from Hawaii by 2,500 miles or more of ocean.

I passed on a popular singer who was getting pure pharmaceutical cocaine from a local dentist. He had the best coke connection in Honolulu, possibly the entire country, a sweet deal that came to a screeching halt when we cut the dentist off over something else. The singer was in real trouble, had a massive coke problem, and visualized himself as the subject of a highly publicized drug scandal that would ruin his reputation with the blue hairs and others who liked his lounge act. He did a lot of begging and pleading but needn't have bothered; as long as he wasn't turning around and selling the pharmaceutical coke, I wasn't going to try and make a case. And he wasn't selling it: all of that 99.4 percent pure coke went straight up his nose. He wasn't giving anything that good to anybody else for any amount of money. We left him alone, eternally grateful, always saying for years afterward that he owed me, anything we wanted, etc., etc. Nah. With the Luminary Law in play, he wasn't at any risk.

I did make a modest effort for a radio DJ who had quite a following in the islands. She wasn't on any of the stations I normally listened to but she had a distinctive, sexy voice and a bubbly personality that earned her plenty of fans. That included our informant, who said that she had a wicked coke habit and paid for it in part by selling some, mostly in quantities of a few grams, up to an ounce. I'd heard similar things about her before but we generally left cocaine cases to the police department or DEA unless we could show (as we did with the popular singer above) it was coming from a doctor or pharmacy. She was pretty small time and a sort of celebrity, so I'd given her the Luminary Law pass.

Although I figured we'd do the same this time, I had the informant make a couple of phone calls, chumming the water, mostly, to see if she'd rise to the bait. She did, but not enthusiastically enough to make me want to break Rule 5, so I passed the information along to HPD's Narcotics/Vice Division and moved on with other more pressing matters. A few years later, HPD caught her selling ounce quantities to an undercover. Under state law, this was a Class A felony, and it carried a mandatory twenty-year prison term when I had taken my earlier brief look at her. Since then, the state legislature had changed the law to allow probation for Class A drug crimes.

She pled guilty in the HPD case and got ten years of probation and a fine as a "first-time drug offender." Of course, she wasn't exactly a "first-time drug offender;" this was just the first time she'd been caught. And if I hadn't given her that Luminary Law break before the statute changed, she'd have spent some time in prison., but it still didn't make sense. She apparently used the experience to clean herself up and get out of her drug habit, so something good came of it.

Even before the law changed, the courts made Rule 5 hard to live by because a person had to sell a lot of dope to get anything more than probation or a suspended sentence in state court in Hawaii. Even the so-called "mandatory sentences" for Class A felonies could be a joke. I bought enough pills to make a Class A felony case down on the Big Island, took the case to court, and went for sentencing, expecting the mandatory prison term after the conviction. The judge said she'd thought about it, but she was going to suspend the sentence anyway.

The prosecutor didn't object, just avoided my sleeve tugging and increasing vocal protests in the courtroom. The judge was looking at me like, *Have you got something you want to say to me?* Yes, I did, but I'm not allowed to talk in these circumstances. That's the prosecutor's job, so outside, I got right in her face. "What the hell was that? The statute says it's an A felony. Mandatory twenty-year sentence. No suspension, no probation. She can't do that."

The prosecutor had the decency to look abashed, but clearly, no guts to go with the shame. "You're getting on the plane to go back to Honolulu. I've got to go back into her court tomorrow," she said.

"Yeah," I told her. "And trust me, I won't be getting back on the plane to help you with any drug cases anymore either."

Today, the Big Island of Hawaii has a massive, out-of-control methamphetamine problem to go with big unemployment and other social issues. I'd made that drug case down in the Puna District, which people call "Hawaii's Wild West." Not too far from where the Kilauea volcano is currently spewing lava and eating houses. A lot of marijuana was grown in Puna, probably more than the rest of the state put together, and the growers and other dealers in the district had guns and knew how to use them. Going undercover there meant working alone and a long way from any potential backup, down gravel roads with no markings, among people whose lifestyles included all kinds of drug use and sales, cockfighting, gambling, and hostility to police. Now, Puna has meth and the problem is ten times worse, but back then, I'd risked my life undercover and taken chances in the Wild West to make that A felony drug case and take it to state court in Hilo. That judge made me break Rule 5 whether I wanted to or not. After 1986, I couldn't see the percentage in working in that system anymore.

Before I left, a name from the past came up, as they often did. Ray Boyer first showed up on the scope in 1978, a small-time dealer of cocaine and marijuana and sometimes forged-prescription suspect. I wasn't working coke or pot cases at the time; we were concentrating on prescription drugs, and we wouldn't have paid much attention to Boyer because he wasn't dealing in pounds or kilos. He was working in a pizza parlor and selling baggies of weed and grams of coke. Not exactly Scarface. These were misdemeanor marijuana cases and very minor coke felonies. Not going to jail for those, so ordinarily, Boyer would have gotten a complete Rule 5 pass, and eventually, I gave him one.

But he popped back up again just after New Year's Day 1986, when his boyfriend rang in the new year with a claw hammer, beating Boyer to death with it. I saw the news articles and remembered the name, recalling the quick look I'd taken at Ray and his buddies back in 1978, guessing maybe he'd gotten killed over drugs. HPD's homicide investigation showed differently; it turned out to be a domestic dispute gone very bad.

The suspect wasn't one of the 1978 associates and HPD picked him up quickly, getting a confession, convicting him, and putting him in prison for twenty years on the murder charge. Case closed, and Ray Boyer was gone and forgotten again.

Why did I care about small-time Ray Boyer and his smaller-time associates if Rule 5 was in effect in 1978? Because of Punahou School. Punahou, founded in 1841, is the oldest English language school west of the Rocky Mountains. It's the biggest independent K-12 in America and one of the country's elite college preparatory schools. Punahou people see themselves as part of a family, at least bonded by the experience, and connected forever by their Punahou ties. Boyer was selling to Punahou kids, part of the family. My family.

It's a big clan; some people you know, most you don't. I didn't know anybody from the class of '79 —or '80, the kids that made up part of Boyer's circle—but I did have acquaintances in other classes. I still knew people on the faculty, including my mom, a Punahou librarian. Selling drugs to Punahou people might be cause for an exception to Rule 5.

By 1978, Punahou kids were no strangers to pot, or even, as Matt Maxwell proved, to harder drugs. Shoot, they weren't strangers in 1971; we'd just come out of the 60s and made it through the Summer of Love with Sergeant Pepper, Jimi Hendrix, orange sunshine LSD, pot, and The Doors. It's an expensive private school and the families who send their children there typically had plenty of money. Some, like me, made it through on a civil servant's paycheck and a Punahou scholarship, but many others came from wealth and privilege, and had all the cash they needed to get high.

I didn't have any illusions about drugs and the school and its alumni, remembering Matt's death certificate: my classmate, dead of a heroin overdose. Dope touches people in all corners of society. That didn't mean I wanted Ray Boyer touching this one.

So I made some "inquiries" and had the informant ask a few questions. The answers sounded awfully familiar from my own days at school. I got the names of the Punahou students, maybe eight of them, juniors and seniors mostly, seventeen or eighteen years old. They were heavily into smoking pot off-campus—in the same places my classmates had smoked it a few years before—probably doing some coke too. A couple of non-Punahou people rounded out the group; Boyer, the main supplier; and at least one kid from Roosevelt High School, just a few blocks down the street. This made sense. Traditionally, the Punahou kids had the money, and the Roosevelt students, especially those from the lower-income Papakolea neighborhood just behind the high school, had the connections to score marijuana and other drugs. Like me, a couple others in Boyer's group lived in the Manoa Valley-Punahou area and would have gone to Roosevelt as their public school if not for Punahou, so they probably knew the "less fortunate" kids from the neighborhood.

Boyer worked at Mama Mia Pizza, not far from the school, very close to the University of Hawaii, and a notorious drug spot. I spent time in and out of Mama Mia, working undercover because some prescription scammers in town sold their take at the pizza parlor. The place attracted other dope dealers too, small-timers, mostly, who hung out there selling to the college students. I didn't have an informant at Mama Mia's at the moment, or a direct line into Boyer, so I briefly considered busting somebody from the Punahou group to flip them on Ray and the pizza place. This wouldn't have been hard; the Punahou kids usually did their smoking in public places close to campus and weren't particularly subtle about it. Catching somebody—or all of them—in possession would have been a cinch and one of them would have flipped, for sure. But ultimately, I passed, and every Barry, Larry, Bobby, Tom, and their supplier, Ray Boyer, got the free pass. Rule 5.

Like many Punahou grads, they went on to bigger things. But it could have turned out differently and even a misdemeanor drug bust in 1979 might have changed American history. Because, after he graduated, one of Ray Boyer's regular customers decided he didn't like being called "Barry" anymore and started going by the name he used on his way to the top. I wonder if he would have made it as far as he did dragging a rap sheet from 1979?

Well, Barack Hussein Obama Jr. can thank Rule 5 that he doesn't have one and never had to find out. You're welcome, Barry.

Chapter 18

The Times, They Are a Changin'

Kenefic, Oklahoma
May 26, 1978
The Morning of Black Friday

Like every other lawman in southern Oklahoma and Northern Texas, OHP Troopers Houston "Pappy" Summers and Billy Young were hunting for Lancaster and Dennis. Just after 10:30 a.m., on a dusty gravel farm road outside of the small town of Kenefic, due west of Caddo, the two troopers found them.

Pappy Summers turned fifty that year, with twenty-five years on the Patrol. He hailed from Woodward in the northwest part of the state, and his partner and friend, Billy Young, was from nearby Enid, where both worked together for OHP's vehicle inspection division. Young, sixty-two, had thirty-two years on the job and was scheduled to retire in just a few days. Both got the call to go to Caddo the day before and Summers had been working a long way off, out west of Beaver in the Panhandle, near the roadblock we'd manned for Kenny Miller's murderers. Summers stopped in Enid to collect Young and they headed south, a six-hour drive for Summers.

On the morning of the 26th in Unit V-54, the two vehicle inspector troopers took an assignment to do a roving patrol on county roads and State Highways 22 and 48, a loop that brought them within four miles of Russell Washington's farmhouse. Rolling west on a gravel country road, they topped a low rise and came face to face with a blue pickup truck stopped in the roadway ahead. Unsure about the truck's occupants, Young got out and walked toward the pickup, about eighty feet away.

All hell broke loose.

Dennis and Lancaster opened up with rifles and shotguns, firing from behind the truck, vastly overmatching the two troopers, who only had their Smith and Wesson Model 66 .357-magnum revolvers, the same gun OBN had issued me. Young got off four shots and made it back to the cruiser without being hit, reloading as the fusillade continued. Summers, half in and half out of the passenger side, was blinded by glass from the exploding windshield and then hit in the side as he tried to radio for help. Young, looking around the car to check on his partner or to locate the shooters, took a rifle round to the forehead as the two killers kept firing.

When Lancaster and Dennis got no return fire, they climbed back into the truck and drove forward, finding Summers on the ground. One of the gunmen, probably Lancaster, walked up and, ignoring Summers' raised hand, shot him at close range with a 12-gauge shotgun. And with that, it was over.

***

Ray Boyer dying at the wrong end of a hammer should have been the last time I gave more than a passing thought to him and his customers of ten years earlier, but of course, history and the presidential election of 2008 fixed that. Barack Obama went on to electoral victory despite the published admissions in his autobiography that he'd used marijuana and cocaine in high school and college, statements that would have doomed any previous candidate for America's highest office. But times had changed in America, and drug use, especially in the younger generations (who had a vote and used it in 2008) had become mainstream and a non-issue.

Everybody in Hawaii knew of him, the local boy who made good—really, really good—and Hawaii voted for its favorite son over John McCain by almost three to one, the only state that him gave more than seventy percent of the vote. I didn't vote for either of them or anybody else. I'd had bad experiences with politicians and was firmly in the "don't vote, it only encourages the bastards" mindset. Four more years hadn't given me any reason to believe that I'd been wrong for the first two decades, so I wasn't planning on voting for Obama in 2012 either. As the election season started heating up, I wasn't paying much attention. It took a reliable confidential informant to get me to the polls.

I'd known Ronnie for years and made a couple dozen good cases, millions of dollars in forfeitures, and quite a few drug seizures behind his information, using him as the source for at least thirty search or seizure warrants. He'd worked for the DEA too, and established a decent track record there. Solidly into one of the local organized crime groups and a career criminal himself, he knew anybody if they worked long enough on the shadier side of the law in Honolulu. It was extremely common for me to meet with him and ask if he knew this person or that one, and never surprising when he started rattling off their histories, sometimes going back a decade or two. When I did the checks to corroborate the information, he always panned out.

Make no mistake, like most informants, he wasn't a "good" guy. He'd done hundreds, maybe thousands of crimes over the years, mostly drugs, theft, and fraud. He had no compunction about stealing from friends or family, used plenty of drugs, and spent time in state and federal prisons learning to be a better crook. But he was *reliable*, which is the standard informants are judged by, not whether they're donating their kidneys, volunteering at hospices, or teaching Sunday school in their free time. And he freakin' knew *everybody*.

We met at a popular local restaurant, Zippy's, the rendezvous for a couple hundred similar get-togethers. I hadn't seen him for a while and we spent some time catching up, talking about his mother, who I knew, and his kids. One of them had gotten into some trouble and he, not being around most of the time during her childhood, and not exactly a model parent when he was, wanted to make it up to his daughter, offering to help. It wasn't a huge thing, pretty minor actually, although it didn't sound like a problem he'd be able to do anything about.

"I called Barry and he had somebody work it out," he said.

"Barry? Who's Barry?"

"Barry. Obama. The president," he said to stunned disbelief and a short, stupefied silence.

"You know Obama..."

"Sure. We come from the same neighborhood. He was the same year as me at Punahou, '79. We hung out."

Like I said, I was used to him saying "I know that guy," but this was an order of magnitude different from that. Or was it? My mind went back to Ray Boyer and his little group of Punahou customers. At that moment, I couldn't remember the names of anyone else in that group, but why couldn't one of them have been Ronnie? Then common sense took over. This wasn't just a local faction hood or somebody pimping crystal meth. This was the freakin' president of the United States we were talking about. Okay, Ronnie knew everybody, but c'mon, man.

"Hang on. You're saying you know Barack Obama well enough you can call him up and ask him for a favor? Is that what you're telling me?"

He shrugged. "We go back. All the way to small kid time. Punahou kids, you know."

"He's supposed to have been doing a lot of dope back then. I heard about it when I was working narcotics. A bunch of Punahou kids and some dealer named Ray."

He nodded. "Boyer. Gay Ray, they called him. Worked at Mama Mia's. Rode a moped and some crappy old car. He was a dick but always had good dope. I heard some dude iced him later."

"Yeah, with a hammer. Did you know all of the kids who were running with Ray?"

"Most of them. Punahou, mostly. One or two from Roosevelt. We all hung out all the time." He named several, but it had been a while and I didn't recognize any of them.

I'd actually read Obama's first autobiography, *Dreams From My Father: A Story of Race and Inheritance*, or at least the parts that talked about his Punahou years. I thought it was a crock but he did freely admit smoking marijuana, "choom" as his little group referred to it, and doing cocaine. I knew that he'd even thanked "the Choom Gang" and "Ray" personally by name in his entry in the 1979 *Oahuan*, Punahou's yearbook. This already provided some backing for Ronnie's unlikely tale and he definitely had his facts straight about Ray Boyer, but I had my doubts and expressed them.

He didn't seem surprised at my skepticism, just dragged out his iPhone and punched up his contact list. Under W, he picked WHITE HOUSE, showed me, and hit dial, holding it closer to my ear so I could hear it ring and the answer of "White House Communications Office." My eyebrows climbed another couple inches toward my hat. Ronnie had the freakin' White House on speed dial.

He asked for someone by name, but the lady on the other end of the line said the party wasn't there. Ronnie said he'd call his cell phone and hung up. "He's not there 'cause he's over in Kailua with Barry and them. I got his cell number. I can call him, but I don't have anything to say, really."

"That's okay, I believe you," I said. It was Christmas time and as usual, Obama and an enormous entourage, the whole presidential Secret Service circus, had been camping for a week or so in a luxury mansion across the island at Kailua Beach. I contemplated the convergence of all these facts, starting to think that Ronnie's story sounded... reliable. It raised the usual question though.

"So I've gotta ask you, man. Did you ever pick up from Obama?" I'd asked him the same thing countless times before, and every other informant too, though never about somebody who was now president of the United States.

He grinned, knowing the next one: "Can you still pick up from him?" and the follow up to that one: "Can you introduce somebody?" The standard CI/undercover 1-2-3 drill, which he'd heard about a thousand times.

"Why? You think maybe he's got an ounce he wants to let go?" he said, grinning.

I laughed. "That'd be kind of a stretch, huh?"

"Yeah. He's got more on his mind now. Running the world and all. But yeah, back in the day. He never had any money, but everybody was the same. If you get stuff, you shared it. He had some black guy he could get weed and coke from. I never met him. Sometimes he got and he shared. I mean, you paid, but nobody was really dealing, making money on it. You know how it goes. He gave to me, but I sold plenty more to him."

"Nobody made money? Even Ray?"

Ronnie grimaced. "Dude was a loser. Surfing and getting stoned. If he got ten bucks, he spent it on weed or coke before he even had a chance to fold it. You gave him money, he could always get something though."

That's pretty much how I remembered the original information. Ray, Barry, and the Choom Gang, nobody in the whole bunch being worth even the small amount of buy money it would have taken to make a case. Rule 5, writ in all caps. Sure, if Barry came into some "pot or some blow," as he put it in his book, he spread the wealth, just like the others did, share and share alike. The America of 1979 was chock full of folks doing exactly that, and it still was in 2012. Those times hadn't changed a bit.

This left me with the question of what to do about the information from a reliable informant. I'd normally write it up along with everything else he told me, the official thing to do. But officially, I didn't care anymore because officially, I'd been retired for two months. Talking with Ronnie had been more of a social thing and a goodbye. And personally, well, I didn't get too fussed about these guys' small-time crimes in 1979 and I certainly wasn't worked up about it thirty-three years later. That just left the decision about telling somebody else who might care. Obama wasn't shy about talking about his druggie days; he'd laid his marijuana and cocaine use out for everybody in a nationwide bestseller. "Pot had helped, and booze; maybe a little blow when you could afford it," he said in *Dreams From My Father*. The 69.5 million people who voted for him in 2008 evidently didn't think it was a deal breaker. I suspected it wasn't much more important for the sixty million who voted for John McCain, who probably never saw a joint or a line of coke in his whole life.

There may have been a time in this country when admitting to being a high school stoner would have been fatal for any political career. That would have gone triple for somebody who'd been selling the stuff, even pot in the tiny quantities Ronnie was talking about, but those times had changed along with America.

I guess I could've made a big deal of it, gone to the Republicans and offered up some dirt on the opposing candidate. That seems to be a popular political pastime. Two practical concerns nixed that idea. First, I doubted that hearsay from a "reliable informant" would cut much ice with Mitt Romney's people, even if I could talk Ronnie into going down and telling his story in person. Second, I'd gotten involved with politicians in a previous case and knew from bitter personal experience with their ilk exactly what I could expect in that situation. Those memories were still fresh and painful even after twenty-six years.

Nope, I might have retired and left law enforcement and undercover work behind forever, but I still lived by the Rules, including Number 5. Barry and the Choom Gang got their second pass.

CHAPTER 19

THE BOXER

CADDO, OKLAHOMA
72 MILES FROM FROGVILLE
11 A.M. ON BLACK FRIDAY

I said at the beginning of this story that it had a sad ending; about the worst I could have imagined. Painful though it is to remember, hard as it is to tell, it deserves to be told. I owe it to him.

Pat and I said we'd keep in touch, and did talk on the phone about the case a couple of times, but although he only worked a couple miles away in northeastern Oklahoma City, we never met after Frogville. On May 26, 1978, I was in the squad bay at the office when we got word that two OHP troopers looking for fugitives Michael Lancaster and Claude Dennis had been killed near a roadblock outside Caddo, down in Bryan County. Every agent in the office immediately started packing gear and heading out toward I-35 South. Not me. I'd shot somebody a week before and was on administrative duties while the shooting investigation concluded. The other agents didn't get far; the dispatcher called to say OHP canceled the lookout for Dennis and Lancaster.

I got the rest of the story later. After killing Bill Young and Pappy Summers, Lancaster and Dennis stole the troopers' weapons and piled back into the truck, setting off for Caddo. An OHP airplane spotted the truck matching Washington's description of the one stolen and began calling for units to head it off in Caddo, only a couple of miles ahead.

Unit V-54, Summers and Young, did not respond to the call but an OHP cruiser with two troopers followed the pilot's directions as Lancaster and Dennis cut in and out of side streets in sleepy little Caddo. They finally turned into a driveway under a big tree, the pilot guessing they were trying to hide from the eye in the sky above. It didn't work. The oncoming cruiser was only a block away, getting updates from the plane and knowing they were close.

Lieutenant Hoyt Hughes, driving, remembered seeing children playing across the street, people out and about on that May morning, a bad place for a gunfight. Innocent lives in the line of fire. But it wasn't his choice, and Dennis wouldn't be taken alive.

Hughes saw Lancaster raise up with a shotgun, ducking as the first slug broke the cruiser's passenger window, hitting his partner. And although he'd been hit in the right shoulder, the side facing the two convicts, Hughes managed to return fire, emptying his .357-magnum revolver at Lancaster, dropping him with fatal wounds. Grabbing a semi-automatic rifle, Hughes emptied that too, not getting Dennis, who came out from cover when he saw Hughes was out of ammunition, walking forward to finish off the wounded trooper.

Lieutenant Mike Williams, rolling up seconds later, ended it all, shooting Dennis seven times and killing him instantly. Lancaster, on the ground and shot in the neck, was alive but only just, dying before they could get him into an ambulance.

And it was too late for Hughes' partner, hit in the head by Lancaster's second or third round from less than fifty feet away. Pat Grimes, my friend, was dead. A good, kind, dedicated man, gone at only age thirty-six. He left his wife, Kay, and a three-year-old daughter, Traci Lynn, a grieving state, and a legion of Oklahoma lawmen inspired by his service.

I wish now I'd gotten to say goodbye in person, Pat. Saying it standing over your coffin at the memorial service in the state capitol rotunda wasn't the ending I wanted or that you deserved, but thanks, Pat, for teaching me how to be a better cop, for your honor and sacrifice, and for giving everything for the people you served and protected. No one could ask for a better example.

I've always felt okay about what Pat and I did to get Tommy back. Overlooked a couple issues and twisted some rules, maybe bent some regulations. Could've done the legal thing and turned those Mexicans over to the 10-5 train down to Brownsville or Laredo but didn't. Could have tried to force the Hatfields to give up the stolen dope, taken it to Oklahoma City and booked it as evidence but didn't. I don't regret it. It was worth it. I'd gotten one of the only real chances I'd ever have as a law enforcement officer to rescue someone, to pull back somebody lost in the high grass. Looking at it from a distance, I think maybe Pat and I had saved someone, gotten him out, even if nobody besides the two of us ever knew how or why.

***

The life mission that began with Franklin and rolled past Pat Grimes, Tommy Hatfield, and thousands of other cops and robbers ended more than three decades later with a guy named Ben. I had dressed up for the end, wearing my best coat and tie for at least the thousandth time, sitting in front of the bar in federal court for my last hearing as a law enforcement officer. Behind me, the usual bunch of local defense attorneys, their thousand-dollar suits putting mine to deep shame, waited for their clients to appear through the door to the marshals' lockup. Two assistant US attorneys chatted up the magistrate's clerk as the court reporter laughed. A couple of deputies talked to a probation officer.

The courtroom was as far as you could get from a ratty shack full of hepatitis and meth on Oklahoma City's southeast side. It was a big, beautifully appointed room, lightly chilled for the comfort of the robed judge and the lawyers in their bespoke jackets. The taxpayers had paneled it with a million dollars' worth of wood from the endangered Hawaiian koa tree, gleaming softly reddish brown above a thick, tasteful carpet. As big as a basketball court with twenty-foot ceilings, the room had been tastefully furnished with comfortable chairs, more koa tables and podiums, and the massive federal judge's bench, also koa. I'd spent weeks in this room for various trials and hearings and felt right at home. Today, the familiar space was filled with accustomed faces, and all of it would be a fading memory in a few more minutes.

Meanwhile, I had one more initial appearance, one last cattle call of arraignments and pleas, one last half hour before I could retire the coat and tie forever. My defendant wasn't one of the scruffier-looking detainees wearing handcuffs, belly chains, detention-center fashion, and baleful looks as the marshals led them through the side door and into the jury box. The deputies parked them there temporarily and spread them out so they could confer sort of privately with their court-appointed lawyers. Seeing them come in, this gaggle rose en masse from the gallery behind me and pushed through the bar, papers and briefcases in hand, plastering earnest expressions on their faces as they took empty seats next to their new clients and started going over the charges.

Ben, the defendant in my case, already had all his paperwork and an attorney, and was dressed in the suit we'd let him put on when we picked him up at his Waikiki apartment that morning. He could have been mistaken for a lawyer himself as he relaxed in one of the padded juror's chairs, waiting for his attorney to pick his way through the real riffraff. Unlike the other defendants, Ben wasn't facing the threat of a no-bail federal dope charge and a mandatory minimum five- or ten-year sentence. The papers he clutched in one hand included an indictment for bankruptcy fraud and for laundering the money he'd gotten from bank fraud—just about the whitest of white-collar crimes. He'd made a full confession before we booked him downstairs and gave him to his five-hundred-dollar-per-hour lawyer.

He was a nice guy, a soft-spoken family man who lived in a handsome condominium in Waikiki, where his daughter went to private school and played violin and his wife cooked and kept a beautiful house. Ben was ambitious though, scheming for a place a little more beautiful in the luxurious Trump International Hotel & Tower nearby. Condos like his at the Trump Tower went for well over a million dollars, some much more; but they do, after all, overlook the most famous beach in the world. And the building featured infinity pools and five-star restaurants and had all of the Trump panache. He wasn't the only person who'd connived a way to get through the golden lobby doors. And probably not the only one whose plan was totally illegal.

His arrest put that plot on hold, and it appeared he'd be downsizing his dream of living in air-conditioned comfort, thirty stories in the sky directly above the glittering lights of Waikiki. Instead of hearing the soft strains of his daughter's Mozart as the sun set over the Pacific, he'd be listening to fellow inmates bitch about the lack of Swiss Miss in the commissary, walking the yard in a federal prison camp on his way to the job in the glove factory. Today, he chatted quietly with his lawyer and gave me a smile and a little wave as I looked over. I waved back, then faced forward and closed my eyes, thinking it sure as hell hadn't started out this way. A lot of water had passed beneath the thirty-five-year-long bridge between Ben and Franklin, and now it was finally time to walk away from the river.

***

On a beautiful weekday morning in late spring, I crossed the grounds of the only official royal residence in the United States in search of pizza. One of Hawaii's most popular tourist attractions, the one hundred and thirty-year-old Iolani Palace sits on a wide, green lawn next to the state capitol. Dozens of visitors milled around, waiting for their guided tour of the home of Hawaii's last two monarchs, and office workers from downtown Honolulu carried their lunches across Richards Street to eat them in the shade of the palace trees. On Fridays, the Royal Hawaiian Band plays concerts on the lawn, and it's an island of serenity in the bustle of the big city.

I saw the girl on the grass, apparently asleep, but she looked wrong. As I got closer, I could see she wasn't stretched out, but had collapsed in a heap, one leg awkwardly folded beneath her, her head resting on a half-crushed McDonald's paper cup. Sadly, homeless people sleeping on the palace lawn are a too-common sight in Honolulu, and residents and visitors used to seeing them walked around and past her, none stopping or sparing more than a glance. But she seemed off to me, so I slowed for a closer look.

The clothes were well worn but clean and the hair covering her face uncombed. Two small backpacks had fallen to the grass at her side and one rubber slipper had come off, lying next to her bare foot. She had a pair of tattoos, amateurish but colorful, on the one ankle I could see, a rainbow above a flower. I didn't think there were too many real rainbows in her life anymore, or flowers either. I checked closer to see if she was breathing.

She was, and I walked on, headed over a block for that pizza. She was still there when I got back ten minutes later.

She'd moved a little, might have tried to sit up and didn't make it. I'd already decided that on this trip past I was going to stop. I was no longer the only one looking at her. Two palace security guards sat on golf carts about fifty feet away, watching both of us but not making any move to get closer.

"Hey. Miss. Can you hear me? Wake up a minute." I leaned in and repeated the message. She finally stirred.

"What?" she said, making it sound like three syllables.

"Can you talk to me for a minute? Are you okay? Do you need some help?"

She lifted her head as if it weighed a hundred pounds, raising her eyes off the ground, seeing me but never focusing, then fading away, gaze falling. "I'm all right," she mumbled to her lap.

She was maybe twenty-five but had traveled a lot of hard miles getting there. The pupils in her heavy-lidded brown eyes were dull, hard, and tiny. Heroin. I checked her forearm for the marks. Yep. There was none of the usual junkie paraphernalia lying around, no syringe, tie-off strap, or bent spoon with a black bottom. She hadn't fired up right there on the spot, which meant she'd probably survive this particular trip down into the heroin mine, especially if she was talking to me.

"You don't seem all right. You sound like you might have got a little too close to the edge. Do you want me to call an ambulance, get the paramedics to take a look at you?"

"No, don't need..." She drifted off, chin dropping to her chest again.

"Miss, hey, miss. Stay with me here. Talk to me. What's your name?'"

"Judy," she said to the ground.

"Okay, Judy, I think you got some good stuff and it knocked you out."

"No, I had a stroke."

"A stroke, huh? No, I'm the one who's had a stroke. I'm gonna say you just shot up some heroin. Your eyes are totally pinned and I can see the tracks."

She looked down at her arm, discovering it for the first time, staring numbly at it, like the arm and the track marks belonged to someone else, wondering how they got there, then blearily back up at me. "In the past, yeah. Don't judge me."

Yeah, like ten minutes past. "Look, Judy, I'm not judging you. I just want to know if you're somebody who needs help. Are you sure you're okay? I can get somebody down here with some Narcan."

"No, don't need any help." She swayed back and forth but didn't fall over, one of those remarkable junkie skills. "I'm just hungry, is all."

"Uh huh. It looks like you just came from McDonalds. Where did you shoot up?"

"Didn't... never..."

"Come on. I just want to know if you did it right here or somewhere else and you walked over. Did you do it in McDonalds? Or here?"

She shook her head slowly. "Across the street."

The YWCA, maybe, about a hundred feet away across Richards Street.

"Okay, so you could walk this far after. I don't think you're gonna die this time. But it's going to get you, you keep doing it."

She contemplated that grim prediction for a minute. "What do you care?" she said finally, sounding genuinely curious.

Good question. Why should I be concerned about this wretch? I wasn't getting paid to care anymore. Trying to keep people like her alive might have been my mission once, decades ago, but standing there in the bright sunshine, surrounded by Japanese tourists and downtown office workers, those days seemed light years distant and the mission nothing more than a lingering dream.

"I had a friend named Matt," I told her. "He died from heroin a long time ago, not far from here. That shit happens. You don't want it to happen to you. Me either."

She raised her head again, looked me straight in the eyes for the first time, held my gaze for a moment, then nodded off without another word.

I went over to the men on the golf carts. "She's messed up. Wasted on heroin. I don't think she's going under today but she could choke if she lays down on her back." We looked over to where Judy sat, head hanging, her face almost touching her knee. Gone girl, gone deep, down into the heroin mine. She'd probably climb back out into the sunlight a little later that day. Or not. I got the feeling it didn't much matter to Judy, or at all to the security guards. "If you see her lying on her back, you gotta roll her," I said, turning to go.

"Do you know that girl?" the guard asked.

"Never seen her before this morning," I said. "Her name's Judy though. And yeah, I've known her almost my whole damn life."

I walked away, acutely aware that nothing I did or said would alter the arc of Judy's transit through her earthly existence by even a fraction of a degree. She was lost in the high grass, and there was nothing I could do to fetch her back. There never had been and there never would be. I carried these desolate thoughts with my pizza, back across the parking lot, into the cool shade under the banyan tree behind the palace, past laughing children and palace visitors from other states and other countries, and wondered at the even sadder reality of it all.

This girl, a few milligrams from becoming a statistic, a stat I knew from personal experience nobody officially cared about, was nodding off a hundred feet from one of the city's busiest tourist attractions. She lay practically underneath the window of the governor in the state capitol and across King Street from Honolulu's beautiful old Federal Building. On the other side of the capitol, in the vital stats office at the Department of Health where they store the state's death certificates, there was a blank paper waiting for her name and a date someday in the future. And across Richards Street, a few steps away, deputy prosecuting attorneys and Honolulu police officers came and went from the front entrance to the city prosecutor's office. Twenty floors above in the same tower was the cubicle where I'd finished out my law enforcement career, all of it now a distant and fading memory. I could see my own office windows from where Judy slept, alone now on the grass with her rainbows, flowers, and heroin.

There's where we are in the War on Drugs in 2022. Forty-five years after I enlisted and ten after I left it, it's an America where the death certificates pile up on bureaucrats' desks by the tens of thousands every year, where parents bury their children while no one else watches. It's a place of odd juxtapositions, where drugs touch everyone from the high and mighty like the King of Rock and Roll in a Memphis bathroom to the lowest like Judy on a real palace lawn in Honolulu. And there's almost nothing we can do about it. Hundreds of thousands at least, probably millions, of people pay their nickels and take their chances every day. Some, like Judy that morning, make it to the next day, to another nickel and another chance. And some, like Matt or Elvis, or one of these days, Judy herself, will lose her nickel and everything else.

It's sad and it's disheartening and more than a little scary, but I believe after those four decades, I found some awful truth to carry away from the royal palace with my pizza.

We're the ones who are lost in the high grass, all of us.

THE END

Photos

Lieutenant Pat Grimes – Official photograph,
Oklahoma Highway Patrol, courtesy of
the family of James Pat Grimes

DEA Special Agent Larry Wallace, courtesy of the
DEA Library, Drug Enforcement Administration

DEA Special Agent Paul Seema, courtesy of the
DEA Library, Drug Enforcement Administration

BOND DEFAULT
WANTED BY FBI

JAMIEL ALEXANDER CHAGRA

FBI No. 153 807 K1

ALIASES: Jim Alexander, Jimmy Chagra, Jim Garcia, Jim Lewis, Jim Moore, Jim Turner, "Diamond Jim," "Jimmy The Shoe" NCIC: POPIPIPOI4POPIP16

Photographs taken 1979

DESCRIPTION
AGE: 35, born December 7, 1944, El Paso, Texas
HEIGHT: 6'1"
WEIGHT: 190 to 200 pounds
BUILD: large
HAIR: black with gray sideburns
OCCUPATIONS: carpet salesman, professional gambler, narcotics trafficker
EYES: brown
COMPLEXION: olive
RACE: white
NATIONALITY: American

SCARS AND MARKS: scar over left eyebrow
REMARKS: An avid professional gambler who has a reputation as a "high roller"; uses private jet aircraft to travel.
SOCIAL SECURITY NUMBER USED: 457-70-4853

CRIMINAL RECORD
Chagra has been convicted of aiding and abetting in the distribution of cocaine, continuing criminal enterprise and unlawfully carrying a weapon.

CAUTION
CHAGRA WHO IS KNOWN TO HAVE CARRIED A .357 MAGNUM HANDGUN IN THE PAST, AND IS REPORTEDLY A NARCOTICS USER, SHOULD BE CONSIDERED ARMED AND DANGEROUS.

A Federal warrant was issued on August 23, 1979, at El Paso, Texas, charging Chagra with violation of Title 18, U.S. Code, Section 3150, bond default.

IF YOU HAVE INFORMATION CONCERNING THIS PERSON, PLEASE CONTACT YOUR LOCAL FBI OFFICE. TELEPHONE NUMBERS AND ADDRESSES OF ALL FBI OFFICES LISTED ON BACK.

William H. Webster
Director
Federal Bureau of Investigation
Washington, D. C. 20535

Identification Order 4850
January 2, 1980

FBI wanted poster for Jamiel "Jimmy" Chagra,
marijuana kingpin and the man behind the
assassination of federal judge John Woods. FBI

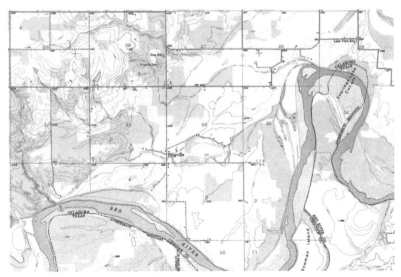

Frogville Quadrangle, from a 1951 U.S.
Coast and Geodetic Survey map of the area.
USCGS map, University of Texas.

Howard Hughes in earlier, drug-free times. From
an interview in 1938. Library of Congress, Prints &
Photographs Division, photograph by Harris & Ewing,
[reproduction number, e.g., LC-USZ62-123456]

John Madinger, on TDY in Africa, author's collection

Clarence "Japan" Handa, cocaine trafficker, informant, and apparently a believer in psychics. Author's collection.

Seizure of sixty pounds of Colombian marijuana. The author (right) purchased the drugs as a sample of what would be a 2,000-pound purchase in Fort Lauderdale, Florida. Any doubts about whether we're winning or losing the war on drugs? That purchase and seizure was the smallest in South Florida that week. Author's collection.

Million-dollar seizure in a crystal methamphetamine case. Also eleven pounds of crystal meth. Author's collection.

Going under with a dentist – purchasing Quaaludes. This buy took place out on the street, but the author talked him into doing the next one in the state narcotics office. Author's collection.

El Paso attorney Lee Chagra represented the ten defendants in the seizure of 17,000 pounds of marijuana in Ardmore, Oklahoma, Jimmy Birdsong's biggest case. Photo from the El Paso Times.

Elvis Presley (seated, front) and Dr. George
Nichopoulos (kneeling, left) Getty Images

THANKS AND ACKNOWLEDGEMENTS

Those deserving of special thanks include:

Agent James Birdsong, Oklahoma Bureau of Narcotics and Dangerous Drugs, a great agent and good man, who shot me once, but I forgive him. He saved me from myself more than a couple of times, for which I probably owe him my life and am appropriately grateful. R.I.P., Jimmy.

Troy Leathers, Agent, OBNDD, who may be the best undercover agent I ever worked with. R.I.P., Troy.

Sydney Zalopany, Agent and Supervisor, Hawaii Office of Narcotics Enforcement, who could buy dope from anybody and was the best partner a cop could have.

Also, James Nobriega, Detective, Honolulu Police Department, who introduced us to "Search Warren."

To the United States Attorneys and their assistants in the District of Hawaii, who over the years capably prosecuted the cases I took to them; it was a privilege working with you all.

And very special thanks to Lieutenant Mike Grimes of the Canadian County Sheriff's Office, Pat's brother, who retired as Deputy Chief of the Oklahoma Highway Patrol and stayed in law enforcement, recently marking fifty-seven years of service. Mike read the manuscript and shared it with Pat's widow and daughter, and I'm grateful for his comments and his dedication to the people of Oklahoma.

For More News About John Madinger,
Signup For Our Newsletter:

http://wbp.bz/newsletter

Word-of-mouth is critical to an author's long-term success. If you appreciated this book please leave a review on the Amazon sales page:

http://wbp.bz/goingunder

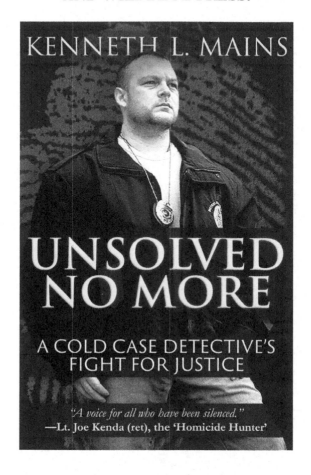

Made in United States
Orlando, FL
14 September 2022

22416015R00157